Notable Encounters

Create Enduring Memories

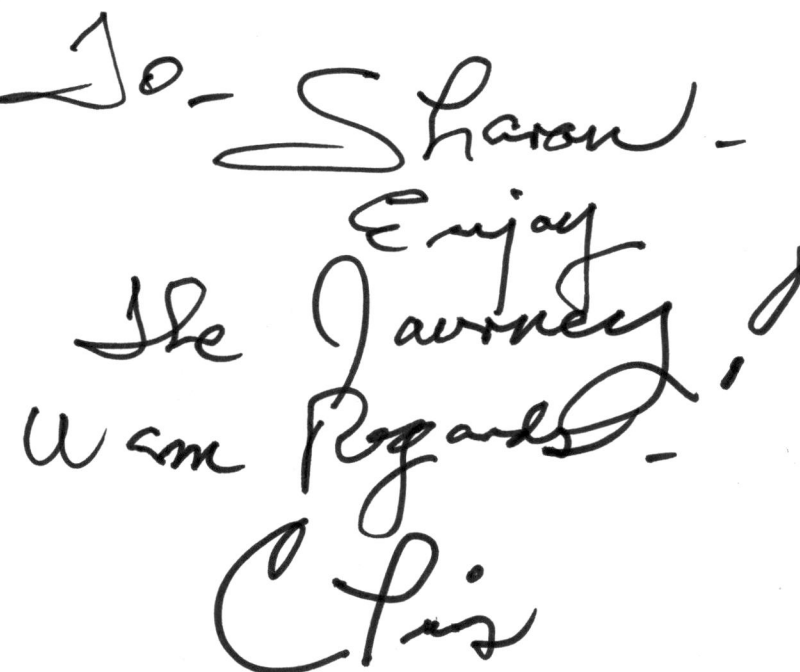

To - Sharon -
Enjoy
the Journey!
Warm Regards -
Chris

Chris Adams
with
Paulette Bridges

ISBN 978-1-64416-070-1 (paperback)
ISBN 978-1-64416-072-5 (hardcover)
ISBN 978-1-64416-071-8 (digital)

Christian Faith Publishing, Inc.
832 Park Avenue
Meadville, PA 16335
www.christianfaithpublishing.com

Printed in the United States of America

Contents

 # **Introduction**

S ome time ago, while watching television, I observed a group of apparently newly introduced people at a gathering, lively exchanging handshakes with one another. As I sat watching the obvious pleasure of the greetings, I turned my attention to my own right hand and the palm. Ruminating, I thought back over the years and the many handshakes that my palm had engaged in greeting new friends and old friends alike, and the many incredible people I have had the pleasure of meeting and greeting. Many of those whom I greeted for first time became and remain friends for life, while other encounters were brief and moved on, but many in exceptional ways are memorable.

Virtually every encounter, meeting, or greeting is initiated with a handshake. The handshake symbol or practice has existed in some form or another for thousands of years. One popular theory is that the gesture began as a way of conveying peaceful intentions. By extending empty right hands, strangers could show that they were not holding weapons and bore no ill will toward one another. Some also suggest that the up-and-down motion of the handshake was supposed to dislodge any knives or daggers that might be hidden up a sleeve. Another description is that the handshake is a symbol of good faith when making an oath or promise. When people clasp hands, they demonstrate that their word is a sacred bond.

I began to recall and reflect on the many people of the present and the past; literally, from all over the world that I have had the pleasure of meeting. I also pondered about how many I could remember, especially the time and the place, as well as the circumstances leading up to the meetings. The more I contemplated the thought, the more

I began to recall and reflect on the people, times and places of those special events, and decided to document them; for whatever purpose, but any event, a good mental challenge and exercise.

When I initially typed the chosen title for this projected work, my very responsive laptop promptly highlighted the synonyms for the term *notable*, which I had planned to use. I was pleased to see "noteworthy, worthy, famed, noted, renowned, etc.," which fit my work title choice. Then I continued with the other term I had chosen, *encounters*, which seemed to fit meeting people. To my dismay, the synonyms, "brush, clash, skirmish, fight, combat, scrap," popped up on the side screen, before *meeting*, finally displayed. It was *meeting* or *greeting* that I was seeking to make the case for a suitable title. I gave considerable thought to the more derisive definitions of encounters, and to choosing an alternative term, but decided that I still preferred *Encounters*. *Notable Encounters* stood fast in my thoughts as a project title choice; especially since the handshake is the most likely gesture to avert a potential *brush, clash, skirmish*, or *fight*!

The handshake is also the most common gesture upon an initial meeting and greeting, offering congratulations, expressing gratitude, completing an agreement, or departing. The purpose of clasping hands is to convey trust, respect, balance, and equality.

"An agreement can be expressed quickly and clearly in words," historian Walter Burkert once explained, "but is only made effective by a ritual gesture: open, weaponless hands stretched out toward one another, grasping each other in a mutual handshake."

As I began to further contemplate putting my thoughts on paper, I recalled once sitting around the table chatting with friends, and as we are prone to do, I began to share the recent experience of a meeting encounter with a substantially well-known individual. Before I delved too much into my storied experience, one of the ladies at the table blurted, "Name dropper!"

The table fell quiet for a moment; a few snickered, and then one of the fellows responded, "It ain't bragging, Chris, if you did it!" Several chuckles resulted, lightening up the situation. I smiled and snickered along with them, letting the story go, electing to

not further describe my celebrity-meeting experience. If you read further herein, you may likely be subjected to that incomplete story.

After considerably more reflections on the past and the surfacing within my thoughts of so many adventures, I decided, for the record, to move forward and share some of my special notable encounter experiences. Many of those have continued long afterward, while others were "touch and go," so to speak. Each encounter began and, more often than not, ended with a sincere handshake, a pleasant goodbye, and a feeling of satisfaction with the meeting. So many of those special encounters, as you will understand, remain indelibly implanted in my memory bank. Last, and most important of all these memories, is that time and space does not permit me to document many and perhaps "most" of you!

I was concerned that recalling and documenting so many exceptional encounters with noteworthy people might become a challenging task of ensuring that the details of the meetings, time, and place are accurately recounted. I quickly discovered, however, that as I began to recall special times, places, and events, I frequently found myself, literally, back then and there, reliving the venture. Many of my encounters are easily recognized names, while others introduced will share the same recognition as you review them. I was also concerned that some might view these series of recollections an ego trip. That being the case, there is a bit of ego in all of us, recalling a quote from someone in the past; "Learn to say no to the things that don't add value in your life, and open your arms and run towards the things that do." Each and every encounter that I have recalled herein added some value to my life's experiences; many, if not most, by coincidence and others where opportunity presented itself and I did not hesitate to *run toward it*!

Once again, I have called upon two special and notable encounters who have become friends for life, to assist me with this work. First, educator, creative writer, exceptional editor for several of my works, and coauthor for this piece, Paulette Bridges. I am pleased to once again have Paulette join me in documenting these many encounter experiences and fond memories. Likewise, gifted and imaginative professional artist, and special friend, Craig Holloway, has once again stepped forward to embellish the work with his brilliantly created cover jacket.

I invite you to also join me in this journey of special notable encounters . . .

1

Notable Leader Encounters

Personal experiences frequently become indelible memories. Noteworthy encounters with some of the truly great leaders whom I had the pleasure of meeting, knowing, and serving during my Air Force days and beyond became those lasting memories. I have also especially enjoyed the privilege of meeting many of you along the way and cherish every developed friendship! I could also write a book about many more of you! But herein I will attempt to single out just a few special seniors who engraved proud memories in my life and career. Some of you perhaps will not recognize all of these, while many of you will have your own memories re-energized as you recall these and others who also impressed your lives and careers. Later in this work, I will highlight others from various backgrounds and professions whom I also had the distinct honor of meeting, remembering, and in several instances, also serving. I will begin the story of these incredible encounters with some notable leaders in the order of the approximate period of my introduction to each and share them chronologically. Lastly, I wish to share who and the backgrounds of these many special encounters so that you may also get to know them. I invite you further to Google up any of those referenced herein if you wish to join me in appreciation of their incredible lives and contributions.

Special encounters with many notable leaders will always remain in our hearts and minds:

Brigadier General Robert R. Scott, USAF (Ret)

I first met then Colonel Robert Scott at Ramey Air Force Base, Puerto Rico, in 1962, where he was Deputy Commander, Operations for the 72nd Bomb Wing, B-52s. I received a call one day from Lt. Colonel Ralph Griffin, Chief of the Wing Command Post, during which, Colonel Griffin said that he was looking for a B-52 qualified pilot to become an Officer Controller in the Wing Command Post., and would I be interested?

I was surprised by his call, but after a few seconds thought, I told him, "Yes, sir," that I would be pleased to come to the command post and become an Officer Controller. After ten years in the cockpit, I thought it would be "a pleasant relief to learn something else about the Air Force!"

A few months later, and in the new job, I was summoned to the DOs, Colonel Scott's office. I had seen and met Colonel Scott briefly on a few occasions when he would pop into the Command Post to review ongoing activities. His secretary escorted me into his office. He greeted me with a pleasant smile and welcome. We shook hands, and then I was surprised when I looked around to see my boss, Colonel Griffin, and several other wing staff members present. As I stood a little bit in shock, Colonel Scott motioned me over to the front of his desk and asked his executive officer, "Read the citation."

I was completely surprised as he read and that I was being awarded the Air Force Commendation Medal for my bomber combat crew duty, the Cuban Crises activity, and so on. My bomb squadron commander had nominated me upon departure from the crew force to the command post. Colonel Scott penned the Commendation Medal on my uniform, gave me another warm hand shake, patted the medal, and I remember his words well, "Congratulations, Chris, I am sure that you will earn several more of these."

In developing this treatise, I am sure that I, as many of you, will remember events and details about times past that the principals involved, other than yourself, would never recall. That has been a fun and pleasure part of this work. The award of the Commendation

Medal that day was to be the unexpected beginning many future notable encounters with Colonel Robert R. Scott.

In high school, Bob Scott says that he knew he had a penchant for aviation and flying. He said that he thought of pursuing a career in commercial aviation. Instead, he chose to join the Army Air Corps to pursue his love for flying, as well as his sense of duty to country. A native of Miami, he attended a military school in Florida from the fourth to sixth grade. There, he was introduced to discipline and commitment at an early age. He remained focused to pursue aviation, took advantage of the advanced courses he had taken in high school, earning two years of college credits, and qualifying him for the Army Aviation Cadet Program. While as an aviation cadet, he married his high school sweetheart, LaVern. After their marriage, she worked to help support them while he continued aviation cadet training. Following completion of flight school, he trained to become a B-17 bomber pilot, and departed for England, where he was assigned to the 92nd Bomb Group in Britain's 8th Royal Air Force. He says, "I was the pilot and commander of a crew of nine. We all survived World War II and came back together. I was the only one who stayed with the military."

During the war, he said that he was promoted from second lieutenant to first lieutenant to captain within forty-three days, due to the combat losses in Europe. At twenty-one, he became the lead formation bomber pilot. After the war in Europe, the bomber planes became carriers of military personnel back to the United States. He said, "We started carrying troops to get them back as fast as we could to retrain them to get back to the Pacific."

Bob's wife, LaVern, moved back to Miami while he was overseas, where she worked as a stenographer and bookkeeper for Pan American Airways. They were reunited after the war, and their son, Randy, was born in December 1946. They moved to Roswell, New Mexico, and Walker Air Force Base in 1947, where Captain Scott was assigned to the 509th Bomb Group, flying the nuclear-capable B-29 bomber. There, he became involved in conducting nuclear weapons testing over the Nevada desert. When the 509th transitioned to the arrival of the newly developed B-36 heavy bomber, he checked out in the mighty aircraft and began flying missions and deployments around the world as the Cold War became the latest challenge to the United States and the military services.

From Walker AFB, the Scotts were transferred to Loring AFB, Maine, in June 1953. There, he was assigned as the operations officer of the 70th Bombardment Squadron. Later, he became operations and training officer, then onward to chief of training, 42nd Bombardment Wing, and finally, commander of the 69th B-36 Bomb Squadron. In 1956 he attended B-52 bomber transition training and directed the conversion of the 69th Bombardment Squadron from B-36s to the B-52.

Lt. Colonel Scott was then transferred to Westover Air Force Base, Massachusetts, in November 1957, where he served with headquarters, Eighth Air Force, as chief, Bombardment Reconnaissance Branch. Later, he became chief, Standardization Division, and finally, Chief, Training Division. Promoted to Colonel, he was transferred to the 72nd Bombardment Wing, Ramey Air Force Base, Puerto Rico, in July 1961, to become Deputy Commander for Operations, and later, Commander, 72nd Combat Support Group.

In June 1964, he was reassigned to headquarters, Strategic Air Command, Offutt Air Force Base, Nebraska, as Chief, Officer Manning Branch, and later Deputy Chief of Staff. In July 1966, he was reassigned as Commander, 390th Strategic Missile Wing, equipped with the Titan II ICBM, at Davis-Monthan Air Force Base, Arizona. In August 1968, he moved on to became commander, 90th Strategic Missile Wing, with Minuteman missiles, at Francis E. Warren Air Force Base, Cheyenne, Wyoming. His wife, LaVern passed away in September 1968, shortly after arriving at Francis E. Warren.

Moving onward, Colonel Scott became commander, 17th Strategic Aerospace Division, Whiteman Air Force Base, Missouri, in August 1969. He married Terry Ratliff that year, a Cody, Wyoming, native and school teacher in Cheyenne. He was promoted to brigadier general in February 1970 and became the first commander of the 4th Strategic Missile Division, back at F.E. Warren Air Force Base, Wyoming.

In June 1972, General Scott assumed duties as Deputy Chief of Staff, Personnel, Headquarters Strategic Air Command, Offutt Air Force Base, Nebraska. I will mention later in my tribute to Lt. General Warren D. Johnson; Generals Scott and Johnson, once to my complete surprise and pleasure, jointly coordinated a transfer for yours truly out of a static position in Washington, DC, and the Defense Nuclear Agency, back to operations in Strategic Air Command. It was a move for which I was, ever grateful, exceptionally enhancing my Air Force career thereafter!

Brigadier General Robert R. Scott retired after thirty-one years active duty, in November 1973. His numerous military decorations and awards include the Legion of Merit, Distinguished Flying Cross, Air Medal with three oak leaf clusters and the Air Force Commendation Medal with two oak leaf clusters. He is a command pilot and wears the Senior Missileman Badge.

This treatise on Robert R. Scott's successful Air Force career and retirement would ordinarily bring to a close a busy and storied life's history, but in the case of this unique and energetic man's quest for living and adventure, departing the Air Force served to open unimagined doors. Terry, his energetic wife, sharing his desire for new undertakings, enthusiastically joined him in their lives' next chapter. I want to interject here, son, Randy Scott, mentioned earlier and whom we got to know during our concurrent tour of duty in Puerto Rico, was a very successful student and high school football player. Randy graduated from the University of Arizona, receiving a commission in the Air Force. Like his dad, he attended flight training, becoming a successful pilot and, like most of us in the '60s, served a tour in Vietnam. Randy was awarded two Silver Star Medals for valor in conducting rescue operations as an A-10 Air Commando pilot. Thereafter, he became a T-38 instructor, flew A-7s and F-16s, served a tour in Korea and retired as a squadron commander, after twenty years active duty. A non-stopper, as is his dad, he continued on to fly as a captain with Delta Airlines for ten years and later, with Citation Shares Executive Airline for an additional five years, before "retiring" to Colorado Springs with his wife, Carol, and three children.

Following retirement from active duty, Bob and Terry Scott moved back to Cheyenne where Bob joined American National Bank as Vice President, Marketing. Not one to sit still in any capacity, he worked successfully with the Air Force and Federal Reserve to locate a subsidiary bank on Francis E. Warren Air Force Base.

Bob remained with American National Bank for fifteen years, transitioning through numerous administrative and management positions, including Vice President, Operation; Senior Vice President, administration and Operations to secretary to the board of directions. Nothing like putting a "retired general" in charge!

As I refreshed my recall of General Bob Scott's "race track" career, I was reminded how our respective flight paths had traced a very similar landing and touch down pattern along the way. From my introduction at Ramey, also to Whiteman, to Frances E. Warren, to Davis-Monthan, to Offutt Air Force Bases, and finally, to succeed this exceptional officer as Commander, 90th Strategic Missile Wing and Cheyenne, Wyoming; to be reunited there with him and Terry was an extraordinary personal journey.

Terry returned to her teaching career in Cheyenne, this time as a professor of humanities, including English, grammar, writing, literature, and poetry. She concurrently completed her long-sought master's degree, before she herself decided to "retire."

Neither Bob nor Terry can come to grips yet today, with "retirement." He has pressed on as an active member of the Chamber of Commerce, Military Affairs Association, YMCA board of directors, Wyoming Heart Association, Kiwanis Club and Daedalians, pro-active and taking lead roles in each. Terry continues in full support as member of the Military Wives Club and the women's PEO chapter. It is such a pleasure to share this notable encounter with these two incredible people, who have yet to say, "Stop! Let's retire!" They haven't, and will not in the near future. They now reside in Terry's hometown of Cody, Wyoming, where they actively participate in hunting, fishing, winter sports, and all the rest and beyond!

Friends for life, Bob Scott, at an ageless ninety-five, continues to ski off the Wyoming and Colorado slopes with ever-energetic Terry. They both enjoy great health and life as it should be lived.

General Benjamin O. Davis, USAF (Ret)

While assigned to the 388th TAC Fighter Wing, Korat Air Base, Thailand, during Vietnam—not as a fighter pilot, but as a C-47 "Gooney Bird" pilot—I was summoned one morning to report to the flight line and to wear my *best* khaki uniform. I chose one of two I brought with me; otherwise, flight suit and fatigues were the uniform of the day. When I arrived at base operations, there was a large crowd of guys, members of the wing staff and several Thai Air Force officers. The wing personnel officer called me aside and told me that I was to receive the award of an Air Medal. I was shocked! I had no idea that I had been recommended to receive the Air Medal, and for what? I had only been shot at and fortunately missed a few times; nevertheless, I was lined up with several others, and stood first, *alphabetically*, in line. Our small wing musical band played a few notes and our wing commander, Brigadier General Chairsell, called the group to attention. Then, an impressive-looking officer, a three-star General, walked out of the base ops building and up to me with a broad smile on his face.

He held out his huge hand, grasped mine, and said, "Hello, Major Adams. Congratulations on your exceptional airmanship!" I had never seen, much less met, Lt. General Benjamin O. Davis, but I recognized him from photographs and stories. He proceeded to pin the Air Medal on my shirt, then held out his hand again and gave me another warm grasp. What a special day and surprise!

Lest we not forget, General Benjamin Davis was the first Air Force African-American general officer. His father had preceded him in graduating from West Point and also was promoted to brigadier general in the Army. General Benjamin Davis immediately took to becoming an aviator as a young officer and one of the first pilots to join the all-black aviator World War II Tuskegee Airmen. Quickly promoted through the ranks to lieutenant colonel, he became commander of the first all-black 99th Pursuit Squadron. Equipped with Curtiss P-40s, the Tuskegee Airmen were deployed to North Africa in the spring of 1943. The Tuskegee Airmen under General Davis compiled an outstanding record in combat against the German

Luftwaffe, completing more than fifteen thousand sorties, shooting down 111 enemy planes, and destroying 273 on the ground. They lost only sixty-six of their own planes. Following combat in Korea, he moved upward and was promoted to lieutenant general. He assumed command of the Thirteenth Air Force at Clark Air Base in the Philippines in 1967, of which the air units in Thailand were assigned.

General Benjamin O. Davis retired from active military service in 1970, following thirty-four years of active duty. He was appointed Assistant Secretary of Transportation by President Nixon in 1971, where he served for three years. In December 1998, he was deservedly promoted to the rank of four-star general, U.S. Air Force (retired), with President Bill Clinton pinning on his fourth star.

By coincidence, twenty years after General Davis honored me with the award of the Air Medal, I happened to be visiting Wright-Patterson AFB, Ohio, on business as a civilian. During my visit, the base was celebrating the fortieth anniversary of the Air Force as a separate service. During the festivities, General Davis was introduced as one of the special guests of honor. I was taken by complete surprise and after a lengthy period during the evening festivities, I finally worked my way to him and introduced myself, reminding him of his pinning the Air Medal on me back in 1967. He broke into a big smile, grasped my hand, and gave me a hug as if he remembered me from that special time in my life. We chatted for a considerable time, his insisting on knowing what had occurred in my life over the years since that day. This special memory of a young Air Force officer remains embedded to this day!

General Daniel "Chappie" James Jr., USAF (Ret)

In May 1967, I flew one of our trusty C-47 "Gooney Bird" World War II vintage transports, from Korat Air Base, Thailand, into nearby Ubon Air Base, to pick up a group of fighter pilots and take them back to Korat for the inaugural meeting of the Red River

Valley Rats Roundup. The idea for the Red River Valley Rats was that of Colonel Robin Olds, Commander, 8th Tactical Fighter Wing (TFW), located at Ubon, during the Vietnam War. The reunion at Korat was to be the first of five succeeding fighter pilot get-togethers, rotating among the other air bases in Thailand, during those war years.

Colonel Chappie James, Director of Operations of the 8th TFW, and twenty-five fighter pilots loaded onto my aircraft. Colonel James came up to the cockpit and introduced himself, thanking us for transporting him and his pilots to the reunion, and remained chatting with my copilot and me until we arrived at Korat. I had heard considerably about this particular Air Force "warrior," who was also a graduate of Tuskegee Institute; to meet him personally was a special treat. He was cordial, friendly, and quizzed the two of us about our backgrounds and our jobs there at Korat.

To digress, the purpose and mission of the Red River Valley Rats organization was directed toward generating awareness of the prisoners of war (POW) and aircrews missing in action (MIA) and killed in action (KIA) fighting in Vietnam and supporting their families. In 1969, then Brigadier Robin Olds called for a reunion to permanently form and incorporate the Red River Valley Fighter Pilots Association. A college scholarship program was a major priority of the organization. The scholarship fund was established at a San Antonio reunion in 1970. The hat was passed at that reunion, and three-thousand-dollar scholarships were initially funded. In August of 1973, after the prisoners of war were returned home, a major River Rats reunion was held in Las Vegas, Nevada, with overwhelming attendance and the coming together of hundreds of comrades who had been separated for years. On April 30, 1975, the organization's name was amended to Red River Valley Association, Inc. The association presently provides scholarships to children of United States military personnel MIA/KIA in armed conflicts from Southeast Asia to the present.

Additionally, dependents of aircrew members killed in military aircraft accidents also qualify for scholarships. Since 1970, The Red River Rats have awarded more than 1,130 scholarship grants with a value of over 2.3 million dollars to the children and spouses of Air Force, Army, Navy, and Marine Corps aircrew members. This incredible association continues to hold reunions and award scholarships annually. Back to my special encounter; General James was born on February 11, 1920, in Pensacola, Florida. He was the first African-American to become a four-star general in the U.S. Air Force. He attended college at the famous Tuskegee Institute African-American school.

During college, General James picked up the nickname Chappie. He became interested in flying and began pilot training through the Civilian Pilot Training Program located at Tuskegee. After completing the program, he applied for and became an instructor pilot. Overcoming racial prejudices in the military at the time, he fought to attend the Army Air Corps flight school. Having already become a civilian pilot, he passed the required tests with ease and completed military pilot training. During World War II, he served as an instructor pilot, teaching other African-Americans in the 99th Pursuit Squadron

When the Korean War started, General James volunteered for combat, flying over one hundred missions and was awarded the Distinguished Service Medal, an award most unusual for a young officer. He was promoted rapidly to the grade of colonel and assigned as director of operations, 8th TFW, at Ubon Royal Thai Air Force Base, Thailand, in December 1966. It was there in May of 1967 that I was privileged to meet him. Shortly after the Red River Rats Reunion, he became vice commander of the 8th TFW. He and Wing Commander, Colonel Robin Olds, became a legend in their own time, becoming known as "Blackman and Robin." They had fun with themselves and others who were privileged to know them, even in combat! Chappie James flew seventy-eight combat missions in Vietnam and was hailed as a hero, leading flight of his young fighter pilots on one mission, shooting down seven North Vietnamese MiGs. It was the highest single mission "kill" of any mission during the Vietnam War.

Following Vietnam, General James's stunning career continued. He was named vice commander of the 33rd TFW at Eglin Air Force

Base, Florida. While stationed at Eglin, the Florida State Jaycees named him as Florida's "Outstanding American of the Year" in 1969. Thereafter, he became commander, 72nd TFW at Wheelus Air Base in the Libyan Arab Republic.

General James became Deputy Assistant Secretary of Defense (Public Affairs) in March 1970 and was designated principal deputy assistant secretary of defense (Public Affairs) in April 1973. Thereafter, promoted to Lt. General, he became vice commander of the Military Airlift Command (MAC), headquartered at Scott Air Force Base, Illinois. He was promoted to the four-star grade of General in September 1975 and assigned as Commander in Chief, NORAD/ADCOM at Peterson Air Force Base, Colorado.

It was my special opportunity and pleasure to meet General James again in October 1975, when I visited NORAD Headquarters as a newly selected brigadier general along with other general officer selectees, as we traveled around to the various major commands as a part of our orientation program, *affectionately* called Charm School. He welcomed us into his office and greeted the dozen of us graciously. As he went around the room, asking each of us about our backgrounds, etc., I chose the opportunity to recall my meeting him back at Ubon, Thailand, in 1967. He smiled, remembering the inaugural Red River Rats Reunion, and thanked me for "taxiing" him and his fighter pilots to the event.

In December 1977, General James was appointed special assistant to the chief of staff, U.S. Air Force, where he served until his retirement from the Air Force in February 1978. He died unexpectedly of a heart attack on February 25, 1978, just two weeks after his fifty-eighth birthday and three weeks following his retirement from the Air Force. He was buried with full military honors at Arlington National Cemetery.

In closing my encounter memories of this notable patriot and great American, General Chappie James was also widely known for his speeches on Americanism and patriotism, for which he was frequently editorialized in national and international publications. When once asked his views and opinion on civil rights movements during a talk about his military experiences and recalling having to make an emergency landing with his aircraft in North Vietnam, he replied, as he further cited in an excerpt from an essay he wrote in 1967, following being awarded the George Washington Freedom Medal, "Look, friend, I'm really not interested in all of that. You see, I consider myself damned lucky to have been able to land my airplane at that emergency strip in one piece. Being asked about militants like H. Rap Brown and Stokely Carmichael, who implied that blacks ought to fight at home rather than in Vietnam," he angrily replied, "with the lawlessness and rioting, men like Stokely Carmichael acting as if they speak for the Negro people. They aren't and set civil rights back one hundred years!"

Vice Admiral Lloyd M. Mustin, USN (Ret)

Returning from my year in Southeast Asia and Korat, Thailand, I was virtually shocked by my follow-on assignment, with only a degree in business administration, to the Defense Atomic Support Agency (DASA) and Joint Task Force Eight (JTF-8), Sandia Base, New Mexico. While serving with JTF-8, I was privileged to meet and work with some of the most interesting nuclear warfare professionals and scientists who would years later re-enter my life. I had also to be even more surprised when I received an early promotion to lieutenant colonel upon my arrival at JTF-8. Then after three years serving with the super classified Agency's Sandia operation, I was reassigned to DASA Headquarters in Washington, DC, which traced its origin from the Armed Forces Special Weapons Project (AFSWP), and its descendant government organizations, from its original founding in 1947. AFSWP was formed to provide military training in nuclear weapons operations. Over the years, its sequential descendant organization became the Defense Atomic Support Agency (DASA).

The Agency was headed by Vice Admiral Lloyd M. Mustin, a 1932 graduate of the U.S. Naval Academy. As the stories were told, he was tutored by Captain, later Admiral Chester W. Nimitz. It was also alleged that he carried with him Nimitz's "tough, take no pris-

oners" motto throughout the remainder of his notable career. His father, Captain Henry C. Mustin, USN, was a pioneer naval aviator who established the first naval air station and launched the first aircraft from a ship underway.

During World War II, Admiral Mustin took part in developing the Navy's first lead-computing anti-aircraft gun sight, which proved of major importance in the air-sea actions during the war. He served aboard the cruiser USS Atlanta during the naval battle of Guadalcanal. His ship was sunk during that action, and with other survivors he landed on Guadalcanal and began serving ashore with the naval unit attached to the First Marine Division. His post war service included several commands at sea with the development and evaluation of weapon systems. He later served as director of operations for the Joint Chiefs of Staff during Vietnam and prior to being appointed director, DASA. Among his and his family's legacies was the naming of a guided missile destroyer in honor of the Mustin name, USS *Mustin* (DDG-89) as well as Mustin Naval Air Station in Pennsylvania.

I arrived at DASA Headquarters, located in the Thomas Building, on the edge of the Potomac, in Rosslyn, Virginia. I felt like I had been dropped off in another jungle, similar to Southeast Asia. I was assigned to the Operations Plans Division under the direction of Army Major General William Shedd. He was a super gentleman and welcomed me into the division, which was made up of Army, Navy, and Air Force officers. I had been at DASA only two months, getting to know my job and the "territory," when one day I was called to report to the admiral's office. Admiral Mustin and his staff occupied the seventh (top) floor of the Thomas Building, affectionately called "The Bridge." I walked up the two flights of stairs from my location on the fifth floor, a little nervous and wondering what was ahead. I was greeted by the admiral's secretary and invited to take a seat to await the admiral's summons to come into his office. The seventh floor area was very pleasant and open with three desks backing the main wall; a secretary occupied the two outer desks with a large center desk in between. The office across the reception area where the three desks were located reflected the name plate of Captain Duran,

USN, Chief of Staff. The Admiral's office door suddenly opened and out walked Admiral Mustin.

"Lieutenant Colonel Adams," he said curtly.

I jumped to my feet and replied, "Yes, sir."

He extended his hand and shook mine. "Come in," he motioned toward his office door. I followed him as he walked behind his desk cluttered with paper and stood in front as he sat down. His secretary closed the door behind me. The admiral motioned for me to sit down. I was confused and extremely uneasy about what this was all about. "What had I done?" I hadn't been in the Agency long enough to screw up, I thought, and General Shedd hadn't mentioned anything to me. The admiral was distracted for a long moment, glancing over a paper on his desk.

He looked up finally, smiled, and said, "This place is crazy! Washington, DC, and all this damned paper!" Then he looked directly at me and said, "Chris, it's good to have you here in the headquarters. Your name kept popping up from out at Sandia from time to time, and it already has since you arrived." I couldn't imagine what was going on and became pensive as all get out! "I want you to be my executive officer," he said abruptly. "I have already advised General Shedd, and he is in full agreement. How do you feel about it?" I was more than shocked, I was stunned with my head swimming. "Well?" he smirked abruptly.

I quickly replied, "Sir, I will be pleased to do whatever you wish me to do. I am deeply honored."

"Good," he replied. "Tell Captain Duran that you are coming upstairs as my exec officer and as his deputy chief of staff. The secretaries will set you up outside and provide whatever you need. Welcome aboard." He stood up, held out his hand across the desk, and shook mine. "We'll discuss details after you get moved in."

That was it. I departed, nodded to the two wide-eyed secretaries, who were obviously curious to learn the outcome. I nodded to them, walked across to Captain Duran's office; his door was open and rapped on the facing. He was sitting behind his desk, obviously anticipating my arrival. He welcomed me to the new position, shook my hand, and offered his support in any way. "Stub," as he was called,

a short and slight built submariner; he and I became lasting friends during my assignment there and years beyond. That was a whirlwind shocker of the day, and from there, it became a roller coaster ride.

I learned quickly that the admiral was predictably unpredictable. The previous note that he was a student and advocate of Admiral Nimitz's demeanor and manner was, as several told me, factual: no nonsense and quick to react. Once in place, I also learned that my "predecessor," also an Air Force lieutenant colonel, was suddenly transferred. This was as much of a surprise to him as others in the staff. With support from his primary secretary, I began to learn how the admiral operated. He was abrupt in his exchanges, expressing disapproval of people, no matter their position or political status. I'll not delve into any particular details regarding his real demeanor, but I did witness more than several reactionary events. As mentioned earlier, his large mahogany desk was continuously cluttered with paper, which drove his secretary crazy and me as well. I marveled at how he would receive a letter or document that he had authored, typed, and was ready for his signature, which he would then spend hours rewriting between the typewritten lines, not once, but perhaps several times. Suspense responses to other agencies and congress meant very little to him—we were the "worry warts" and managed the persistent queries from all directions. I take pride in the fact that I was able to work well with the admiral and worked around outside issues. He was likewise exceptionally pleasant with me and, more often than not, invited me to sit in his office during meetings with high-level military and government officials.

A notable event occurred when the admiral summoned me into this office one morning and advised that "we" were going to change the name of the Defense Atomic Support Agency. He told me that he had discussed his idea with the chairman, Joint Chiefs of Staff, and they approved the name change to Defense Nuclear Agency (DNA). Then he told me to "Go make it happen." It was an arduous bureaucratic coordination challenge that took about six months. I won't go into the details, but both outside and within the Agency, it was a learning experience! I had been working for the admiral for little more than a year when one day, while he was swimming in the Pentagon, a frequent lunchtime habit, another swimmer collided headfirst with him, causing him to lose an eye. He was quickly medically retired thereafter. This was a very sad consequence to the career of a true professional senior officer. His retirement, however, did not deter him for very long; once he recovered from the healing of his eye injury, he was elected president, National Rifle Association. He passed away at age eighty-seven in January 1999.

Lt. General Carroll H. Dunn, USA (Ret)

General Dunn was promptly assigned as the director, DNA, replacing Admiral Mustin following his accident and retirement from active duty. General Dunn had begun his thirty-five-year Army Engineering career in 1938, which took him from a second lieutenant through lieutenant general, U. S. Army. His career included a battalion commander at age twenty-six with eleven months combat in World War II. He served in the 30th Infantry Division as division engineer and battalion commander, 105th engineer Combat Battalion. His unit deployed to England in June 1944, where he participated in the invasion of Omaha Beach. He was wounded by a German mine in the attack on Saint Lo and sent back to England to recuperate for two months then back to his unit for the final push in the defeat of Germany. A highly distinguished engineer, following the war, General Dunn supervised construction of numerous projects: the National Aeronautics and Space Administration (NASA) Manned Spacecraft Center at Houston, the Arkansas River Navigation and Flood Control Project, and the Titan II Missile Base construction and the Ballistic Missile Early Warning System for the Air Force. He served as director of construction and logistics for the Military Assistance Command in Vietnam and deputy chief of the Army Corps of Engineers before becoming director of the Defense Nuclear Agency.

General Dunn arrived at DNA headquarters and promptly introduced himself around those of us in his new office. He was exceptionally polite and forthcoming, greeting each one of us with

a warm handshake, asking our names, our position and brief background. Working for him became a special pleasure and far removed from the operating manner of Admiral Mustin. He was an engineer all the way. He was precise in every detail regarding the Agency's operations. His first instruction to me was to always deliver letters, documents, and so forth to him ready for signature. I was to ensure they were properly completed before he received them. That procedure alone brought considerable relief for the entire Agency staff; it also placed the burden of responsibility on all of us to ensure accuracy and final completion. It was an incredible learning experience for everyone. He brought his own aide with him, a young Army major, Tom Kelly, who also eased smoothly into the office operation. Tom and I became good friends and working partners in supporting the general. In his first year, General Dunn desired to learn all about the Agency, nuclear weapon responsibilities, etc. I was pleased and honored to accompany the general and Tom Kelly, first to Europe and U.S. weapons facilities in the UK, Spain, and Italy. It was a great learning experience for me!

The next trip was an experience of a lifetime. The Air Force chose to use a retired Air Force One, the VC-118A Liftmaster, which was used initially to support the president of the United States. It was still fully outfitted with elaborate sleeping quarters, dining facility, and all the conveniences. President Kennedy's specially constructed orthopedic chair was still in its fixed position near a window where he could sit comfortably and look out on the world. Of course, we all took our turns checking it out during our journey to the Far East, Japan, Korea, and Guam on return. The plane is presently on display at the Pima Air & Space Museum adjacent to Davis-Monthan AFB near Tucson, Arizona.

About a year after General Dunn arrived, I received some great news from the Air Force that I was to be promoted to full colonel! General Dunn arranged a very formal "pinning on" ceremony, inviting all within the headquarters to come to the seventh floor for the event. I continued on as his exec officer for a period, and then he informed me that he was reassigning me to become the Director, Plans and Policy, heading up the office from where I first began my assignment. I commented to him that several of the officers in that directorate outranked me. He smiled and said, "That was before you got promoted; you are now the senior officer in there." I moved back to the fifth floor and assumed my new position back with my previous office Air Force, Army, and Navy office mates. They welcomed me "home," and we resumed our working relationships. Earlier, General Shedd received orders to depart for a new assignment in Germany.

General Shedd was replaced by Major General Warren D. Johnson, USAF, the previous Chief of Staff, Strategic Air Command (SAC). I had no idea that my own career path was also about to change as well. Shortly after General Johnson arrived, he began to call in each directorate head to brief him on their respective office functions and responsibilities within DNA. When it became my turn, I was considerably surprised by his introductory questions to me. "What are you doing here in this agency anyway? With your background in SAC and newly promoted, you need to be back in the field." He continued on to tell me that he had reviewed my assignment records and strongly suggested that I return to "your parent command, SAC."

I told him that I would like that very much, since I had been in DASA/DNA for almost five years, but I also had been treated very well with two promotions. (To be continued.)

I was invited on another occasion to accompany General Dunn and Tom Kelly on a facility inspection journey, this time to Europe. We flew to Germany via a PanAm, first class, dining room service aboard the mega 747 airliner along with full-size sleeping bunks. After visiting military units in Germany, we traveled on to Vicenza, Italy, and the U.S. Army facilities there. The armored battalion commander invited us to take a staff car trip to visit Venice where he also arranged for a tour of the Venice canals via the U.S. ambassador's private boat. The boat tour was special in itself, but that evening, the colonel escorted the three of us along with another colonel and their wives to the Riviera Restaurant in Venice. I have shared this story many times about the ambiance and fanfare at this restaurant adventure. The wait staff seated the seven of us around a huge round table, already set with china, silver, and linen napkins, but the most noticeable feature was forty-nine wine glasses: seven at each place setting. The glasses were graduated in size from the smallest, less than half an ounce, to mega goblets. My first thought was, "Are we going to be served 'something' in each of those glasses?" Long and wonderful evening story, short, they actually served a touch of a different wine in each glass before the elegant dinner evening was over. The good news was for all, that the wine samples accompanied each course of the dinner servings, and no one over-imbibed. They added to perhaps the most elegant dinner event I ever attended. Another indelible memory!

General Dunn continued on as director DNA for another year before retiring and beginning a second career in 1973. General Johnson was promoted to lieutenant general and succeeded General Dunn as director. General Dunn returned to his engineering-favored engineering world, serving as senior vice president for construction, engineering, and environmental affairs for Consolidated Edison Company of New York. He was responsible for upgrading and expanding power generation and high voltage transmission for the New York City metropolitan area. Among General Dunn's awards were the Silver Star and the Purple Heart. He also received the Chief of Engineers Award for Outstanding Public Service for contributions to the Army and the nation as an engineer officer and civilian. For service as a member, and later as Chairman of the NASA Safety Advisory Board, he received the NASA Public Service Award. Until his death in 2003, General Dunn was a fellow in both the American Society of Civil Engineers and the Society of Military Engineers. He was a published author and member of the National Academy of Engineers, the National Academy of Construction, a fellow of the American Society of Civil Engineers, and the Society of American Military Engineers.

Lt. General Warren D. Johnson, USAF (Ret)

I will continue here with my preceding introduction of General Johnson. He was a giant of a man: tall, heavyset, and completely bald with intense gazing eyes. From the time you met him, he had your attention. "He was not a high-maintenance general," said retired Lt.

Col. Jay Tutterow, a longtime friend. "He didn't give orders. He led people using respect and charm. You had to screw up more than once to get in his doghouse."

I fully concurred with Colonel Tutterow's appraisal. General Johnson had enlisted in the Army as a private in 1942, shortly after World War II began. Even though he had only a high school GED diploma, he was selected for officer candidate school, then flight training and spent the 1940s and '50s advancing through the ranks. He served in personnel, logistics and squadron command roles while continuing to fly bombers, including the B-29, B-47, and the Mighty B-36. He loved to fly and allegedly flew a B-47 under the Mackinac Bridge in Michigan, according to his daughter, who said he told his copilot and radar operator to "Close your eyes because I don't want to get you in trouble for what I am about to do." I will leave that to the history books.

As I commented previously, General Johnson captured my attention immediately when I went into his office the first time. He immediately stood up from behind his desk, held out his large hand, and grasped mine. "Hello, Chris." He greeted me with a smile. "Have a seat and tell me what you do here."

Before I could respond, as mentioned earlier, he interrupted my response and asked why I was there in DNA in the first place. I responded with a brief synopsis of my SAC B-36 and B-52 flying days, Korat Air Base and JTF-8 Sandia, thence to DNA. We continued with a friendly chat and finally got around to describing what my division responsibilities were in DNA. I noticed that he was holding a large paper pad while I was talking and appeared to be drawing or sketching, not taking notes. I was later to learn that he was a very accomplished pencil artist drawing mostly patterns and odd forms. I still have several that he later shared with me.

As I departed his office, he smiled and said, "We need to work on your future." That left me wondering, but not for long. A couple of weeks later I received a call from Air Force Personnel advising that I was being reassigned to the 351st Strategic Missile Wing (SMW), Whiteman AFB, Missouri, as Director of Operations. I was very pleased with the notice; it would be good to get out of the Washington environment! When I went to advise General Johnson, he smiled, stood, and congratulated me, as if he wasn't already aware! He told me that he had a brief chat with General Bob Scott, Strategic Air Command Deputy Chief of Staff, Personnel and that everything fell into place. I commented that I knew General Scott from my days at Ramey Air Force Base. He smiled, knowingly.

I will proceed herein to continue the next quick in succession actions in my Air Force career. I reported to the 351st SMW as the wing DO, six weeks later, I received a call from 15th Air Force personnel advising me that I was being reassigned to the 90th SMW, F.E. Warren AFB, Cheyenne, Wyoming, as Vice Wing Commander—my "mentors," Generals Johnson and Scott, still at work! Fast forward to conclude this segment and get back to the principle theme. After a year as wing vice commander, I assumed the position as wing commander. The following year I was promoted to brigadier general.

The first congratulatory call I received was from General Warren D. Johnson! "Well, I kicked your fanny through the door and you did the rest," he chuckled over the phone. "Now get to work!"

General Johnson succeeded General Dunn as director, DNA, receiving his third star. He retired from the Air Force in 1977, joining Baxter International as a corporate officer. His activities were varied ranging from facility planning, telecommunications, and aviation to Baxter's operations in South Africa, finally recommending divestment of the company's interest in that country. He chaired Baxter's Crisis Management Team before retiring in 1990. We continued to keep in touch via a couple of visits, e-mail, and an occasional phone chat until he became ill, passing away on January 23, 2007, leaving behind a special legacy, wonderful personal contributions to his family, and many grateful personal memories for yours truly.

General Russell E. Dougherty, USAF (Ret)

General Russell Dougherty became commander in chief, Strategic Air Command (SAC) in 1974, the same year that I assumed command of the 90th Strategic Missile Wing at F.E. Warren AFB, Cheyenne, Wyoming. I was privileged to meet him at the annual commander's conference that same year. He was perhaps the most informal and genuinely comfortable general officer I had ever seen or met. General Dougherty greeted each of us with a welcome smile, warm handshake, and cordial words of welcome. It was at that first commander's conference that he surprised all of us in attendance with the introduction of his WWII B-29 navigator, Tennessee Ernie Ford! A special treat to remember, as Tennessee Ernie sang several songs accompanied by the Strategic Air Command band. What an evening! It is virtually impossible to capture all of the incredible attributes and accomplishments of General Russell Dougherty! I will attempt to highlight the many dimensions of his magnificent career and his impact on my own.

General Dougherty graduated from Western Kentucky University and the University of Louisville Law School. After serving with the FBI and the Kentucky National Guard, he entered active military service as an aviation cadet at the outbreak of World War II. During the war, he served as an instructor pilot and later as a B-17 and B-29 combat crew. He served in the Far East Air Forces, flying with the 19th Bombardment Wing, concurrently serving as the staff judge advocate for the wing onward as assistant JAG for the Twentieth. After the war, he served as the assistant JAG for FEAF in Japan; returning to the United States, he was assigned to Air Materiel Command as chief of the Appeals Litigation Division.

In December 1952, General Dougherty elected to leave the JAG Department and take an assignment with Strategic Air Command. He took refresher training in both the B-29 and KC-97. Recognized as a future commander-to-be, he began successive assignments as operations in the 303rd Air Refueling Squadron, commander of the 303d Armament and Electronics Squadron, deputy chief of operations, 303rd Bombardment Wing, and commander 358th Bomb Squadron, all at Davis-Monthan AFB, Arizona. He later became deputy director of operations at headquarters, Fifteenth Air Force, March AFB, California.

Following his graduation from the National War College in 1960, General Dougherty was assigned to the deputy director for war plans in headquarters, USAF, where he helped develop Air

Force positions on matters under consideration by the Joint Chiefs of Staff. In April 1961, he was appointed deputy assistant director of plans for joint matters, and in February 1963, became assistant director of plans for Joint and National Security Council Matters. In 1964–1965, he was the deputy director for plans and operations (J-3), headquarters, U.S. Command in Paris. During that time, General Dougherty was the American planner for the successful U.S.-Belgian rescue operation at Stanleyville in the Congo. In August 1965, he returned to Washington as director, European Region, International Security Affairs, in the Office of the Secretary of Defense. In July 1967, he returned to Europe once more and served as director of plans and policy (J-5), at headquarters U.S. European Command.

In September 1969, General Dougherty served as assistant deputy chief of plans and operations in Headquarters USAF; he was promoted to lieutenant general and named deputy in February 1970. Then, in April 1971, he was named commander of the Second Air Force (SAC), at Barksdale AFB, Louisiana. It was the Air Force's largest numbered air force, consisting of the majority of SAC's B-52 bombers and KC-135 tankers.

On May 1 1972, General Dougherty was promoted to four-star general and chief of staff, Supreme Headquarters Allied Powers Europe (SHAPE). On August 1, 1974, he was appointed commander in chief, Strategic Air Command, becoming a legend within SAC and the Air Force. The enduring legacy of General Dougherty was his "officership, leadership, and gentleman-ship." He possessed the brilliance and skill to lead, guide, and direct with a touch of a genius of his familiar clichés: "It doesn't take a bull whip to get a horse to move; a few gentle words of encouragement will usually do."

Pleasant experiences become indelible memories and of which I had the special pleasure of several such with General Dougherty. I was on temporary duty at SAC Headquarters once to fly my turn on the airborne command post, Looking Glass. It was late one evening, and General Dougherty called me into his office to discuss an issue paper; he wanted my views and ideas. The meeting was typically cordial as all were with him. It was around midnight when we finished the discussion; he thanked me, and I started to depart his office when he called my name, "Chris."

I turned and responded, "Yes, Sir?"

He grinned and said, "Ain't it fun?" An evening never to forget!

On the day before Thanksgiving in 1975, I had just walked into my home at lunchtime, when my handy-talky phone rang. I answered, and the voice on the other end, greeted, "Chris, Russ Dougherty, am I interrupting your lunch?"

"No, sir!" I quickly blurted!

He continued, "How would you like to move to Tucson and take command of the 12th Air Division at Davis-Monthan?" I was thunderstruck; goose bumps ran all up and down me. That meant a promotion to brigadier general!

I regained my composure and replied, "Sir, whatever you want me to do."

"Good," he replied. "Make arrangements to be out there on this Friday for a change of command. And, congratulations!"

His thoughtfulness was unmatched. Upon my promotion, the local newspaper displayed a photograph of my young son, Christopher, and the wording, "Son is 'generally' proud of his dad." The news release found its way to General Dougherty who promptly wrote him a letter with a five-dollar bill and a note that read, "Your dad's promotion means an automatic allowance increase for you, so show him this five-dollar bill to get you started."

General Dougherty was considered an air power visionary; following his retirement from active duty, he served on various government and commercial defense-related boards and commissions. He was the executive director of the Air Force Association. The Air Force Association Board Chairman, Bob Largent, said, "General Dougherty was an incomparable leader, a true icon for the United States Air Force and the Air Force Association. Always displaying an infectious smile and ready with a quick story to illustrate a cogent point, Russ Dougherty made a significant impact upon everyone with whom he came into contact. He served our nation with great honor, and we will continue to benefit from his leadership and his wisdom for an eternity."

Later in my post-Air Force career while serving as an associate director, Los Alamos National Laboratory, I decided that the requirement for a senior executive board to convene periodically was necessary to address critical military and national defense issues that faced our nation during the Cold War. I formed and chartered such a board of notable leaders and scholars, to which General Dougherty graciously accepted an appointment. Once again, I was able to witness the cordial and intellectual genius of this truly great man whom I was blessed to encounter within my lifetime.

My lasting memory of this extraordinary leader among many occurred at the Strategic Air Command-2000 Reunion and the commemoration of that historic Cold War military command. The hosts of SAC-2000 invited me to present a book report at the event of my first publication at the time, *Inside the Cold War: A Cold Warrior's Reflections*. I agreed, and when the time came on that day's agenda, I was overwhelmed with the audience that assembled in the Hilton Hotel Ballroom. Moreover, I was taken by surprise with the dignitaries who showed up! On the front row sat General David Jones, retired Chairman of the Joint Chiefs of Staff, General Dougherty, General Dick Lawson, General Jack Chain, and General Lee Butler. When my turn came up on the agenda, I was more than surprised, shocked, when General Dougherty rose from his seat and walked up on the stage to the podium! He began and gave the most gracious and humbling introduction of yours truly, which literally brought me to my knees. When he finished his remarks, I walked nimble-legged up to the stage where he grasped my hand and pulled me to him, whispering, "God love ya', Chris," and a bear hug that I remember to this day as I scribe these notes. I hardly remember anything of the remainder of that day's event except looking down at the five four-star Air Force generals sitting on the front row, looking up at me—along with 1,500 former SAC warriors and friends in the audience. Memories!

We lost a singularly great leader in General Russell E. Dougherty with his passing at age eighty-seven in 2007.

General Richard H. Ellis, USAF (Ret)

General Ellis succeeded General Dougherty as commander in chief, Strategic Air Command and director of the Joint Strategic Target Planning Staff (JSTPS). Shortly after he assumed command, I was notified that I was being reassigned from commander, 12th Air Division to SAC Headquarters as deputy chief staff for operations. I found General Ellis to be quite the opposite and of a much different personality than his predecessor. His manner was stolid, but cordial and short on conversation. He greeted me pleasantly, welcomed me to the headquarters, and I saw very little of him after that first introduction. There was one early interaction, when I suddenly looked up from my desk one morning, and General Ellis was standing in the door of my office. "What are you doing in this cubby hole?" he asked. "I thought this room was a safe down here?"

I stood up and responded, "Sir, General Watkins assigned this room to me as my office; he elected to not share the DOs with me as his deputy." General Ellis shook his head, shrugged his shoulders and departed. In all the previous years, the DCS, Operations, and his deputy shared the same office. Jack Watkins, the present DO, decided that he wanted to singularly occupy the spacious office as his own. Memories. After all, a young brigadier general among a dozen or more in the building made little difference or caught much attention unless you goofed up! I served in deputy position for less than a year when one day I received a call to report to the CINC's office. Jim Enney, a fellow brigadier, arrived there with me. General Ellis was behind his desk when the secretary ushered us in. He stood, with a sober smile and simply said, "Congratulations, gentlemen, you have been promoted to major general." He walked around and shook our hands and that was it. Of course, within Jim Enney and myself, there was considerable jubilation; we just didn't display it until we were out of his office!

General Ellis, as did his predecessors, in addition to serving as CINCSAC, also served as the director of the Joint Strategic Target Planning Staff (JSTPS) and the Joint Strategic Capabilities Staff (JSCS). The JSTPS coordinated the United States nuclear war

plans and developed the nation's Single Integrated Operational Plan (SIOP) while the JSCS analyzed strategic connectivity systems and procedures and ensured the compatibility and commonality of the strategic command, control, and communications systems. His deputy director for the two additional responsibilities was a Navy vice admiral. It was shortly after my promotion to major general that General Ellis appointed me Deputy Chief of Staff Operations Plans/ Deputy Associate Director, JSTPS, which meant that I would then report jointly to him and the associate director, JSTPS, the Admiral, who was at the time, Vice Admiral Kenneth Carr.

General Ellis, as was General Dougherty, was a unique Air Force officer. He held a bachelor of arts degree in history from Dickinson College and juris doctorate degree from Dickinson School of Law. Later in his career, he was awarded an honorary doctor of science degree from Dickinson College, and honorary doctor of laws degrees from Dickinson School of Law, the University of Akron (Ohio) and from the University of Nebraska, Omaha.

During World War II, General Ellis served with the 3rd Bombardment Group in Australia, New Guinea, and the Philippines, and flew more than two hundred combat missions in the Pacific area. He served as a pilot, squadron commander, group operations officer, group commander, and deputy chief of staff, Far East Air Forces, in the Philippine Islands and Japan. After the war, he practiced law until he was recalled to active duty in 1950, serving in numerous senior operations positions.

In 1961, General Ellis became executive to the chief of staff, U.S. Air Force, General Curtis LeMay. From time to time, he shared many stories about his experiences working for LeMay. He was an extraordinary officer and commander, having been appointed an incredible number of senior command positions throughout the Air Force in Europe and the United States prior to becoming commander in chief, Strategic Air Command.

Having never served in SAC prior to his appointment, General Ellis was eager to learn all about the command, both in the United States and overseas. In doing so, he began traveling extensively, taking members of the SAC staff with him. Traveling with him aboard the

CINC's VC-135 (converted Boeing 707) was a unique experience. Located at the rear of the aircraft were private quarters for the CINC. The next section forward on the left side of the cabin was configured with two wide seats facing forward separated by a table and two seats facing aft. The CINC always occupied the seat facing forward and his wife, who always accompanied him, occupied the seat across the table facing to the rear of the aircraft. Across the aisle from the CINC's seating were two seats facing forward and two facing the rear of the aircraft with a table in between. The chief of staff, SAC, was assigned the seat across from the CINC and facing forward. The configuration permitted the chief of staff to be nearby to the CINC to discuss anything that might come up during a flight. Across from the chief of staff's seat and the table, the two seats facing to the rear were occupied by the next two ranking staff officers. I was privileged to always sit in one of the two seats, which was not always the desired place to be, in the direct line of sight of potential question from the CINC!

As mentioned, General Ellis's wife virtually always accompanied him on the journeys, especially those overseas. Affectionately, "Peg" Ellis was someone to know and remember! She always arrived at the aircraft upon departure from our home base of Offutt AFB, wearing her own personally designed "flight suit." The flight suit was of lightweight material, powder blue in color with four "red hearts" on the epaulets (designating her "four stars"). Peg was something to behold and remember! Those of us traveling with the CINC on a trip arrived and boarded the aircraft first. The CINC came aboard and nodded as he strolled down the aisle to his seat. Peg came aboard and headed for the jump seat behind the pilots for takeoff. She usually remained awhile, chatting with the pilots and then entered the main cabin stopping along the way to visit with various staff members. She then came back into the rear area of the plane, assertively so, stopping for conversation with one or more of us and on into the private quarters where she soon returned. She was either in casual dress for a long journey or in a fashionable outfit for the soon-to-be stop ahead. The more experienced travelers with the CINC had a private joke among us; when we expected her arrival down the aisle, we always appear to be absorbed in a newspaper held up in front of us. Having Peg Ellis on board was always a learning experience as well, especially for those of us across the aisle from her seat, as she was not immune to sharing her observations or opinions with her husband about individuals or places we had just visited. On occasion he would noticeably signal her to shush her comments. Memories . . . Traveling with General Ellis, especially overseas, was always a special experience.

Serving General Ellis otherwise also provided for occasional unexpected events. Once while attending an evening social event, I happened to encounter him at the snack table when he casually said, "Chris, come by my office in the morning, I have something I'd like to discuss with you."

I replied, "Yes, sir, I'm scheduled to depart on leave early tomorrow, but—"

He casually interrupted, "That's okay, come on by," and strolled away. I changed our departure leave plans, put on my uniform, and was in his outer office before he arrived the next morning. By the end of the day, leave plans were on hold to address and coordinate the issue he had mentioned.

Once I happened to be accompanying General Ellis down a corridor to a meeting when he slowed his pace, turned, and said, "Chris, I would like to establish a bilateral working relationship with the French Department of Defense to discuss our mutual nuclear ICBM operations."

As I was absorbing his statement and about to respond, he made an abrupt turn into an office along the corridor. I stood outside in the hallway for a moment, my thoughts about his comment whirling around and then proceeded onto the meeting. I had learned over time that once he made a statement or request, it was not wise to reengage the subject with him. I returned to my office and began to contemplate the challenge! I was aware that France had dropped out of NATO in 1966 and while also a Cold War foe of the Soviet Union, they operated militarily separately in their defense planning and strategies. They had also developed their own strategic nuclear missiles, but there was no coordination with the United States or its allies. So, my question was, "Where do I begin with his stated objective?"

Finally, my internal system turned on, and I called an old friend of mine from flying days, Brigadier General Walter Ratliff, whom I knew was stationed in the Pentagon. I told Walt about the CINC's statement. We noodled our thoughts back and forth for a while, and he then suggested that he would call the French embassy there in Washington and try to engage the military attaché. He did, and a few days later I flew to Washington. Walt had invited the French attaché, a sharp-looking colonel in the French Air Force, and who by coincidence had also attended flight training with the U.S. Air Force in the United States. We hit it off well and began to develop a strategy to initiate discussions on the issue of French-U.S. nuclear weapons planning and coordination. From there, things moved faster than I could have ever guessed they would. Within two months, we had arranged for the then acting French Minister of Defense (MOD), Joel Le Theule, to fly to Washington and then onward to Omaha, Nebraska, and SAC Headquarters. Everything would be carried out very low key, including the Minister of Defense flying to Omaha with only the attaché as his escort and no fanfare. The meeting was to be between General Ellis and the French MOD to discuss whatever they might. An interesting side note was that this event occurred in November 1980, only a few days after Ronald Reagan had been elected president. During an informal reception for MOD after his arrival, the attaché commented to me that the MOD was impressed with all of the apparent joy and frivolity among the Air Force members present. I told him, jokingly, that this was a dual celebration— the French MOD's visit and that Ronald Reagan was to be our new president. Carter was out! He told me later that the MOD was *very* disappointed with the election results! Positive results accrued after the visit and several doors of cooperation were opened between our two military services, including interactive visits between our own SAC missile personnel and the French. Mission accomplished and good memories. France, however, was not to join NATO again until 2009.

General Ellis's achievements were superior among many: a command pilot, awarded the Master Missile and the Parachutist badges. His awards and decorations included the Distinguished Service

Cross, Distinguished Service Medal with three oak leaf clusters, Silver Star, Legion of Merit with two oak leaf clusters, Distinguished Flying Cross, Air Medal with four oak leaf clusters, Purple Heart, and Grand Officer of the Italian Republic. He was awarded the State of Delaware Distinguished Service Medal by Governor Bacon in 1946. In September 1980 he was presented the Air Force Association's highest honor, the H.H. Arnold Award for significant contributions to national defense. As the recipient of this award, General Ellis was also named as the association's National Aerospace Man of the Year. He also received the Korean Order of National Security Merit First Class (Tong Il Jang) on May 13, 1981, at the Korean Ministry of National Defense in Seoul. This award was the highest honor given by the Republic of Korea to a foreign military leader. This pillar of a great leader passed away in 1989 at the premature age of 69.

General Bennie L. Davis, USAF (Ret)

A native American, born in Oklahoma, General Davis assumed command of SAC upon the retirement of General Ellis in July 1981. He was also my last Air Force senior leader. He played football for four years under Coach Earl Blaik at West Point and the great Army teams for the late '40s. Following graduation, he attended pilot training at Vance Air Force Base, Oklahoma, earning his pilot wings in August 1951. He completed B-29 Superfortress combat crew training in October 1953, and reported to Okinawa as a B-29 aircraft commander with the 307th and later the 19th Bombardment Wing. He returned to the United States with the 19th Bombardment Wing in June 1954, and served as a B-47 Stratojet aircraft commander and instructor pilot at Pinecastle Air Force Base, Florida. Onward to B-52 combat crew training in 1961, he become a B-52H instructor pilot with the 93rd Bombardment Squadronat Kincheloe Air Force Base, Michigan. He was a graduate of the Armed Forces Staff College and the National War College where he also earned a Master of Science degree.

General Davis flew the B-57 tactical bomber during Vietnam, completing 142 missions. In August 1968, he was assigned to the

Organization of the Joint Chiefs of Staff in the Pentagon as an operations officer and later as chief of the Current Operations Branch, Strategic Operations Division. In August 1970, he was assigned as the Air Force member of the Chairman's Staff Group, Office of the Chairman of the Joint Chiefs of Staff. In 1969, he attended the advanced management program at the Harvard School of Business.

Continuing his highly varied and successful career at Randolph Air Force Base, Texas, in 1972, General Davis served as vice commander of the Air Force Military Personnel Center and later commander of the Air Force Recruiting Service and Deputy Chief of Staff, Air Training Command. In July 1975, he was assigned as director, Personnel Plans, Headquarters U.S. Air Force. Promoted to general in 1979, he became commander of Air Training Command at Randolph Air Force Base. He assumed command of SAC in August 1981.

It became apparent early on that General Davis was not personable in the manner of his predecessors; he was direct and quick to the point in discussions, and it was not unusual for him to abruptly walk away or leave the room with a subject still open. He appeared to be frequently preoccupied or bored during briefings or discussion sessions. My personal experience began late one night while I was flying aboard Looking Glass, the SAC Airborne Command Post. Looking Glass was required to have a general officer on board on every mission, each flight of which was scheduled for approximately nine hours, or until relieved by the succeeding Looking Glass aircraft when it became airborne.

The well-known SAC Red Phone on my console startled me, and I promptly answered. "Chris, General Davis," his abrupt voice sounded tired, "come to my office first thing in the morning. You are going to be the Chief of Staff."

I was shocked and promptly responded, "What happened to Andy Pringle?"

He replied sharply, "He's no longer the chief of staff; you are. See you in the morning." Click, he hung up.

"Yes, sir," I replied to the dead phone, leaning back in my seat with my thoughts circling overhead. I was well aware that trouble was brewing over a breach of security incident issue within the command, but I'll not delve into that side story. I had engaged General Davis only a few times since he had become CINCSAC and each of those were fairly routine, except one! On that occasion, the present chief of staff and two other senior SAC officers had called a meeting with General Davis in an attempt to dismiss a war planning project that I had initiated. That's another long side story.

During the called meeting, it became apparent that the general was not at all interested nor inclined to cancel the program project that I had previously briefed to him and received approval to proceed. As the first briefer got up to speak, General Davis abruptly dismissed the meeting, inviting the chief of staff to his office. That was the end of that discussion.

The abrupt change and elevation in my job assignment came about smoothly after the initial shock. I was able to adjust to the new position and responsibilities and got along reasonably well with General Davis, adjusting, of course, to his operating manner, etc. I had served as his chief of staff for little over a year, when I decided quite suddenly to retire from the Air Force to accept an "out of the blue" appointment offer to become an associate director, Los Alamos National Laboratory. I took him by complete surprise when I went in to tell him of my decision. It was not a pleasant meeting. He was one that did not like surprises unless they were at his calling.

Anytime a senior staff positioned officer departed, it meant the staff dominoes would have to fall and be readjusted to replace the departing individual—me. He was visibly and verbally upset, and among his sharp remarks commented that there were "bigger things in the making" for me and that I would be giving them up. There was no explanation and I didn't pursue his statement, nor did he elaborate. I left the teasing remark hanging. In the end, it was an honor to have served in such a prestigious position as chief of staff, Strategic Air Command, but I had made a decision to move on. As always there are many anecdotal experiences and tales to reflect, but suffice to say, it was a distinct honor to have been chosen by General Davis to serve in that position. Memories. General Davis passed away suddenly at age eighty-four in 2011.

General Curtis E. LeMay, USAF (Ret)

I was privileged to meet the legendary General Curtis LeMay on two occasions during my tour of duty, and his visits to Offutt Air Force Base and SAC Headquarters. In spite of his reputation, he was always cordial with a warm handshake and looked you right in the eyes, as if to see if he recognized you. General Ellis, his protégé from earlier years, would invite him back to the headquarters to recall their former years and to keep the general informed of ongoing events. Without a doubt, General LeMay was the most controversial senior leader in Air Force history. He was also heralded as the most perceptive and creative leader in the Air Force; the architect of strategic air power, he advocated that the United States must be willing to use nuclear weapons if and when necessary. General LeMay had directed the massive B-29 air assaults over Japan in the final days of World War II and was the commander in the Pacific in charge of the missions that dropped the atomic bombs on Hiroshima and Nagasaki.

Years after relaying the orders from President Harry S. Truman to drop bombs on Japan, General LeMay said the actions were not necessary. "We felt that our incendiary bombings had been so successful that Japan would collapse before we invaded," he said in a 1985 interview with the *Omaha World-Herald*. "We went ahead and dropped the bombs because President Truman told me to do it. He told me in a personal letter."

After World War II, General LeMay commanded the Berlin airlift and quoted at the outset of his assignment, "I want to see all my key staff officers at least once a week," he said in his first staff meeting in Germany in 1947 while he was heading the Berlin Airlift. "Don't bother to knock, just walk in. If I'm busy, I'll tell you to get out. I want men of action in my organization who can make their own decisions." Then he added, "If you make an occasional wrong one, I'll back you up."

General LeMay became commander in chief of Strategic Air Command in 1948 and remained until 1961, convincing the Department of Defense that SAC should become the dominant nuclear bomber force and became instrumental in the acquisition

of the largest fleet of new strategic bombers along with a supporting aerial refueling operation. He also initiated the development of a strategic ballistic missile force and established an unprecedented command and control system and readiness response capability for all SAC forces. With the Cold War threat increasing in intensity, he initiated the twenty-four-hour alert force program for bomber and tanker combat crews, which meant that crew members would be housed in alert facilities near their aircraft and prepared to respond at any time. Alert crew duty would last from three to seven days depending on base locations. This author can attest to having served on B-36 and B-52 bomber alert force tours from its beginning in 1957 until 1963, and then on twenty-four-hour missile combat crew alert from duty 1963 to 1966.

General LeMay instituted an Air Force survival school program that was located in the mountains near Colorado Springs; the purpose was to train aircrew members with the skills and will to escape and evade if they were to be shot down behind enemy lines. The story is told that on one bitterly cold night as some bomber crew members were huddling in their tents cobbled together out of parachutes, one of the guys began to shout out loudly, "Who thought up this frigging deal anyway?" Out of the flaps of another improvised tent emerged the unmistakable cigar and the four stars of the commanding general, Curtis LeMay. Likely that concluded the evening!

I can also give testimony to survival school, having attended the three-week training and outing in the cool Colorado mountains and again in the Philippines en route to Vietnam. The latter experience resulted in a short fall off a cliff, dislocation of a knee cap, and helicopter retrieval from the jungle. I was tempted to ask, "Who thought up this frigging deal anyway?" for whatever good it might have done!

Those of us who served in Strategic Air Command, especially during the General LeMay years, can attest to his absolute requirement for rigorous training and the highest standards of performance. This applied to *all* SAC personnel, officers, enlisted men, aircrews, mechanics, and administrative staff. "I have neither the time nor the inclination to differentiate between the incompetent and the merely unfortunate," he was frequently quoted.

Following SAC, General LeMay served as Vice Chief and Chief of Staff, U.S. Air Force under Presidents Kennedy and Johnson from 1961 to 1965. He convinced President Kennedy to initiate airborne nuclear bomber flights around the world during the Cuban Crisis, which convinced Khrushchev to retreat from the island and cease the development of missile facilities. He was hawkish on the Vietnam War and an outspoken advocate of manned air power based on a willingness to use nuclear weapons. In his book, *Mission with LeMay*, published by Doubleday in 1965, he wrote of the North Vietnamese, "My solution to the problem would be to tell them frankly that they've got to draw in their horns and stop their aggression or we're going to bomb them back into the Stone Ages." Where is Curtis LeMay today with regard to North Korea? And, one might ask, "Who's listening?"

General LeMay retired from the Air Force in 1965 and entered politics briefly in 1968 as the running mate of George C. Wallace with the former Alabama Governor's unsuccessful campaign for the presidency. When Wallace introduced him as his running mate on the American Independent Party ticket, General LeMay called for use of any available means, including nuclear weapons, to end the Vietnam Conflict. Later, he visited South Vietnam on a fact-finding mission and called for renewed bombing of North Vietnam, especially the harbor at Haiphong. Nicknamed the "Iron Eagle," LeMay was avid anti-Communism and held strong conservative views. "I don't believe there are good Communists and bad Communists," he was quoted, "I just think they are Communists and they all have the same basic principles involved, which I think are basically wrong."

He was known to be tough and an outdoors type, more often than not, appearing gruff, dominating, implacable, and unduly blunt, to summarize the opinion of many. One story that circulated about him was that when a group of colonels invited him to dinner, he replied with a scowl, "A man should have dinner with his friends, and the commanding general has no friends."

I will close this memorable pleasant recall of General LeMay with the last event I witnessed during which he visited Headquarters SAC in the summer of 1980. Following President Carter's decision to cancel the much-desired and needed B-1 strategic bomber, General Ellis directed several of us on the staff to work on an alternative notion he had employing the FB-111 bomber. His notion was to have the aircraft industry extend the fuselage of the bomber by a sufficient length to accommodate additional or larger nuclear bombs. We had all but completed the concept, and General Ellis felt that during General LeMay's visit would be a good opportunity to "try out" the idea with him based on his vast experience and knowledge of strategic air warfare.

General Ellis invited me and two other staff officers to join General LeMay and him in the conference room. He mentioned briefly to General LeMay that he wanted to share an innovative bomber idea with him. General LeMay nodded, adjusted his hearing aid, got out of his chair, and moved up to the end of the staff table and closer to the video screen. When the briefer signaled to begin the presentation and a huge photograph of the FB-111 showed up on the screen, General LeMay got up out of his chair and turned to General Ellis, "Dick, LBJ shoved that F-111 up my ass the first time, and no one else is going to do it again; anything else you want to talk about?"

The room fell deathly quiet. General Ellis rose out of his chair and escorted General LeMay out of the conference room. It would have been something else to be a fly on the wall back in the CINC's office afterward . . .

The legendary man of steel, General Curtis LeMay, who was known for the cigar clenched in his teeth, was seen as tough, blunt, but also fair. He died of a heart attack at the age of eighty-three in 1990. Lest we forget our many and fortunate notable encounters!

General David C. Jones, USAF (Ret)

I met and was in the company of General Jones several times along the way. A native of North Dakota and graduate of Minot State College, he joined the Air Force and became a SAC bomber pilot. His successful career led him to become chief of staff, U.S. Air Force and chairman, Joint Chiefs of Staff. His is another incredible story of commitment and service to the nation. He served as a bomber pilot in Korea and moved swiftly up the career chain. He was assigned to Strategic Air Command headquarters during SAC's build-up period, initially as an operations planner in the bomber mission branch until he was selected by CINCSAC, General Curtis LeMay, as his aide and promoted to colonel.

Capping a career that had included operational and command positions in bomber, tanker, training, and tactical fighter units as well as headquarters staff positions, General Jones became chief of staff of the Air Force in July 1974. Jones pursued a policy of developing high-technology weapons systems. In addition, he reorganized the Air Force command structure and substantially reduced headquarters staffs. He supported and ordered the modernization of the F-15, F-16, the A-10, and the E-3A. Much of the modernization program was focused on the European area, where the United States developed initiatives in response to Department of Defense and congressional interest for an increase in the capability of NATO. On May 31, 1978, Jones was awarded the Order of the Sword, the Air Force enlisted force's highest honor for officer leadership.

As chairman of the Joint Chiefs of Staff in the Carter and Reagan administrations, General Jones served longer than any predecessor on the Joint Chiefs, 1978–82. It was under his watch during the Carter administration that a mission to rescue fifty-three American hostages in Iran ended in disaster. He was highly criticized for the debacle, but also were several others at lower levels of command down to the detail planning. No one was held personally accountable for the sad disaster.

During my brief introductions, I found him to be a very affable officer and gentleman all the way. As mentioned previously, he was present at the SAC-2000 Reunion where I presented the book review. He congratulated me warmly and later sent me a very gracious letter saying that he had read my book and was very appreciative. He passed away in October 2013 at age ninety-two.

General John D. Ryan, USAF (Ret)

I was at the Pentagon once doing business of one kind or the other and went into the Air Force Headquarters Distinguished Visitors Office to make some phone calls. As I walked into the lounge, I looked up and spotted a distinguished-looking gentleman leaning back in one of the mega chairs. As I was about to nod and speak to him, he greeted me, "Come on in, General; where are you from?" I then recognized him from photos as retired General John D. Ryan.

"Chris Adams, sir, SAC Headquarters at Offutt."

"What do you do out there?" he asked.

"I'm with SAC DCS/Ops," I replied. He stood up from his comfortable chair and held out his hand.

"Ryan," he said.

"Yes, sir, General," I replied as we shook hands.

"So, you wear 'two hats,' SAC and JSTPS," he smiled.

"Yes, sir, I do," I replied.

"Who's the admiral you report to in JSTPS?"

"Vice Admiral Ken Carr," I replied.

"Have a seat," he motioned to the lounge chair across from his and nodded to the steward standing nearby, indicating a coffee refill. "Bring me up to date on how things are going out at SAC Headquarters."

We had a pleasant chat over coffee, with his asking me questions about the Command. I gave him a brief rundown of ongoing activities, not that he likely knew most of it anyway. Finally he said, "I know you have business to do, so I won't hold you up."

As I was preparing to depart to one of the protocol offices to make my calls, he smiled and said, "Tell Dick Ellis to watch out for those damned Navy people, or one day they will be sitting at his desk."

"Yes, sir," I replied.

General John Ryan had been the seventh chief of staff of Air Force. He was a West Point graduate, class of 1938, and decided to go Air Force instead of the Army. He rose in rank rapidly at the beginning of World War II, commanding the 2nd Bombardment Group in Italy and later operations officer for the 5th Bombardment Wing. He returned to the United States in April 1945, and became deputy air base commander, Midland Army Air Field, Texas. In September 1945, General Ryan was assigned to the Air Training Command where he remained until April 1946, when he assumed operations officer duties with the 58th Bombardment Wing and participated in the Bikini Atoll atomic weapons tests.

For the next ten years, General Ryan served in various capacities moving up in responsibilities in Strategic Air Command as air operations officer, squadron, and wing air division commander. He became director of materiel for the SAC in June 1956, and in 1960, assumed command of SAC's Sixteenth Air Force in Spain. He became Commander, 2nd Air Force at Barksdale Air Force Base, Louisiana, in 1961. In August 1963, he was assigned to the Pentagon as Inspector General for the Air Force. One year later he was named Vice Commander in Chief, Strategic Air Command, and in December 1964, he became Commander in Chief. Three years later, he was reassigned to become Commander in Chief, Pacific Air Forces, in February 1967. Perhaps having the most varied career ever in the Air Force, he was appointed Vice Chief of Staff of the U.S. Air Force in August 1968, and Chief of Staff in August 1969.

As Chief of Staff, U.S. Air Force, General Ryan served in a dual capacity as a member of the Joint Chiefs of Staff and principal military adviser to the president, the National Security Council, and the Secretary of Defense. He retired from a very active and distinguished military career in 1973.

A year or so after bumping into General Ryan that day in the Pentagon, I attended the celebration dinner of the annual SAC bombing competition at Barksdale AFB, Louisiana, and was assigned to host one of the dinner tables. As I stood waiting for the guests to arrive at my table, I noticed one of the name cards, General John D. Ryan. About that time, up he walks.

He smiled and said, "I know you."

I held out my hand, "Yes, sir, General; Chris Adams, welcome." There were eight seated at the table, and as the dinner and evening

proceeded, the conversation became more fluid. I reminded him of his admonishment about the Navy taking over SAC one day, and he retorted, "Watch my words." We all chuckled.

General Ryan passed away in October 1983, at age sixty-seven.

Postscript: In 1998, I was invited to attend the change of command ceremony at United States Strategic Command (USSTRATCOM) at Offutt AFB, Nebraska, where Navy Admiral Richard Mies was assuming command of the major joint force headquarters. USSTRATCOM had replaced Strategic Air Command when the major command was retired in June 1992. All of the former SAC facilities at Offutt AFB were then transferred to STRATCOM. During the reception prior to the change of command ceremony, I noticed the chief of staff, U.S. Air Force, General Michael E. Ryan, standing with a small group. When it appeared appropriate to do so, I moved over and introduced myself, congratulating him on his appointment and the first of a son following his father to become chief of staff of the Air Force. I then took the opportunity to tell him about my conversations with his dad years before and the senior General Ryan's admonishment that if the Air Force wasn't careful, the Navy would someday occupy the senior commander's desk at Offutt . . . and, "That day had now arrived." He got a huge charge out of the story. Memories . . .

Lt. General Edgar S. Harris, USAF (Ret)

An encounter I shall never forget and will savor the many memories to follow was when I was sitting at my desk one twenty-degree wintry Saturday morning at F.E. Warren Air Force Base, Cheyenne, Wyoming, and the phone rang.

Before I could barely utter, "Hello, this is Colonel Adams," a thundering voice on the other end loudly blurted, "Who in the hell is in charge out there? Who are you?"

I responded, "This is Colonel Adams, vice commander."

The voice bellowed again, "Where's Guthrie?"

I knew by then that this was a serious call and I replied, "Sir, Colonel Guthrie is in the hospital with pneumonia. Can I help you?"

That brought another retort, "This is General Harris, 15th Air Force! I want to know what happened with the CINC's visit out there yesterday!"

I knew then I was speaking with the Chief of Staff, 15th Air Force and a "tiger" by reputation.

I responded, "Sir, we thought General Meyer's visit went very well. I escorted him around the base for an hour, answered his questions, and he departed. Was there a problem reported?"

General Harris fired back, "You damn right there was. General Meyer said that when he visited your Maintenance Control facility, the guys in there were lollygagging around in short sleeve shirts with the thermostat set at eighty degrees and it was twenty degrees outside! Don't you idiots know that we are in an energy conservation program?"

I replied, "Yes, sir, we do, but—"

Before I could complete my "excuse," he hung up on the other end. I thought to myself, "What a way to start the day! What should I do next?"

Later in the day, I went over to the base hospital to see my boss, Colonel Bobby Guthrie, 90th Strategic Missile Wing Commander. He was feeling much better and in good spirits until I relayed my morning's experience. He mused for a while and then said that he would call out to 15th on Monday and try to calm things down. Thereafter, the subject never came up again. We made sure that everyone in the wing understood President Carter's energy conservation edict and thereafter ensured compliance.

That was my introduction to then Brigadier Edgar S. Harris. As the next thirty plus years have evolved, I could relate dozens, perhaps hundreds of Big Ed Harris stories, and I shall briefly share a few herein. But at the outset, so as to not misrepresent this memorable encounter and others along the way, nor offend his blessed family in any way, I want to assure all that General Edgar Harris and I have developed and continue to enjoy a deep and abiding friendship for life! Many of these anecdotal stories are a sincere tribute to this officer's great leadership, teaching and his unrelenting commitment to ensuring professional performance by all within the U.S. Air Force.

Those who know him so well will smile and chuckle as they also recall their extraordinary personal relationship and experiences with this great officer and commander.

Lt. General Edgar S. Harris was born in Danville, Virginia, in 1925. A southern gentleman, he carries with him to this day his southern, no offense, accent. He graduated from the United States Military Academy, West Point, with a bachelor of science degree in 1946. He chose the Air Corps over the Army and was accepted for pilot training. He graduated and received his pilot's wings. Following multi-engine training, he was assigned to the Bombardment Wing at Davis-Monthan Field, Arizona flying the B-29 bomber. Over the years, he accumulated piloting experience in the B-29, B-47, and B-50 bomber aircraft before moving on up to staff positions. Thereafter, he piloted most all the aircraft in SAC.

General Harris spent the majority of his Air Force career in Strategic Air Command. Over the years, he has served as a staff officer at various command levels and twice as a SAC wing and air division commander. He also had two assignments with the Organization of the Joint Chiefs of Staff. He received a master's degree in International Affairs from The George Washington University while attending the Naval War College.

Among General Harris's many varied assignments was Beale Air Force Base, California, as commander, 14th Air Division where he had responsibility for B-52, KC-135, U-2, and SR-71 aircraft units and operations. From there he was assigned to March Air Force Base, California, as chief of staff, 15th Air Force. During that period he was sent to Guam on temporary duty to command the 57th Air Division at Andersen Air Force Base. From 15th Air Force, he moved to Headquarters, Strategic Air Command, as assistant deputy chief of staff for operation, thence he returned to March Air Force Base as Vice Commander, 15th Air Force.

In August 1976, he returned to Headquarters SAC as chief of staff, a position he held until December 1977, when he was promoted to lieutenant general and appointed vice commander in chief, Strategic Air Command. In June 1978, he was transferred to Barksdale Air Force Base, Louisiana, and assumed command of 8th Air Force.

General Harris retired as a command pilot following thirty-five years active duty on August 1, 1981, with more than 7,900 flying hours. He has been awarded the Master Missileman Badge having served with the Titan and Minuteman missiles. His military decorations and awards include the Distinguished Service Medal, Presidential Unit Citation emblem with oak leaf cluster, Air Force Outstanding Unit Award ribbon with three oak leaf clusters, and the Republic of Vietnam Gallantry Cross with palm.

Following that noteworthy introduction back in 1973, General Ed Harris, whom many refer to him to this day as Big Ed, has served as a godfather and teacher to me and others in so many varied ways—you might say *his* way. His illustrious Air Force career being highlighted, I want to not only pay special tribute to my friend for life but have some fun in good faith with our memorable friendship.

Major General Harris, then Vice Commander, 15th Air Force, made a staff visit to F.E. Warren AFB shortly after I had been elevated to wing commander. Following an afternoon visiting the base and wing facilities and dinner with the staff, I drove him to our distinguished visitors' quarters, Quarters 74, an elegantly restored 1800s two-story brick home on the base. The next morning, I arrived in my staff car to pick him up for breakfast. When I entered the downstairs living area, he was sitting in one of the comfy chairs drinking coffee with the newspaper in his lap.

As I was in the process of greeting, "Good morning, Sir."

He responded with, "Good morning, Chris. Say, your guys flunked flag last night."

Confused, I said, "Sir?"

He smiled and repeated, "Your troops failed to bring the flag in from the porch last night. They should never leave the flag out overnight."

"Yes, sir," I replied. The security police were supposed to take the flag out of its staff socket and return it in the mornings. They failed on this night! Following his visit I had a small floodlight installed to ensure that the flag, if not removed, was always lighted overnight.

Another memorable event with Big Ed always jovial and joking, occurred at a dinner party at Headquarters SAC where he was serv-

ing at the time as vice commander in chief, Strategic Air Command. During the reception, my wife and I were visiting with others when up walks General Harris.

We all stepped back and greeted him as he smiled and looked us over. Then he said to me, "Chris, my wife, Ethel, is ill this evening, so may I have the honor of Miz Adams joining me as my guest at the head table?"

Taken by surprise, we had little to say and my wife smiled, "Yes, sir, I would be honored."

General Harris then looked at me with a wry smile, "I guess you can find somewhere else to sit." He was a joker, always seeking an opportunity to shock us with a surprise and a smirky smile.

A special tribute was tendered to General Harris as he approached his time to retire from the Air Force. While I was serving as commander, 12th Air Division at Dyess AFB, Abilene, Texas, in cooperation with the city and the Air Force, we were able to secure a long since retired B-47 strategic bomber from the storage depot to bring to Dyess Air Force Base and to be placed alongside several other military aircraft of the past in our drive by museum along the main entrance to the base. The Air Force also agreed that General Edgar Harris could pilot the bomber from the storage depot to Dyess, where he had served as the bomber wing commander in past years. He was greatly respected and admired by the city fathers of Abilene and it was to both their special delight and an honor for him to fly the mighty bomber to its final resting place. The city turned out by the thousands for the event and a great day in his honor!

When I decided to retire from active duty to accept an appointment at the Los Alamos National Laboratory, I wrote letters to several friends that I was retiring to accept an incredible opportunity offer. I also wrote a letter to General Harris. I received a handwritten letter in response from him that I retain today. Therein, he expressed his great appreciation and trust, and for our friendship, which had grown stronger over several years. He also admonished me seriously that he regretted to see me retire and also that he . . . knew that I would go out there and make him even more proud."

We have kept in touch over the years, and he called once and asked if I was going to attend a forthcoming event at SAC Headquarters to which we were both invited. I told him that I hadn't given it much thought, but it sounded interesting. He said that he had flight reservations and would be flying via DFW in Dallas on his way and invited me to meet him and go to the event. I met him at DFW and we traveled on to Omaha. He had made plans that evening to meet an old West Point retired general friend of his at the Offutt Officers Club that evening for dinner and invited me to join them. I accepted, and during the course of the dinner, he and his old buddy exchanged West Point stories.

After a while, his friend looked at me and asked, "What class were you in, Chris?"

I promptly replied, "'52, General."

General Harris looked at me, a bit taken back.

"That's great," his friend responded and they kept on exchanging war stories.

Following dinner and strolling back to the base quarters, General Harris stopped and looked straight at me, "Why in the heck did you tell him that you were in the class of '52? You didn't go to West Point."

"Well," I replied, "no, sir, I didn't. I was Class of '52, East Texas State Teachers College. He didn't ask me what school I went to."

General Harris smiled and slapped me on the back. "You got the best of me with that one!"

There are numerous anecdotal tales I could relate herein and with each story shared in great respect for a superb Air Force leader, whom it was my pleasure to serve, learn, and honor.

I will digress in closing my characterization and tribute of this tough-minded military disciplinarian that so many viewed him to be, to the man I came to know and enjoy over the many years of our bonding and so many special times along the way. General Ed Harris was, and is to this day, a dedicated, fun-loving family man, filled with heart and soul. His lovely late wife, Ethel, and three daughters loved him as husband and father always being supportive, funny, sweet, and a hands-on family man. He planned family outings, took

his girls roller skating, ice skating, and all-day sledding trips in the frigid Omaha winters. He was the homework dad that ensured that his girls understood their assignments and turned them in on time. That, to some perhaps, is in contrast to what many on active duty observed. I have had the great fortune of remaining in touch with him during these latter years of his failing health and yet vibrant attitude when we talk, in person and on the phone. He was, and is, the greatest, according to his daughters. He set the bar high for his family and encouraged them all along the way, just as he did for all of who were blessed to know him and serve under his brilliant tutelage.

At age ninety-three, Lt. General Edgar Harris, great Air Force Leader, husband and father, with a few medical issues, continues to be a beacon of light and life to all of us and to his beloved daughters and grandchildren with whom he resides in Texas.

Vice Admiral Kenneth Carr, USN (Ret)

Admiral Carr was the fourth Navy admiral I had the pleasure of serving during my Air Force career. Admiral Mustin, previously cited, was followed by two predecessors to Admiral Carr. The two previous admirals served only brief periods in the Joint Strategic Target Planning Staff (JSTPS). An assignment for a senior naval officer to Omaha, Nebraska, was not the best of career objectives in their minds, so they either shortly retired or requested reassignment. Admiral Carr saw the opportunity differently and took the assignment as Vice Director, JSTPS, seriously. At the time, I was serving in two capacities: first as Deputy Chief of Staff/Operations, reporting to CINCSAC, and I wore the other hat as Assistant Director, Joint Strategic Target Planning, reporting to Admiral Carr, who also reported to CINCSAC/Director, Strategic Target Planning. It was confusing to some, but clear to us who wore the respective hats.

Vice Admiral Carr came to JSTPS, Offutt AFB and Omaha from his previous assignment as commander, Submarine Force, Atlantic Fleet. He had enjoyed an exceptional naval career and was known as an icon of the Navy's submarine fleet. He enlisted in the Navy during World War II, serving on an assault landing craft in the Pacific Theater. During the war he earned an appointment to the U.S. Naval Academy, graduating in the class of 1949. After serving as an assistant gunnery officer, he entered Submarine School. He served on the diesel submarines USS *Flying Fish* and the USS *Blackfin*, until 1953, when he was assigned to the commissioning crew of the USS *Nautilus*, the world's first nuclear-powered submarine.

Following his service as a crew member on the Nautilus, Vice Admiral Carr moved on as the executive officer of the USS *Scorpion* and the USS *James Monroe*. He was the first commanding officer of the USS *Flasher*, and later, became the Commander of the USS *John Adams*. His shore assignments included the office of the Chief of Naval Operations and the senior member of the Naval Nuclear Propulsion Examining Board. In 1972, he was assigned as chief of staff to the commander, Submarine Force of the U.S. Atlantic Fleet and promoted to rear admiral, thence becoming military assistant to the Deputy Secretary of Defense.

His was an ideal appointment to be vice director, JSTPS, since the directorate was the primary nuclear planning and targeting agency for the Navy's sea launched nuclear ballistic missiles as we were for all of the Air Force's strategic bomber and ICBM targeting. Admiral Carr's presence also made the other naval officers assigned to JSTPS happy, including my Navy deputy, Captain Ernie Toupin. The admiral and his wife, Molly, by coincidence, moved next door us on the Offutt Row, as it was known. There were some twenty plus flag officers assigned to various organizations at Offutt with most living in the beautiful late 1800's three-story brick mansions of the time. Having your boss living next door might make it tedious for some, but the Carrs made great neighbors, socially and otherwise. The admiral enjoyed playing tennis, as did I, and we played frequently during lunch hours, when we could get away, and some afternoons during the Omaha spring and summer days. Molly was a bit of a hoot in that she wasn't as comfortable as was he, being surrounded by Air Force people and very few Navy with whom to associate. She frequently commented as such that his assignment was not as dignified or at the level of his previous position. All in all, we all got along well. I did so, especially working with him.

I preceded the admiral in retiring from active duty to accept the appointment as associate director, Los Alamos National Laboratory, and he followed two years later departing from active duty with the Navy to be appointed as a commissioner with the US Nuclear Regulatory Commission (NRC). He became chairman, NRC, in 1989, remaining until his retirement in 1991. We visited frequently during that period, either during my visits to Washington or his coming out to Los Alamos.

The admiral was highly decorated with his awards, which included two Defense Distinguished Service Medals, the Distinguished Service Medal, the Defense Superior Service Medal, the Legion of Merit with one Gold Star, the Meritorious Service Medal, a Presidential Unit Commendation with Gold "N," Navy Unit Commendation, Meritorious Unit Commendation and the American Campaign medal, Asiatic and Pacific Campaign medal with two Engagement Stars, the World War II Victory Medal, the National Defense medal with one bronze star, the Korean Service medal, the Korean Presidential medal, and the United Nations Service medal.

Losing a good friend, Admiral Carr passed away in 2015, at the age of ninety, preceded by his beloved wife, Molly, in 2014.

Lt. General Lincoln D. Faurer, USAF (Ret)

Former Director, National Security Agency, Linc Faurer was a valued friend for many years. I first met him by contacting him directly while I was serving as an associate director, Los Alamos National Laboratory. One of my laboratory divisions was tasked with intelligence gathering research and analysis of suspicious foreign technologies. I cannot delve into that particular subject, except to share that I felt the requirement to acquire some expert technical observation, evaluation, and advice concerning this sensitive activity. General Faurer readily agreed when I explained my plan and that I had already recruited General Russ Dougherty, retired CINCSAC, and two other senior officers. Earlier in my Air Force days, I also reminded him that I had previously served with his brother, Judson, in SAC missile operations. He said that he remembered.

Lincoln Faurer graduated from West Point in 1950 and received a commission in the Air Force. He received a master's degree from Rensselaer Polytechnic Institute in 1964. He also attended the National War College in 1968, concurrently earning a master's degree in international affairs from George Washington University. Afterward, he served as director of J-2, United States Southern Command, in the Canal Zone. In August 1977 he was assigned as director, J-2, U.S. European Command in Germany and in August 1979 became deputy chairman of the NATO Military Committee. He was promoted to lieutenant general September 1, 1979, and served as director of the National Security Agency and chief of the Central Security Service from 1981 to 1985.

In 1985 President Reagan presented Lieutenant General Faurer with the National Intelligence Medal of Achievement in recognition of his service to the national intelligence community. He retired on April 1, 1985, after thirty-five years active duty. Additionally, his military decorations and awards included the Air Force Distinguished Service Medal, Defense Superior Medal with oak leaf cluster, Legion of Merit, National Defense Service Medal with one bronze service star, Meritorious Service Medal, Joint Service Commendation Medal with oak leaf cluster, and Air Force Commendation Medal with oak leaf cluster.

Never one to retire, Lincoln Faurer served as chairman of the Association for Intelligence Officers and consulted Congress on national security issues. He also served on the Board of Directors of several corporations and Chairman of the Board of Directors of the National Cryptologic Museum Foundation. As mentioned, he served on my Laboratory Technical Advisory Counsel as well as working together with Dr. Ray Cline and me on several close-hold projects.

With great sadness, I lost a notable encounter and dear friend with the passing of Lt. General Lincoln D. Faurer, on November 7, 2014. He was preceded by his wife of fifty-nine years, Virginia.

Lt. General Phillip J. Ford, USAF (Ret)

I first met Phil Ford by chance in the summer of 1986 while passing through Barksdale Air Force Base. Phil was a colonel, and vice commander, 2nd Bomb Wing at the time. I had departed my position at Los Alamos National Laboratory and was en route to accept a new job in Dallas. We enjoyed a brief visit, stayed overnight in the base quarters. Time and events race through our minds as we become busy and absorbed in our own activities. Some three years later, I heard that Phil Ford had been promoted to brigadier general and was assigned as the inspector general, Strategic Air Command. I recalled being impressed with our first meeting encounter and delighted to hear that he was moving onward and upward. Some years later, I was at Offutt Air Force Base for an event and invited to visit Phil and his wife, Kris, in their base quarters. By this time he had become Deputy Commander in Chief, United States Strategic Command and a lieutenant general. He assumed this present position after having served as commander, Eighth Air Force, and its multiple mission responsibilities.

In catching up on his most interesting and accomplished career, I learned much more about the young colonel I had encountered by coincidence years earlier. Phil Ford had met the challenges of an Air Force calling that would be the envy of most everyone. As the Cold War came to a close, relations between the United States and the Soviet Union warmed considerably. I know from my own experience of working in the former Soviet Union thereafter for five years. As Vice Commander, 2nd Bomb Wing and years later, Commander, Eighth Air Force, Phil had the opportunity to participate in numerous visits and aircraft operation exchange programs with Russian Air Force Leaders. While visiting the former Soviet Union, Phil was invited to fly the Russian Tupelov 25 bomber. Later, he invited several senior Russian Air Force officers to come to the United States to visit our facilities.

Phil Ford enjoyed an illustrious Air Force career with a range of duty assignments that covered the spectrum ranging from aviator with 4200 flying hours in a variety of aircraft, including the

KC-135R, RC-135, B-52G/H, B-1B, T-39, and the B-2, to a graduate of the Air Force Command and Staff College, the National War College, and the Harvard University Senior Executive National and International Securities Program.

His awards and decorations include among others: the Defense Distinguished Service Medal, the Distinguished Service Medal, Defense Superior Service Medal, Legion of Merit with oak leaf cluster, Meritorious Service Medal, Legion of Merit with oak leaf cluster, Aerial Achievement Medal, Joint Service Commendation Medal, and Air Force Commendation Medal with oak leaf cluster.

Phil Ford retired from Air Force active duty on May 1, 2000. General Ed Harris and I were invited and privileged to attend his retirement ceremony. Retirement from the Air Force did not quell Phil's call to serve. He was selected to become general manager/CEO of the Brazos River Authority (BRA) of Texas on July 1, 2001. Taking on the new and different role of managing the largest river basin in Texas, reaching from the New Mexico border in the Panhandle and extending 1,050 miles to the Gulf of Mexico, created a whole new world of management challenges. Perhaps, he laments, "Serving a twenty-one-member 'civilian' Board of Directors, with backgrounds ranging from lawyers to bankers to educators and beyond, along with managing the activities of 350 employees, while addressing a continuum of evolving State directives, mother nature and beyond . . . ," became a whole new world. The greatest of which, perhaps, "the continuous roll-over and political appointment of new board members, many of whom couldn't spell *water*!"

By coincidence, I was appointed by Governor Rick Perry to serve on the Brazos River Authority Board of Directors, soon after Phil assumed his new position. I considered it to be my good fortune to work with a former Air Force comrade and did so for thirteen years. After sixteen years of honorable service, Phil decided it was time to retire from the Brazos River Authority. In commemorating his years of service and loyalty to the BRA, the Chairman of the Board cited Phil:

"The year was 2001 when Phil accepted the responsibility of managing the Brazos River Authority. His first act was to assemble a team that would take action to ensure the BRA's mission of providing water for an ever-expanding Texas population was accomplished. And, over the past sixteen years, Phil has led the way in accomplishing the goals to ensure that success. It has not been easy, as some of you know. Some of the challenges and accomplishments of Phil Ford are:

"Decommissioning of the Hydroelectric plant at Possum Kingdom Lake. Addressing issues at the SWATS facility.

"Possum Kingdom divestiture, an enormous effort to the BRA that was directed by the Texas Legislature to get BRA out of the land management business.

"System Operation Permit, probably the most innovative and complex water rights permit in Texas history—this one has touched all of us around this table and the directors for the past thirteen years.

"Graham Project, another flood control activity that involved partnering with other governmental entities over the course of the last decade to address flooding issues in Graham, Texas.

"Remediation of the Williamson County Regional Raw Water Line after extensive construction issues.

"And, just think of the number of directors that have come on board during his term—sixty-seven to be exact . . .

". . . the list of Phil's accomplishments goes on and on and on . . .

"Texas and the Brazos River Authority have benefited greatly from Phil's vision for the future and his leadership in taking us there. In conclusion, I would like to extend our deepest appreciation and thanks to Phil Ford for his inherent leadership, integrity, dedication, service, and all that he has accomplished for the BRA and the State of Texas.

"Phil, on behalf of the Board of Directors of the Brazos River Authority, thank you for your service!"

Sincere respect and appreciation to a notable encounter and his lovely wife, Kris, friends for life.

Chief Master Sergeant of the Air Force James M. McCoy, USAF (Ret)

I first met Chief "Jim" McCoy in 1975 when I visited SAC Headquarters for my initial orientation to fly the airborne command post, Looking Glass, duty. At that time, he was the senior enlisted adviser, Strategic Air Command, reporting to CINCSAC, General Russell Dougherty. I found Chief McCoy to be a most gracious and hospitable gentleman in every regard. He, along with Ms. Dorene Sherman, to be notably recognized herein later, guided me around the headquarters, introducing me to the various staff members and office heads. As the years passed, I had numerous opportunities to meet, interact, and appreciate Jim McCoy's qualities and deeply embedded sincere substance.

Chief Jim McCoy was born in Creston, Iowa, graduating from Maur Hill High School, Atchison, Kansas, in 1948. He entered the U.S. Air Force in January 1951, after attending St. Benedict's College in Atchison and St. Ambrose College in Davenport, Iowa. He received a Bachelor of Science degree in business administration from Centenary College of Louisiana in 1966. He is an honor graduate of the Second Air Force Noncommissioned Officer Academy and a graduate of the first class of the U.S. Air Force Senior Noncommissioned Officer Academy in March 1973.

After basic training at Lackland Air Force Base, Texas, Chief McCoy served with the Air Defense Command as a radar operator and instructor until 1956. He then returned to Lackland. In 1957 he transferred to Clark Air Base, Philippines, where he served as the base training non-commissioned officer. During the Taiwan crisis of August 1958, he was instrumental in establishing and operating the wing command post that coordinated all inbound combined Air Strike Force aircraft. In 1959, Chief McCoy was assigned as the assistant commandant of cadets, Air Force Reserve Officer Training Corps, Detachment 225, University of Notre Dame, Indiana.

Chief McCoy was assigned as commandant, Strategic Air Command Noncommissioned Officer (NCO) Preparatory School in 1960. Two years later he became an instructor with the Second

Air Force NCO Academy at Barksdale Air Force Base, Louisiana, where he supervised the development of course studies for non-commissioned officer leadership schools. Thereafter, he became the academy's sergeant major. He transferred to the 41st Aerospace Rescue and Recovery Wing, Hickam Air Force Base, Hawaii, as non-commissioned officer in charge of operations training. He supervised and monitored all training programs for the H-3, H-43, H-53, and HC-130 helicopter crews assigned throughout the Pacific and Southeast Asia. He also served as senior enlisted adviser to the wing commander.

In April 1973, Jim became chief, Military Training Branch, Headquarters Pacific Air Forces. He revitalized the on-the-job training program and represented the command at several worldwide conferences that helped improve Air Force-wide training programs. During this assignment, he was selected as one of the twelve Outstanding Airmen of the Air Force in 1974.

Returning to the Strategic Air Command in March 1975, Chief McCoy became its first senior enlisted adviser. He served as the personal representative of the commander in chief to the enlisted men and women of SAC. In addition to traveling extensively throughout the command, he also served as chairman of two worldwide senior enlisted adviser conferences for the Air Force Association. Their efforts helped identify issues affecting quality of Air Force life. In 1979, Chief McCoy became the sixth chief master sergeant of the Air Force. In that capacity, he served as adviser to Secretary of the Air Force Hans Mark and Chief of Staff of the Air Force General Lew Allen Jr., on matters concerning welfare, effective utilization and progress of the enlisted members of the Air Force.

Chief James McCoy retired from active duty following an exceptional sterling Air Force career on November 1, 1981.

Chief McCoy's awards and decorations include among many the Legion of Merit with oak leaf cluster, Meritorious Service Medal with two oak leaf clusters, Air Force Commendation Medal with two oak leaf clusters, Air Force Outstanding Unit Award with oak leaf cluster, Air Force Outstanding Airman of the Year with bronze service star, U.S. Air Force Civilian Exceptional Service Medal, U.

NOTABLE LEADER ENCOUNTERS

S. Air Force Recruiting Service America Spirit Award, Air Force Association Presidential and Special Citations, Hoyt S. Vandenberg and Stortz Individual Membership Awards, and the Boy Scouts of America District Award of Merit, Silver Beaver Award, and Silver Antelope Award.

As with many and most military retirees, Jim McCoy was not one to permit retirement to curb his zest for life and energies. He continues to serve above and beyond as a member, Board of Directors, Air Force Association, Board of Directors, Airmen Memorial Foundation, Chairman, Air Force Retiree Council, Air Force Sergeants Association, Aerospace Education Foundation, American Legion and Disabled American Veterans.

A notable encounter and friend for life, Jim McCoy, who also honored our friendship by endorsing my 2009 publication, *Deterrence*, with a blog on the cover.

Chief Master Sergeant Joseph M. Sewell, USAF (Ret)

Technical Sergeant Joe Sewell was among the first to greet me when I arrived at Korat Air Base, Thailand, in October 1966. I had been back at Clark Air Base, Philippines, going through jungle survival school during which I encountered an accident, dislocating my right knee cap. That's a whole other story, but I finally arrived at Korat, not feeling very well. Joe met the air transport plane when we landed and helped me with my luggage to my assigned quarters: a four-bedroom "hootch." I put my gear in my assigned room and Joe drove me to Base Operations where I met my new boss-to-be, Lt. Colonel Johnson, who promptly told me that he would be departing for the States soon and that his replacement should be in shortly, either before or after his departure. To complete that part of the story, his replacement never showed up and I became the director of operations for the Combat Support Group for the next year. It was a heady job for a young Air Force major, but I grew into it—with the exceptional support of my assigned non-commissioned officers, of whom

Joe Sewell became my champion! Although there were four other officers, all captains and several NCOs, including a master sergeant, Joe was my choice above all. This young sergeant was at work before everyone else and remained until everything was done for the day.

Joe was a chunky, redheaded fellow in his early thirties at the time. He appeared to be happy every day, no matter the work to be done, the weather, good or bad food in the mess hall. That was Joe. He had preceded me by just a few weeks in arriving at Korat, but he arrived ready to go to work. That was his nature, always smiling, happy, and ready to take on anything to be done. About a month or six weeks after I arrived, he came in one morning and told me that he had received a letter from his wife, Donna, and that she was expecting. He lamented that he had left her not in the best of circumstances. I told him to not worry, that when the time came, he could take emergency leave of absence and return home to look after her.

Korat Air Base was in the Vietnam war zone. There was an F-105 fighter wing located on the base, and those kids flew out day and night on combat missions into North Vietnam. Most came home safely, but frequently some did not. I had five C-47 "Gooney Birds" assigned to me, to respond to any and about every requirement handed to us: from Vietnam, Cambodia to Laos. Virtually every time I flew out on a mission, Joe Sewell asked to accompany me, to do whatever might needed to be done. He made a great crew chief, although he wasn't certified to be one. Joe Sewell's many virtues and commitment to his military service are beyond all of my recall, but I would like to share a few during our South East Asia tour.

At my six-month duty time, I took a ten-day respite and caught a flight back home to Texas, the family, kids, and my parents. It all happened too quickly and when I returned and walked into my once shabby sheet rock paneled office, I was startled to see that the office had been completely renovated, vinyl wood-like paneling, carpeted floor, freshly painted window frames, etc. Joe followed me in and when I turned around, he was smiling ear to ear. He had done it all. But that wasn't all!

A few days later, the Combat Support Group commander and my boss unexpectedly dropped by base operations and stuck his head in my office. I looked up from my desk when he walked in and immediately stood up to greet him. He strolled in slowly and began to take in all the upgraded embellishments. As he looked around and back at me, I began to explain, "My guys did all of this, Colonel, while I was away. All the materials came from the scrap yard."

He just nodded his head and walked out without speaking. The issue never came up thereafter, and I suggested to Joe not to be so "upscale" in his projects from then on. "This is a war zone," I told him. He smiled.

About eight and a half months into his tour of duty, Joe came into my office smiling. "Sir, we have a baby girl!" I congratulated him and told him to get out and go catch a hop to the States. He objected for a moment and then nodded, "Yes, sir." I also told him to go and take all of his personal belongings, go to the nearest Air Force base personnel office, and find a new job back home, because his tour of duty there at Korat was all but done. He objected and then finally agreed to do so. We shared a big hug and he departed.

Ten days later, Joe walks into my office with his familiar big toothy grin. I was surprised but not shocked. He told me that he just couldn't leave like that; he had another month and a half to complete his tour of duty. That was Joe. Our respective tours of duty finally did come to an end, and he received orders to the Air Force base near Little Rock and I departed for my assignment in New Mexico.

We said goodbye in October 1967, and it would be eight years later when I am sitting at another desk at Davis-Monthan AFB, near Tucson, Arizona, as commander, 12th Air Division, and my secretary calls and tells me that a Chief Master Sergeant Sewell wishes to see me. It took me a flash of a second to jump up as in walks Chief Master Sergeant Joe Sewell. We exchanged hugs, I looked at him, and he looked great. I asked him, "What are you doing here?"

He smiled and replied, "I've come to work for you, General."

We sat and did eight years of catching up, finally concluding that, indeed, he had a job right there. I made the necessary arrangements and once again had Joe Sewell at my back. The Tucson assignment turned out to be brief for me. After six months in that position, I was advised that the Air Force wanted to transfer me, the Air

Division Headquarters, et al, to Dyess AFB, near Abilene, Texas. All of my staff members agreed with the move and we relocated to Dyess. Joe, his lovely wife, Donna, and eight-year-old daughter moved right along with us. Our tour of duty in Abilene was great and Joe continued to be by my side. There were many social functions associated with my job, mostly with the gracious city of Abilene. Joe became the "hosts of hosts" as we entertained various groups from within the city and visitors from without. And then that tour of duty came to an end in two more years when I was reassigned to Offutt AFB, Nebraska. Joe elected to not make that transfer and remained in Texas.

Years passed, and soon after I had retired from the Air Force and then at the Los Alamos National Laboratory, Joe and Donna dropped by for a visit. It was obvious that Joe wasn't well, but there was no mention of his being ill. A few months later, Donna called and told me that Joe had passed away peacefully with a heart condition. I flew out to Tucson where they had retired and attended the funeral of a great encounter friend for life. A further sad ending to this tribute to Joe was another call from Donna Sewell in the spring of 1987 with the tragic news that their daughter had been killed in Tucson, hit by a vehicle as she crossed the street during her noon lunch break. Donna also asked if I could come to the funeral service and provide remarks for friends and remaining family. I agreed, and that final visit with Donna and her siblings and friends leave lasting memories of a long and wonderful notable encounter and relationship.

2

Notable Hero Encounters

*H*ero is virtually defined as one noted for courageous acts, exceptional character, special achievements and abilities; a role model. He or she may be or was an illustrious warrior, one who demonstrated extraordinary qualities, great courage, and nobility of purpose. Heroes have frequently been known to risk or sacrifice his or her life without regard for the potential consequences. The notable hero encounters with whom I have had the exceptional pleasure of meeting demonstrate each and all of those traits and are patriots of extreme admiration and devotion. I want to begin this next series of encounters with a hero who paid the full price for his dedication, commitment, and service to our great nation.

Lt. Karl W. Richter, USAF

I met First Lieutenant Karl Richter shortly after I arrived at Korat Royal Thai Air Base, Thailand, in the fall of 1966. He was an F-105 fighter pilot with the 388th Tactical Fighter Wing tasked to fly missions over North Vietnam. I bumped into him one evening at the officers club and struck up a conversation. He was a very personable young officer and looked the part of a strident fighter pilot in his green flight suit. He was a very pleasant, soft-spoken, and mild-mannered officer. He was also very respectful. I held the rank of major at the time; while most all aviators in the war theater at the time were overly casual, neither did rank count for a whole lot. Richter and I chatted for a while over Heineken beers, and I learned that he had graduated from the Air Force Academy just two years before in the class of 1964. He was very modest about his flying experience, but he told me that he had gotten to Korat and the 388th via ferrying a replacement F-105 fighter directly from Nellis Air Force Base, Nevada. He said that on arrival, he received a quick combat flight checkout and began flying missions over North Vietnam. Thereafter, I saw him from time to time after we first met and heard other pilots in the wing speak highly of his flying skills.

The stories that grew from this young aviator's commitment and flying skills were talked about all around the base. It wasn't long after his arrival in the spring of 1966 that Karl Richter quickly became an exceptional fighter pilot and sought every opportunity to fly a mission. With only two years' Air Force flying experience, he became an element leader. Once, when he was granted R and R leave, he turned down time off to go to Bangkok or Hong Kong. He chose instead to go to Nakhon Phanom Air Base there in Thailand where he flew additional combat missions in the Cessna O-1E Bird Dog observation aircraft, "Just for the fun of it," he said.

On September 21, 1966, Karl Richter was flying an F-105 as element leader, near Haiphong, North Korea, looking for surface to air missile (SAM) sites. As he was about to fire his aircraft cannons at a SAM site, two North Korean MiG-17 fighters suddenly made a pass at him. He immediately turned away and pulled in behind the MiGs and began firing his 20mm cannons striking one of the enemy aircraft.

The story was told that just as Richter's gun went empty, the MiG's wing broke off and he saw the MiG pilot eject. Back at home base, Korat, he told his pilot friends, "In a way, I was happy he got a good chute. I guess that's the thought that runs through all our minds. He's a jock like I am, flying for the enemy, but he's flying a plane, doing a job he has to do."

At the age of twenty-three, Karl Richter became the youngest American pilot to shoot down a MiG over North Vietnam. He went to Saigon to receive the personal congratulations of Lt. General Momyer, Commander, 7th Air Force and awarded the Vietnamese Distinguished Service Medal by South Vietnamese Premier Nguyễn Cao Kỳ.

As Richter approached flying his one hundredth combat mission over North Vietnam and an automatic return home to the United States, he requested permission to fly a second one hundred missions before returning. He said that he believed that his combat experience could be used when he did return home to train younger pilots. His request to remain in the combat zone was denied and he returned to the States. Some two months later, I bumped into him back at Korat Air Base. He told me that training pilots was boring and had made another appeal to return to combat, which was granted.

Shortly after his return, on April 20, 1967, while leading a flight of F-105s over North Vietnam, his flight pinned down a battery of enemy AAA and SAM sites. He let his flight in under heavy fire and destroyed an important railroad target. He remained in the dangerous zone, leading his flight in spite of intense enemy fire and storming weather. He was awarded the Air Force Cross for his skill and heroism for that mission.

On July 28, 1967, flying with a new pilot, Richter spotted a bridge and instructed the trainee pilot to stay above him and to keep an eye out as he flew his F-105 toward the bridge target. Before he knew it, North Vietnamese anti-aircraft gun suddenly opened fire, hitting Richter's plane and forcing him to eject. The trainee pilot said later that he saw Karl's parachute disappear into the fog bank. A rescue helicopter picked up Richter's parachute beeper signal, flew in, and rescued him. He had been critically injured during his bailout. Some speculated later that he likely crashed into the side of a sandstone cliff during his descent. Karl Richter died from his injuries on board the helicopter en route to the field hospital.

Late that same evening, I was returning to Korat from a flight to Saigon with my operations officer, Dick Osborne. As we approached Korat Air Base, Dick called the tower for landing instructions. The tower operator then asked if we had sufficient fuel to land at Korat and fly on to Bangkok to transport a casualty. I replied that we did

and asked if the casualty was wounded or otherwise. The tower operator responded that the casualty was deceased and needed to be transported to the military morgue. I then asked if he was one of our pilots.

The operator replied, "Yes, sir, he was killed up north and recovered by one of our helicopters."

"Can you tell us who he is?" I asked.

The tower operator replied, "I'm not supposed to reveal his name, sir, but it is Lt. Richter."

Dick and I looked at one another in shock, and I trembled all over. We didn't speak another word to the tower or each other. I landed the sturdy old C-47 and taxied up to the ramp in front of base operations where a drab green military ambulance was parked. Dick got out of his copilot's seat, went to the rear of the aircraft, and opened the side door. I sat in shock in my seat and observed out the window as the corpsmen removed a litter supporting a rubber body bag from the ambulance and placed it on the gritty floor of our aircraft. They stepped back and saluted as Dick secured the door and returned to his seat. I taxied out, and we took off for Bangkok Airport. We landed and taxied up to an ambulance parked on the ramp, waiting to take the young hero to the morgue and subsequently back to his home in the States. That day ended with one of the saddest experiences in my life.

"Notable Hero" modestly describes Karl W. Richter who was born October 4, 1942, the youngest of three children. He graduated from high school in Holly, Michigan. From a very young age, he was interested in flying, and by age eighteen, he had learned to fly and developed into a highly skilled pilot. Encouraged by his sister, he applied for an appointment to the United States Air Force Academy, which he received out of high school and graduated in June 1964, with a commission as a second lieutenant in the Regular Air Force. At the time of his untimely tragic death, Lt. Karl Richter had flown more missions over North Vietnam than any other U.S. Air Force pilot: 198!

A bronze statue of his likeness stands at Maxwell Air Force Base in Alabama, with the engraved in stone inscription: "Whom shall I send, and who will go for us? Here am I. Send me" (Isa. 6:8).

This author has visited Maxwell, viewed his memorial statue, and took a photograph in memory. I am sharing my photograph of his memorial herein. A statue of his likeness also stands on the Mall of Heroes at the U.S. Air Force Academy in Colorado and his former high school in Holly, Michigan, is named for Karl W. Richter who paid the ultimate price.

General James H. Doolittle, USAF (Ret)

It is an exceptional pleasure to share an unexpected special encounter with a hero whose name became a household word throughout World War II and far beyond. I enjoyed the distinct honor of meeting General "Jimmie" Doolittle twice. The first encounter was in 1976, and by sheer coincidence of being in the right place at the right time. I had just parked my car and was in the process of unloading my clothes bag and travel items in the visiting officers' quarters parking lot at March AFB, California, when I noticed a slight built fellow who appeared to be walking around a bit confused. Upon closer observation, I recognized him to be General Jimmie Doolittle, our guest-of-honor-to-be at the 15th Air Force Commanders Conference which I was there to attend. I walked over to him, held out my hand, and introduced myself. He smiled, and we shook hands as I asked him if I could assist him. He said that he was looking for the Distinguished Visitors Quarters where he and his wife were to stay that night. I directed him to the building next door and where to park his car. He was exceptionally shy and gracious, and thanked me. When I offered to assist him and his wife to their quarters, he declined with a warm smile. I strolled on back to getting my business done, reeling over the fact that I had just met *the* famous Jimmie Doolittle!

Later, those of us in attendance at the dinner enjoyed a pleasant evening where General Doolittle spoke very briefly and humbly, mostly thanking everyone for the invitation to be there and the gracious hospitality. I was to meet General Doolittle again in the coming years, but first I want to review, refresh your memories, and share the background of this great American hero.

James Harold "Jimmie" Doolittle was born in Alameda, California, in 1896. He was educated in Nome, Alaska, Los Angeles Junior College and a year at the University of California School of Mines. He enlisted as a flying cadet in the Army Air Corps Reserves in 1917 and commissioned as a second lieutenant in 1918. He received a regular commission in 1920 and promoted to first lieutenant.

In September 1922, General Doolittle made the first of many pioneering flights that earned him the first of many major air trophies and international fame. He flew a de Havilland two-seat biplane equipped with basic navigation instruments, in the first U.S. cross-country flight from Pablo Beach, Florida, to San Diego, California, in twenty-one hours and nineteen minutes. He made only one refueling stop at Kelly Field, San Antonio, Texas. He was awarded the Distinguished Flying Cross for this historic feat. In the same year he received his Bachelor of Arts degree from the University of California, Berkeley. Driven in many directions, he entered Massachusetts Institute of Technology in 1923 and graduated the following year with a Master of Science degree in engineering. One year later he received a doctorate degree in aeronautics.

In 1925, General Doolittle went to the Naval Air Station in Washington, DC, for special training in flying high speed seaplanes with the Naval Test Board. He won the Schneider Cup Race, the World's Series of seaplane racing that year, with an average speed of 232 miles per hour in a Curtiss Navy racer equipped with pontoons. This was the fastest a seaplane had ever flown. The next year he received the Mackay Trophy for this feat.

In 1926, General Doolittle was granted a leave of absence from the Army to go to South America to conduct aircraft demonstration flights. In Chile, he broke both ankles but still put his Curtiss P-1 through stirring aerial maneuvers with his ankles in casts. He returned to the United States and was confined to Walter Reed Hospital for these injuries for a year.

Returning to Mitchel Field in September 1928, General Doolittle assisted in the development of fog flying equipment. He helped develop the now almost universally used artificial horizontal and directional gyroscopes and made the first flight completely by instruments. He attracted wide newspaper attention with this feat of "blind" flying and later received the Harmon Trophy for conducting the experiments.

General Doolittle resigned his regular Army commission in 1930 and became a major in the Specialist Reserve Corps. He was then named manager of the Aviation Department of the Shell Oil Company. He also went on active duty with the Army frequently to conduct aerial tests, setting the world's high-speed record for land planes in 1932. Along the way, he won the Bendix Trophy and the Thompson Trophy Race in a Gee Bee racer with a speed averaging 252 miles per hour.

On January 2, 1942, General Doolittle was promoted to lieutenant colonel and assigned to Headquarters Army Air Force to plan the first aerial raid on the Japanese homeland. He volunteered and was given approval to lead the attack of sixteen B-25 medium bombers from the aircraft carrier Hornet, targeting Tokyo, Kobe, Osaka, and Nagoya. The daring one-way mission that occurred on April 18, 1942, electrified the world and boosted America's hopes following Pearl Harbor. Doolittle and his crew bailed out after they dropped their bombs and fortunately landed in a rice paddy in Chu Chow, China. Several of the other flyers lost their lives on the mission.

General Doolittle, following the successful mission, received the Congressional Medal of Honor, presented to him by President Roosevelt at the White House: "For conspicuous leadership above and beyond the call of duty, involving personal valor and intrepidity at an extreme hazard to life. With the apparent certainty of being forced to land in enemy territory or to perish at sea, Lt. Col. Doolittle personally led a squadron of Army bombers, manned by volunteer crews, in a highly destructive raid on the Japanese mainland." In addition to the nation's highest award, he also received two Distinguished Service Medals, the silver star; three Distinguished Flying Crosses, bronze star; four Air Medals; and decorations from Great Britain, France, Belgium, Poland, China, and Ecuador.

General Doolittle was also promoted two grades, from lieutenant colonel to brigadier general. Thereafter, he became Commander, 12th Air Force in North Africa. A year later he was promoted to major general and commander, North African Strategic Air Forces.

Thereafter, Doolittle commanded the 15th Air Force in the Mediterranean Theater in November and 8th Air Force in Europe and the Pacific until the end of the war. Following General Doolittle's promotion to lieutenant general, he decided to revert to inactive reserve status and returned to Shell Oil as a vice president and later a director. In 1951, he was appointed as special assistant to the chief of staff, U.S. Air Force, for ballistic missile and space programs.

General Doolittle retired from Air Force duty February 28, 1959, but continued to serve his country as chairman of the board of Space Technology Laboratories. He also was the first president of the Air Force Association, in 1947, assisting its organization.

Fast forward to 1981 and an event at Offutt AFB and Strategic Air Command Headquarters, honoring several military notables including General Doolittle. It was my pleasure and honor to be chosen to be his host for the evening program. I introduced myself and reminded him of our previous meeting several years before at March AFB. He acknowledged as if he "remembered." I escorted him throughout the reception period as dozens, if not hundreds, came up to him, introducing themselves and lauding his incredible service. He modestly and humbly acknowledged each and every one with a smile, never appearing tired, but maintaining his overly quiet demeanor. We enjoyed the festivities during dinner where again, he spoke very little, fatigued by then I am sure, generally responding to my comments and others at our table with a smile and nod. With the evening over, I escorted him to his quarters on the base, and we exchanged a cordial "good night," and farewell handshake. Another encounter of a lifetime with a hero known for his many exploits, but above all the Doolittle raid on Japan that is remembered all over the world.

On April 4, 1985, Congress approved General Doolittle's promotion to the grade of general. President Reagan and Senator Goldwater pinned on his fourth star, making him the first officer in Air Force Reserve history to wear four stars.

An American Notable Hero of the ages, General Jimmie Doolittle passed away peacefully at the age of ninety-six in 1993.

Lt. General John P. Flynn, USAF (Ret)

Colonel John Flynn arrived at Korat Air Base, Thailand, in August 1967, to become vice commander of the 388th Tactical Fighter Wing. I had been at Korat for almost ten months prior to his arrival. As director of operations for the 338th Combat Support Group, I met him right away and was superbly impressed with his pleasant temperament and his Irish humor. Those were tough times for everyone, especially the F-105 fighter pilots assigned to the Wing. We were losing one or more pilots being shot down over North Vietnam every week. The enjoyable spirit that Colonel Flynn brought to the base and the 338th Fighter Wing was a welcomed pleasure. Combat was not new to him; he had already served two tours during the Korean conflict and was battle-tested, if there is such a thing? I enjoyed the positive stimulus of interacting with and reporting to him on a near daily basis during the two fast-moving months before I rotated back to the States. Neither will I ever forget the meaningful goodbye he said to me when I departed for home on October 24, 1967.

I arrived back home a day later, on October 25th, and began preparing to relocate the family to my new assignment at Sandia Base, New Mexico. I had been at Sandia for roughly two weeks when I received a call from another Korat Air Base returnee who told me that Colonel Flynn had been shot down over North Vietnam and was presumed dead or to have been taken prisoner. He had been shot down the day I departed for home. Several months later it was confirmed that Colonel Flynn had survived and taken prisoner. I had come to know numerous pilots who had been either shot down, killed, or taken prisoner, but Colonel Flynn's tragedy hit me particularly hard and stuck with me throughout the forthcoming years until he was finally released along with some 591 other American POWs in March, 1973. He was among the fortunate ones who came home. The U.S. had listed almost 2,500 military men and women as either prisoners of war or missing in action. There were 1,200 Americans reported as killed in action and their bodies not recovered. The fate and mystery regarding the others remains today.

Colonel Flynn was the highest-ranking U.S. Military officer held in captivity during the Vietnam War. We learned later from other returning POWs how he distinguished himself by creating the "4th Allied Prisoner of War Wing, Hanoi, North Vietnam," within the prison. As commander of the organization under the eyes of the North Vietnamese guards, he suffered constant life-threatening assaults from the enemy officers and guards. He was heralded by the other American prisoners for his leadership under the most dire conditions. Returning POWs told that the effectiveness of his initiatives and the wing organization and the impact of his leadership was most effective against prisoner exploitation and torture. He had the courage to stand up against the guards on many occasions and survived! They were baffled by his audacity and frequently just walked away from punishing him. Others placed him and members of his chosen staff in solitary confinement for periods of time. It is told that the prisoner wing organization was so well grounded that there was never a loss of continuity during his solitary confinement absences. His goal during their extended confinement was to look out for his fellow prisoners, do what was best for each individual and finally bring his men home with honor and dignity. The incredible distinctive accomplishments of Colonel John Flynn displayed the highest degree of leadership during a period in his life that no one else except those who witnessed his feats could understand.

The Air Force also maintained trust in this unique officer by promoting Colonel John Flynn to Major General immediately upon his release and return home where he became Commander, Air Force Military Training Center, Lackland Air Force Base. I had an opportunity to attend an event at Lackland in the fall of 1973. I spotted General Flynn speaking with a small gathering in the dining room area and proceeded to walk over in his direction, just to say hello. As I approached the group surrounding him, he looked up at me and to my shock blurted, "Chris Adams! How in hell are you? It has been awhile!"

General Flynn stepped away from the group and gave me a huge bear hug. A true story! I shall remember that evening for the remainder of my life. I have never been so honored! I had been told by several former Vietnam POWs that many of them worked diligently during quiet hours alone, and for the many years in captivity, ran names and faces over and over in their memories. They said that it was especially so for their family members, but also friends and acquaintances. They also said that it was remarkable after their return that they could recognize people near their age, much more so than children. Most were shocked when they returned that their children that they had tried to develop in their minds had grown up! I asked General Flynn how on earth he remembered me.

He replied, "Easy, I never forgot who you were."

We chatted for a brief time, catching up and recalling over five years of missing history. There were dozens standing by to speak with him that evening, and we parted with firm handshakes and hugs. I had the opportunity to see him one other time a few years later in Washington, where he had become the inspector general of the U.S. Air Force and promoted to lieutenant general.

He retired from the Air Force to a military retirement community in San Antonio and passed away after an extended illness in March 1997, leaving behind his beloved wife, Mary Margret, and five children.

Lastly, the military honors, decorations, and awards bestowed upon him during and at the close of his extraordinary service career speak volumes: the Silver Star, Legion of Merit with an oak leaf cluster, the Distinguished Flying Cross with six oak leaf clusters, the Air Medal with fourteen oak leaf clusters, and the Purple Heart with one oak leaf cluster. An encounter that never was to be forgotten of that remarkable man who remembered me after those years and all that he had endured!

Honorable Samuel R. Johnson
U.S. Congressman, Texas,
Colonel, USAF (Ret)

I had just taken my seat aboard an American Airlines flight at DFW Airport in Dallas, bound for Washington National Airport. As

other passengers were getting seated, I glanced over my right shoulder and with a double-take, I recognized the fellow across the aisle in the seat next to the window. I had never met Congressman Sam Johnson but recognized him from the newspaper and television. He had just sat down and was gazing out the window. After we were airborne and at cruise altitude, I decided to introduce myself to the congressman. I got out of my seat and made sure that he wasn't busy with paperwork or otherwise preoccupied, which he wasn't. He was still looking out at the window at the dark sky.

I leaned over the vacant aisle seat beside him and held out my hand, "Hello, Congressman, I'm Chris Adams. Hope I'm not interrupting you."

He smiled, held out his hand, and responded, "Hello, Chris, how are you?"

I didn't want to appear awkward and quickly replied, "I'm retired Air Force also and just wanted to say hello, thank you for your service and especially now that you are still serving."

He smiled again and nodded, "Sit down a minute and tell me about yourself."

I sat down beside him, briefly introduced my Air Force background and quickly acknowledged his service and his North Vietnam POW time. I jokingly chided that I was stationed at Korat Air Base not far from Ubon where he was flying out of when he was shot down.

"I might have been able to come pick you up had I known you were down," I chided.

He chuckled, "Wish you had'a been!"

Truth be known, he had actually been shot down over North Korea and taken prisoner some six months before I even arrived in Thailand. We all tell war stories, it's part of the culture.

My first inclination was to record my encounters with Congressman Sam Johnson along with other political notables whom I have been privileged to meet, but then after a brief brain flash, there was no decision to be made to decide between a politician and a true war hero!

Sam Robert Johnson was born on October 11, 1930, in Dallas. He graduated from Woodrow Wilson High School and Southern Methodist University with a degree in Business Administration. He received a commission in the Air Force and graduated from flight training to become a highly skilled fighter pilot and flew the F-100 Super Sabre with the Air Force Thunderbirds precision flying demonstration team. He served twenty-nine-year careers on active duty, including almost seven years as a prisoner of war in North Vietnam. He is a combat veteran of both the Korean and Vietnam Wars as a fighter pilot. During the Korean War, he flew sixty-two combat missions in the F-86 Sabre and shot down one MiG-15. During the Vietnam War, he flew the F-4 Phantom II.

On April 16, 1966, flying his twenty-fifth combat mission over North Vietnam, his aircraft was hit by a surface-to-air missile and he had to bail out. He suffered a broken arm and back as a result. He was taken prisoner and remained so for nearly seven years, including forty-two months in solitary confinement where he was repeatedly tortured. He tells of being identified as a part of a group of eleven U.S. military prisoners known to themselves as the Alcatraz Gang and separated from other captives for their resistance to prison rules. They were held in "Alcatraz," as he refers to it, a special facility about one mile away from the Hỏa Lò Prison, notably nicknamed the "Hanoi Hilton." Sam Johnson, like the others, was kept in solitary confinement, locked nightly in irons in a windowless three-by-nine-foot concrete cell with the light on around the clock.

Sam Johnson was finally released on February 12, 1973, during Operation Homecoming and continued his Air Force career, rising to the grade of full colonel. He served as director of the Air Force Fighter Weapons School and commanded the 31st Tactical Fighter Wing at Homestead AFB, Florida, and the Air Division at Holloman AFB, New Mexico, before retiring after twenty-nine years of Air Force active duty, including his POW years. He walks with a noticeable limp nowadays, due to his wartime injuries. His Hanoi prison experience is described in detail in his autobiography, *Captive Warriors*.

Colonel Sam Johnson's military awards and decorations include the Silver Star with one oak leaf cluster, the Legion of Merit with two

oak leaf clusters, the Distinguished Flying Cross, the Bronze Star, two Purple Hearts, the Air Medal with three oak leaf clusters, the Air Force Commendation Medal with one oak leaf cluster, the Korean and Vietnam Service Medals among numerous others.

Following retirement from the Air Force, he established a homebuilding business in Plano, Texas. Shortly thereafter, he ran for election as a Republican to the Texas House of Representatives in 1984, and was re-elected four times. He then ran for the U.S. House of Representatives in Texas's 3rd Congressional District in 1991. Taking along and employing his Hanoi Alcatraz experience, he continues to honorably serve, having been reelected twelve times. His congressional district includes much of Collin County, an affluent suburban county north of Dallas. He has served in several Congressional leadership positions, including acting Chairman of the House Committee on Ways and Means and Chairman of the Social Security Subcommittee. I have had the pleasure of interacting with Congressman Sam Johnson on numerous occasions over the years, usually at one of Allen Clark's Combat Faith luncheons or with the Military Officers of America (MOAA). He is always affable and in good humor, telling a humorous story or such.

A humble notable hero, Sam Johnson lost his beloved wife, Shirley, after sixty-five years of marriage, in December 2015. He announced in January 2017, that he will not seek another reelection to Congress.

Colonel Kenneth Cordier, USAF (Ret)

I met Ken Cordier at a luncheon hosted by Allen Clark. An Air Force fighter pilot, Ken's F-4C Phantom jet was shot down by a surface-to-air missile over North Vietnam on December 2, 1966, forcing both he and his copilot to eject. Ken was captured immediately and became a prisoner of war shuttling around four different prisons in and around Hanoi. He was finally released with other American military servicemen on March 4, 1973, after six years and three months as a prisoner of war.

Ken is a native of Akron, Ohio, and a 1960 graduate of the University of Akron where he earned a degree in Mechanical Engineering and received a commission via the Air Force ROTC program. He went on active duty following graduation and commissioning and on to pilot training. As the war in Vietnam escalated, he was assigned to the Ubon Air Base, Thailand, in 1965, where he flew fifty-nine combat missions in the F-4C over North Vietnam and Laos. Following his tour of duty at Ubon, he volunteered for a second assignment, this time at Cam Ranh Bay, South Vietnam. When he was shot down, he had completed 175 combat missions.

Following convalescent leave, Ken Cordier requalified to fly jet aircraft and resumed his Air Force career flying the F-4C Phantom once again. As his career advanced, he was assigned to USAFE Headquarters at Ramstein Air Base, Germany, as chief, War Plans Division. Thereafter, he became deputy commander for operations at Sembach Air Base, Germany, in 1979, and later, base commander, where he was tasked to plan and execute the reactivation of Wiesbaden Air Base. His last Air Force assignment took him to London as air attaché to the U.S. ambassador to the United Kingdom. As the air attaché he advised the ambassador on all issues relating to the U.S. Air Force presence in-country and acted as liaison between the Embassy and Third Air Force Headquarters at RAF Mildenhall. He maintained close coordination with the State Department on political-military issues during the politically sensitive period of the first Cruise Missile deployment. Daily professional and social contact with top Ministry of Defense officials and senior RAF staff officers resulted in close relationships that greatly facilitated agreement on cooperative defense issues. Frequent contact with Allied and Warsaw Pact diplomats enabled him to enhance his knowledge of multinational relationships.

After Ken Cordier's retirement from the Air Force in 1985, he returned to the U.S., where he worked for British Aerospace in Washington, DC, as director, Military Aircraft. Ken will tell you that while serving in the U.S. Air Force and as a prisoner of war under the most difficult circumstances, he developed a strong personal philosophy relative to perseverance, goals, and accomplishment. In spite of the brutal regimen of confinement and deprivation of food and contact with fellow American POWs, Ken Cordier made a distinction between the regular Vietnamese people and those in the North Korean army personnel, who took pleasure in abusing the POWs under their control. He bears no malice toward the Vietnamese people, and believes that the United States should engage in constructive dialogue with our former enemy. As part of the healing process, Cordier has made two trips back to Vietnam. On the second visit, he led a group of thirteen former POWs to visit several of the prisons in the Hanoi area where they were held. They also toured northern and southern cities and cultural sites in the country. He views the trip as a success in that it not only helped former POWs bring closure to their war experiences but served as a model for other former POWs. I've had the pleasure of visiting with Ken several times over the past few years, always enjoying his upbeat and positive view of life. An exceptional speaker, I invited Ken to share his incredible experiences with those of us in attendance at the Texas A&M University-Commerce Air Force Reunion in 2016. He pulls no punches in describing the tortuous life he lived and that of his fellow prison mates during the incredible number of years they were held

Ken Cordier holds a Master of Science in Management degree from Troy State University, Alabama, along with his professional military education including Squadron Officer School, the Armed Forces Staff College, the National Security Management Course, and Defense Attaché School. He is a command pilot with more than two thousand flying hours in fighter aircraft. His military decorations and awards include two Silver Stars, Defense Superior Service Medal, Legion of Merit, Distinguished Flying Cross, two Bronze Stars with "V" Device for valor, Purple Heart, Meritorious Service Medal, seven Air Medals, Prisoner of War Medal, National Defense Service Medal, Vietnam Service Medal, and the Republic of Vietnam Campaign Medal.

Ken has also been awarded the prestigious National Society Daughters of the American Revolution Medal of Honor. The highest award presented by the DAR was bestowed on Ken Cordier based upon his demonstrated leadership, trustworthiness, patriotism, and service to the local community and nation. He was presented with the Freedoms Foundation at Valley Forge honor award in 1973 and was selected by the American Fighter Aces Association as an honorary member in 1985.

A special notable hero in my memory book, Ken Cordier and his wife, Barbara, an extraordinary neat couple (Barbara comically refers to themselves as "Ken and Barbie" of Barbie Doll fame), currently reside in Dallas, Texas.

The Honorable Allen B. Clark

I first met Allen Clark in response to his invitation to attend a luncheon he hosted on behalf of his Combat Faith lay ministry in Dallas. I had heard of Allen but knew little about this incredible hero until attending that first luncheon meeting and others to follow, including a special luncheon discussion visit with just him and his lovely wife, Linda. I was hooked on a friendship with this incredible man of survival and spirit.

To lend considerable credence to my impressions and feelings, permit me to share with you his story of faith, perseverance, and endurance. Allen himself will tell you that "Faith" is his middle name. Allen Clark graduated from the United States Military Academy in 1963, receiving a commission in the Army Corps of Engineers. Three years after graduation from West Point, he headed to Vietnam as a Military Intelligence officer with the Fifth Special Forces Group. With just weeks remaining to complete his year tour, he sustained critical injuries in a mortar attack at the Dak To Special Forces Camp in June 1967. His injuries resulted in the amputation of both legs below the knees. However, this was not all bad news! He turned this negative in future years to a positive by increasing his height from five-eight to six-two with successive artificial prosthetic limbs, so that he "grew in all his jobs."

While adjusting to his tragic combat wounds and learning to walk on prosthetic legs, Allen was separated from the Army. Determined *not* to be deterred, he entered Southern Methodist

University in Dallas, Texas, and acquired an MBA degree in finance and investments. Thereafter, he was hired by Ross Perot to manage his personal investments, but, his tenure was cut short by recurrence of post-traumatic stress, that originally struck him in 1968, necessitating then a fourteen-week stay in a closed psychiatric ward at Brooke Army Hospital. Later business experiences led him into oil and gas exploration, real estate marketing, and mortgage lending. Therein he served as a bank vice president, president of oil service companies and cofounder of a real estate investment company. In demonstrating his will to live a normal life with prosthetic legs, he also took up dancing and skiing as a means of good physical therapy.

Allen Clark became impassioned with public service and helping disabled veterans recover from injuries, which led in 1979 to his appointment as special assistant for administration to Texas Governor William P. Clements Jr. In 1981, he was President Ronald Reagan's selection to be the deputy administrator for the Veterans Administration, but, for personal reasons he was unable to serve in that capacity. In 1981, he was one of two Texans selected to represent his state in ceremonies celebrating the International Year of Disabled Persons. He was later nominated by President George H.W. Bush and confirmed by the United States Senate to be the assistant secretary for Veterans Liaison and Program Coordination at the U.S. Department of Veterans Affairs. Thereafter, he served as director of the National Cemetery System until the end of the President George H. W. Bush administration. Allen Clark's dedicated efforts to support veteran's causes at the national and state levels were recognized with his selection in 2011 by the Texas State Disabled American Veterans organization as their Outstanding Disabled American Veteran of the Year.

In 2005, Allen created his present Christian lay ministry organization, Combat Faith Ministry (www.combatfaith.com), which is involved in outreach efforts to help active duty military personnel and veterans recover and heal from the traumas of combat injuries and adverse wartime experiences as has he. Allen participates in many community and civic activities, including regularly speaking at warrior transition battalions, military post chapels, high schools, colleges, service and veteran groups, youth conferences, and churches. He is relentless in his pursuit to assist military veterans to recover physically and emotionally from the wounds of war. He also graciously accepted my personal invitation to speak at the Texas A&M University-Commerce Air Force Reunion in 2014, impressing veterans and students alike with the importance of military service and sacrifices for America.

Allen Clark's autobiography, *Wounded Soldier Healing Warrior*, was published by Zenith Press in 2007. The book's website (www. woundedsoldierhealingwarrior.com) includes an interview by Larry King. His second book, *Valor in Vietnam* (www.valorinvietnam. com) was published in 2012 by Casemate Publishers. He was the 2014 Military Writers Society Bronze Award winner in the History Category.

In his books, Allen cites, "Every war continues to dwell in the lives it touched, in the lives of those living through that time, and in those absorbed by its historical significance." The Vietnam War lives on famously and infamously dependent on political points of view, but those who have "been there, done that" have a highly personalized window on their time of that history. *Valor in Vietnam* focuses on nineteen stories of Vietnam, stories of celebrated characters in the veteran community, compelling war narratives, vignettes of battles, and the emotional impact on the combatants. It is replete with leadership lessons as well as valuable insights that are just as applicable today as they were decades ago. It is an anecdotal history of America's war in Vietnam composed of firsthand narratives by Vietnam War veterans. His reflections are intense, emotional, and highly personal reflections of war. With a foreword by Lt. Gen. Dave R. Palmer, U.S. Army (Ret), his *Valor in Vietnam* presents a historical overview of the war through the eyes of participants in each branch of the military services throughout the entire course of the war. Allen Clark's living stories serve to reflect the commitment, honor, and dedication with which America's veterans performed their service. His current literary effort is a trilogy titled *Soldiers Blood and Bloodied Money*, the introductory foreword written by Lt. Col. Allen West.

Allen Clark's awards include the Silver Star for Gallantry in Action, Purple Heart, and Combat Infantryman's Badge. Not one to slow down, he is an active member of the American Legion, Association of the U.S. Army, Disabled American Veterans, Military Order of the World Wars, Military Order of the Purple Heart, Military Officers Association of America, Sons of the American Revolution, Special Forces Association, Veterans of Foreign Wars, Vietnam Veterans of America, and the West Point Association of Graduates.

A compassionate notable hero, Allen Clark and his wife Linda, an author in her own right, *My Name Is Mary*, *Mary of Bethany/Mary Magdalene*, (https://tinyurl.com/MyNameIsMaryBethany-Magdalene), continue their respective good works in Dallas, Texas.

Colonel Lacy W. Breckenridge, USAF (Ret)

I take no greater pleasure than acknowledging and honoring a notable Texan, college classmate, fellow aviator and friend for life, Lacy Breckenridge. In Lacy's own words, "I was born on October 28, 1930, the only child of Chester W. and Essie Naomi Breckenridge giving me twenty-nine years, two months, and three days to participate in the battles of the 1960s and beyond. Significant events leading up to that period included becoming a Christian, graduating from college, marrying my 1954 beauty queen Rita Jo Davis of Lufkin, Texas, becoming a fighter pilot in the United States Air Force, flying the F-100 Super Sabre for eight years including air refuelings to England, France, Spain, Turkey, Japan, Korea, Okinawa, Thailand, and the Philippines."

I met Lacy when we became freshman at the then small two-year junior college, John Tarleton Agricultural College. The name of the school was misleading in that it was also a compulsory military training college for the male students. Founded in 1899 by its namesake, John Tarleton, it became a part of the Texas A&M University System in 1917. The Army Reserve Officer Training Corps (ROTC) required male students to wear their provided uniforms seven days a week, participate in military academic training, marching drills instruction and weekly formations. There were also strict penalties for violation of the established rules of conduct. Female students made up a small fraction of students and were not a part of the military training program. The ROTC program developed a natural camaraderie among male students. The military training frequently motivated them to continue the training on into universities that provided ROTC programs, which led to commissions upon graduation into either Army or Air Force. Texas A&M was a natural transition for the majority to continue ROTC training.

Lacy was not only absorbed and took military training to heart, he also participated in activities across the campus at Tarleton, including a member of the college rifle team, platoon guidon bearer, and becoming an expert foil swordsman on the fencing team. The latter may have attributed later on to his fighter pilot prowess.

Completing two years at Tarleton, he continued on to Texas A&M. I opted to transfer to East Texas State College and their Air Force ROTC program as a result of being tendered a scholarship from the Masons sponsored by a benevolent uncle. Lacy Breckenridge became a "dyed in the wool," maroon and white, Aggie at A&M and remains even more so today. Gig'em is his and all true Aggie's salutation, hello and goodbye shout with a thumbs-up signal. My roommate at East Texas State was an A&M transfer, so I received and have had my Aggie indoctrination. Okay, 'nuff on A&M and Aggies! Just kidding; I love 'em all.

Following graduation from A&M, receiving a commission in the Air Force and marrying his Lufkin, Texas, sweetheart, Rita, Lacy leaped off to pilot training. Upon graduation, he became a first-class fighter pilot. As stated by him earlier, he spent his first eight years flying the F-100, virtually all over the world: England, France, Spain, Turkey, Japan, Korea, Okinawa, Thailand, and the Philippines. Lacy transferred to the 8th Tactical Fighter Wing, Itazuke Air Base, Japan, in 1960, taking Rita and their young son with him. He was assigned to fly the F-100D, known as the *Hun*, for the next three years. The primary mission of the 8TFW was to protect Taiwan, Okinawa, Japan, and South Korea from China, Russia, and North Korea. The Status of Forces Agreement prohibited the United States from deploying nuclear weapons to Japan, placing the responsibility of deterrence on tactical fighter units.

He took his family to Cannon Air Force Base, New Mexico, his follow-on assignment after Japan, where he spent the next four and one-half years with the 523rd Tactical Fighter Squadron, continuing to fly the F-100D. The "Battles of the 1960s," as he put it, finally arrived and were much more intense than expected as Lacy had lamented. Once again, he left his family at home and in 1966, departed for Ubon Air Base, Thailand, and the 8th Tactical Fighter Wing. He had previously checked out and flown the F-4 Phantom II for the 33rd TFW at Eglin, AFB, Florida. The mission of the 8th TFW was to attack targets in North Vietnam and Laos.

On his 49th mission since arrival at Ubon, Lacy departed with another pilot, Lieutenant Joe Merrick, in the rear seat of the F-4, along with a flight of three other fighters, to destroy an oil storage facility north of Hanoi. Halfway to the target area, the mission was canceled due to bad weather over North Vietnam, and his flight was diverted to conduct an air strike on a target along the Ho Chi Min Trail in Laos. A truck park had been discovered by Forward Air Controllers (FAC). A FAC alerted Lacy's flight that the area had some enemy .57 mm guns in the area but were thought not to be a major threat.

The FAC marked the target area with a smoke rocket and Lacy proceeded to establish a dive bomb pattern with the other F-4 pilots in the flight. On his third bombing pass, both engine throttles in the F-4 stuck in the rear position providing, only 70 percent RPM on each engine. He informed the lead F-4 pilot of his problem and alerted Lt. Merrick, in the back seat, to standby for a possible ejection.

Lacy jettisoned F-4's fuel tanks and zoomed the aircraft up to six thousand feet. He leveled off at three hundred knots airspeed while attempting to correct the throttle malfunction. Attempts to advance the throttles were futile. As the airspeed indicator dropped below 230 knots, he ordered Lt. Merrick to eject, and he ejected immediately. Lacy ejected safely from the aircraft and began his descent into the thick jungle below. Lacy landed into the top of a tall tree and near the trunk. He said that he was afraid that the limb he was sitting on might break, and then what? He could hear small arms fire and took out his handgun, just in case. He said that he then heard the rotor blades of a Jolly Green Giant rescue chopper.

Lacy characterizes the storied event as, "Up a Laotian Tree," and relates it as follows:

"While the Jolly Green was positioning to pick me up, I really expected the limb I was sitting on to break and I would go crashing to the ground. I began thinking that if it did break, maybe I could spread-eagle and catch some lower limbs to stop my fall. My helicopter rescue was an interesting ride in itself. I had never seen a tree penetrator until it was lowered to me while I was sitting in the top of the tree. It is a metal tube about six inches in diameter, about six feet long with three fold-down seats. The entire tube was covered with a zipper cover that encloses several nylon straps that can be secured around your body. When I first saw it, I did not have the slightest idea how it worked.

"I unzipped the zipper and all of these straps fell out and I thought surely I am not supposed to just entwine myself in these things; then I noticed the three folded up seats, so I unfolded them, mounted one, and stuck my arms into the straps. All this time the airman operating the hoist in the chopper was trying to give me hand signals. The jungle penetrator was probably extended down about one hundred feet from the chopper.

"When I thought I was secure on the seat, I gave the hoist operator a thumbs-up signal. The chopper had to back up a little so I would not be pulled up through some thick vines. As soon as I was clear, the chopper went up vertically until I was clear of the tops of all of the trees and away we went toward home base with me suspended in midair hanging onto the penetrator. The chopper's altitude was probably about one thousand feet before they hoisted me up and pulled me into the open door.

"Just as I was clear of the trees, the hoist operator also had a gun mounted near the door, fired several rounds toward the area we were leaving. Later he said he saw some ground forces moving into the area we had just departed, so it was very close. As soon as I was safely inside the chopper, the hoist operator and another airman helped

buckled me into a regular seat. It had been bright outside and it was a little dark inside the chopper, so it took a few seconds for my eyes to accommodate, and when they did, I saw that the chopper was full of other men and I thought, they sure carry a large crew on these rescue units still not knowing they were survivors from the downed chopper that got shot down after picking up Joe Merrick.

"Then I saw Joe and did not immediately recognize him. A medic had taken off his G-suit and combat boot where he had sustained a bullet wound in his foot from ground fire while he was being rescued. Another crew member gave me a shot of whisky and I settled down for an uneventful ride to Nakhon Phanom (NKP), in Northern Thailand.

"When I stepped off the chopper at NKP, the first person I saw was Captain Robert Havard of Lufkin, Texas, my hometown. He was stationed there at NKP as a FAC and did not know I was on the chopper. For something better to do, he had come down to see who had been rescued. While Merrick was at the hospital getting his wound dressed, I had a couple of beers and a good chat with my friend, Robert. He also had left his family in Lufkin while he was in SEA (Southeast Asia). He and his wife were in my wife's high school graduating class. What a small world! We had a lot to talk about. After Merrick's wound had been dressed, they flew us back to Ubon in a Beaver, a small single engine, high wing utility airplane. About halfway back, I looked back at Joe; he was smoking a big cigar, all stretched out with a smug look on his face, so I said 'Joe, you know, that was pretty close wasn't it . . . it's great to be alive!'

"He said, 'Yes!' Then I said, 'You know, I was not really worried.' That got his attention, and he asked why. "I said, 'Well, I always send a decoy out first.'"

After one hundred missions over North Vietnam, Lacy returned home to his family and reported to the Pentagon in March 1967. This was his first full-time staff job after being in the Air Force for fifteen years. He says that the first thing he learned at the Pentagon after his combat tour was that the actual "war" was between the United States Army, Navy, Air Force, and Marines over the Department of Defense budget. He said that he volunteered for another combat tour to get away from the boredom of the Pentagon; his request was disapproved because the Pentagon was a controlled four-year tour. But he was rewarded with promotion to lieutenant colonel in the "secondary zone," meaning one year ahead of his contemporaries. Lacy and his family settled down in the Washington, DC area; son Robert became eligible to be a Boy Scout. Lacy researched the requirements to establish a new troop to accommodate thirty-five boys on a waiting list and formed a new troop in his neighborhood. His wife, Rita, became a Webelos Leader and he helped her with the program.

After Lacy graduated from the Air War College (AWC), he served two years as deputy commander for operations, 1st Tactical Fighter Wing (TFW) at MacDill AFB, Florida followed by two years as vice commander and base inspector general for the 3rd TFW at Clark AB, Philippines. He retired on February 1, 1977, in the grade of colonel. His awards and decorations include Command Pilot, US Army Parachutist Badge, Silver Star, Distinguished Flying Cross, Purple Heart, Air Medals (ten oak leaf clusters), Joint Service Commendation Medal, Air Force Commendation (two oak leaf clusters), AF Combat Readiness Medal, Vietnam Service Medal, and the Marksmanship Medal.

As the old saying goes, Lacy repeated to himself upon retirement, "You can take the pilot out of the airplane, but you cannot take the airplane out of the pilot." Thereafter, he says that he learned how civilian pilots operate and flew small airplanes for some local companies for four years after which he flew jet aircraft for Temple-Inland, Inc. for seventeen years.

Lacy shared these thoughts about his wife, Rita, and their family: "Rita is an Air Force wife. She says an Air Force wife can do anything. I believe it! During our sixty-three years of marriage, my job required me to be away from home at least 50 percent of time during which Rita provided extraordinary care and devotion as a partner, a mother, a teacher, and a surrogate father to our three sons. First and foremost, she is a Christian with great compassion, consideration, interest, and love for everyone. With a charismatic personality, she has always been very active in military and civilian functions such as Officers Wives Clubs, church and Sunday School, charity and social events, two bridge clubs, mah-jongg, and two garden clubs. I could not have performed my job without her total support for which I am most grateful. It is interesting to note that every time I was promoted, she was promoted one rank higher, so now Rita is a general!"

Lacy Breckenridge, notable hero and friend for life.

Major General Patrick J. Halloran, USAF (Ret)

Pat Halloran and I bumped elbows off and on throughout our respective Air Force career days, eventually ending up stationed together as members of the Headquarters, Strategic Air Command Staff at Offutt Air Force Base in the early 1980s. Pat was and remains a friend of all who know him: happy, jovial, always smiling Irishman, with a pleasant warm greeting.

In tracing his remarkable career; Pat flew combat missions in the F-84 during the Korean War. In 1956, he was one of the first group of pilots chosen to fly the new, top secret U-2 aircraft. For the next nine years, he flew high altitude reconnaissance missions around the world, accumulating over 1,600 hours in missions over Cuba during the Cuban Crisis and over Vietnam in the U-2. Pat says that his most dangerous missions in any aircraft, were in the U-2, because of the critical nature of flight in a single engine plane at altitudes seventy thousand plus feet. The U-2 cockpit only pressurized to twenty-nine thousand feet, which requires space suits to be worn in the event of a flameout or a bailout. There was always a concern for the critical oxygen supply and the aircraft handling characteristics at those altitudes. Airspeed control had to be maintained with an eight- to ten-knot window between stall and Mach limit. On one mission, Pat says his space suit helmet oxygen breathing hose disconnected at high altitude, and he immediately began to lose consciousness. With only seconds to spare, he was able to locate the loose hose and make a last-second reconnection.

I chided Pat once about how fortunate he was to be of his relative five feet plus stature so as to be able to sit comfortably in the cockpit of the U-2. I told him that when I once took an orientation flight in the U-2, my long legs barely fit under the yoke and instrument panel, and that I had momentary claustrophobia. I told him that when we leveled off at seventy thousand feet, I could see the curvature of the earth. He smiled and said that all of that was just "routine."

In December 1965, Pat was assigned to Beale Air Force Base, California, and became one of the first pilots to check out in and fly the supersonic SR-71 reconnaissance aircraft. In 1969, he was appointed commander of the 1st Strategic Reconnaissance Squadron. He later served as deputy director of operations for the 9th Strategic Reconnaissance Wing. In July 1972, he returned to Beale Air Force Base as vice commander of the 9th Strategic Reconnaissance Wing and later became commander. He was assigned to Andersen Air Force Base, Guam, in July 1975, as vice commander of 3rd Air Division until July 1976, and then to March Air Force Base, California, where he became chief of staff, Fifteenth Air Force. In June 1977, he was assigned as SAC inspector general and in May 1979, became the command's assistant deputy chief of staff for operations.

It is my pleasure to share the following continuing exceptional story about this extraordinary notable encounter and friend for life, Pat Halloran, who reflects the depth, determination, and endurance of an exceptional man:

> Air Force Legend Is Happy to Be Back in the Cockpit
>
> Air Force Retired Major General Pat Halloran is one of one of only 10 pilots in the Air Force who flew operation missions in both the U-2 and SR-71 high altitude reconnaissance aircraft. For a man who flew harrowing combat missions during the Korean War and piloted the latest and greatest of the nation's spy planes during 34 years in the Air Force, it seemed odd that an accident during a casual morning walk in Colorado Springs would ground him.

Air Force General Pat Halloran, 90, a legend in flying circles, mixes the story of his adventurous life with a bit of quirky Irish humor. A Minnesota native, Halloran never dreamed as a young man that he'd end up as a decorated pilot, one of only 10 pilots in the Air Force who flew operation missions in both the U-2 and SR-71 high altitude reconnaissance aircraft. The SR-71 is a lightning-quick aircraft that cruised at a speed of 2,000 mph and an altitude of 80,000 feet. The aircraft set a record from New York City to London in one hour and 51 minutes.

After graduating from high school in 1946, Halloran aspired to become a music teacher. A drummer in several bands, he attended MacPhail Conservatory of Music in Minneapolis when his mother called one day and told him he'd been drafted. Halloran figured he'd serve a couple of years and get the GI bill to pay for the remainder of his schooling. It would all work out, he thought. Both of his brothers had served in the U.S. Army during WWII, and Halloran intended to serve in the Army, too. But while waiting outside the office of an Army recruiter, Halloran's fate forever changed.

"This guy, he was wearing the new blue uniform. He was a good-looking guy with a band of ribbons," Halloran said. "He asked me if I wanted to be a part of the Aviation Cadet program and become an officer and a pilot. I had never been on an airplane in my life but 20 minutes later, I had signed up for the Air Force. It was a total freak switch.

"Once I got flying air planes, I thought 'this is it. I love it,' and that was the end of my musical career." Halloran flew more than 100 combat missions in F-84 fighter jets over North Korea in the early 1950s, and when a photographer showed up at one of the air strips, a photo of Halloran and his buddy appeared on the cover of Newsweek magazine in 1951.

During his nine years with the U-2 program, General Halloran flew missions from nearly a dozen forward operating locations overseas and accumulated more than 1,600 flying hours in the high-flying reconnaissance aircraft.

In December, 1965, he was assigned to Beale Air Force Base in California and became one of the first pilots to fly the SR-71 aircraft. He flew the U-2 over Cuba and the SR-71 Blackbird and the U-2 over Vietnam. He was appointed commander of the 1st Strategic Reconnaissance Squadron and later served as deputy director of operations for the 9th Strategic Reconnaissance Wing. He progressed through a number of high staff positions with a final assignment on the staff of the Joint Chiefs of Staff in the Pentagon. "I was just getting the hang of it when they said 'time's up.'" Halloran said.

After he retired from the Air Force, Halloran spent two years flying around the United States looking for a place to live. When he found a townhome at the base of Cheyenne Mountain in Colorado Springs, he knew he'd found a place to call home. "As soon as I got here, I said, 'This is it. I made some modifications and I love the location and I love the town. It was the best decision I ever made to come to Colorado Springs.'"

He turned an office in the new place into a mini-museum with old black-and-white photographs, aviation books, models of the airplanes he has flown and the cover of Newsweek maga-

zine from 1951. He became a regular at air shows, and had annual speaking gigs at the legendary air show in Oshkosh, Wisconsin. He kept in touch with Kelly Johnson, an aeronautical design and engineering genius from Lockheed, who is recognized for his contributions to a series of important aircraft designs, most notably the U-2 and SR-71 Blackbird.

He flew his experimental kit airplane often from Meadow Lake Airport, east of Colorado Springs, traveling often to see friends throughout the United States and attend Air Force reunions. He took walks daily to stay healthy and last June 22, 2017, what he calls a "day that will live in infamy," he was struck by a car while walking across Star Ranch Road and Highway 115 intersection in south Colorado Springs. "I was fortunate I wasn't killed," he said. "This guy came around the corner, and I had walked about half way through the crosswalk and pow! He knocked me eight feet in the air."

Halloran floated in and out of consciousness. He remembers people hovered over him while he lay in the street. One woman held his head in her hands and offered words of encouragement.

"She sat with me until the ambulance came. She was really my protector. I have no idea who she was but she told me, 'It's going to be all right. Don't move. I've got you.'"

An ambulance arrived and rushed him to UCHealth Memorial Hospital Central, where southern Colorado's only board-certified fellowship-trained orthopedic trauma surgeon, Dr. Peter Fredericks, was waiting. General Halloran had a punctured lung, nine broken ribs, a broken clavicle and serious injuries to both hips: bilateral

acetabulum (hip socket) fractures. Fredericks, who is known for patching people back together who have suffered multiple injuries and severe trauma, did a total hip replacement surgery on one hip with the help of Dr. Dennis Phelps and fixed the other hip in a separate surgery by placing three screws and a plate.

Halloran spent three days in the Intensive Care Unit—days that he says were "pretty fuzzy" before he was moved to a live-in physical rehabilitation facility to learn how to walk again. While in rehab, he lost 20 pounds. "I was on so many medications, I couldn't eat anything.

"They induce pain," he said of rehabilitation, "And I told them: 'That is what I want because I know I'm doing something.'"

When he got back home, where he lived alone, he was not able to drive and could barely get around. A longtime friend moved in to his home and took him to outpatient rehab and doctor's appointments.

"He really saved my bacon," Halloran said. Eventually, though, he recovered enough to walk four miles with a walker, and then progressed to walking 1.5 miles with only a cane. A friend sent him an Irish shillelagh walking stick, a gift that he cherishes. By November, he was able to walk on his own, without a cane or assistive devices.

"I feel like I have really progressed a tremendous amount," Halloran said. Before Thanksgiving, he went to Meadow Lake Airport. Two of his fellow pilots helped him get up on the wing and into the cockpit of his plane, and he took off for the skies, taking in the iconic sites of the Pikes Peak Region—Garden of the Gods, The Broadmoor Hotel and the Air Force Academy. "It was so nice,"

he said, "to be airborne again," back in the saddle that made him a legend in the sky. (Erin Emery, Content Manager, Marketing, Communications and Media Relations University of Colorado Memorial Hospital Central, March 9, 2018)

Major General Pat Halloran is a distinguished graduate of the Air Force Air War College, a command pilot with more than eight thousand flying hours, including six hundred hours in SR-71s. Among his military decorations and awards are the Defense Distinguished Service Medal, Distinguished Service Medal, Legion of Merit with oak leaf cluster, Distinguished Flying Cross with oak leaf cluster, Meritorious Service Medal, Air Medal with eleven oak leaf clusters, Air Force Commendation Medal, and Army Commendation Medal.

State Trooper Earl "Dub" Gillum, Texas Highway Patrol

On October 1, 1998, State Trooper Dub Gillum was patrolling Highway 377 near Granbury when he observed a reckless driver who was also speeding—doing 85 mph in a 55-mph zone. Gillum stopped the pickup truck; the driver, a disheveled young twenty-three-year-old, named Charlie Cook, turned out to be a wanted felon with seven outstanding felony warrants and a known user of methamphetamine. Without getting out of his truck, the driver fired at Gillum, hitting him ten times in less than three seconds as Gillum approached the driver's side door. The first shot struck Gillum's hat above the forehead, the second shot hit him in the left temple piercing the left eye and then entered the nasal cavity where it exploded and shredded his right eye. The third, fourth, and fifth shots struck Gillum in his left forearm. The sixth and seventh shots entered Gillum's left hip (one of those bullets traveled across the pelvis to right femur and down to the right knee), and finally, the eighth, ninth, and tenth shots were to his back. Gillum credits the bulletproof vest he was wearing that night with saving his life.

The shot to the temple immediately blinded him, so Gillum was unable to return fire, Cook's vehicle struck Gillum as it sped off knocking Gillum to the hard surface of 377 dislocating his right shoulder. Two vehicles had to swerve to avoid hitting the trooper as he lay bleeding on the highway. A third vehicle, driven by a local, witnessed the shooting and stopped his pickup truck and trailer to block the traffic until the ambulance was able to arrive. While lying there, Gillum used his handheld radio to call for backup, then relied on years of training and faith to remain calm. Twenty-five hours later, the Fort Worth Canine Tactical Unit and Texas Rangers tracked the shooter to a wooded area in Fort Worth where the shooter fired at authorities injuring the K-9 officer and killing the police canine, which had been taken out of retirement to assist with this chase. The pursuing officers returned fire, killing the wanted felon. While on the run from the law, Cook had called his father and told him he had shot and killed a highway patrolman. This was more than likely the cause of his father having a heart attack.

In an amazing twist of fate, the father of the young perpetrator ended up in the hospital room right next to Dub Gillum. The father improved and was later released. The Ft. Worth police officer earned a Medal of Valor for his actions.

Dub Gillum stayed in the hospital for the next two weeks. He was off duty for a total of fourteen months and went through ten eye surgeries to retain his sight. Dub Gillum credits the Good Lord, his wife, and his mother with the gift of eyesight today. His wife and mother were at his bedside for the entire two weeks, constantly changing the cold compress on his eyes. He said they rotated these compresses every five to ten minutes during that first two weeks. Dub was told by a surgeon that he would never see again. Dub dismissed this doctor and said he would find another that would help recover his vision. He frequently says that he is grateful to God, his family, friends, and the wonderful surgeons for his miraculous recovery. The retina surgeon Dub credits with his "miracle work" has since retired, but the friendship has long remained, as has the friendship with the Ft. Worth police officer and his family.

Interestingly enough, his wife went back to school stating if she could "nurse Dub back to health, she would definitely like to become a nurse." Dub still has three bullets in his body; located in his right knee, his left arm, and his forehead. During the fourteen months he was off work, Dub Gillum, who has worked as a K-9 handler himself, helped to raise money for the purchase of a canine to replace one that died in the line of duty. Dub also worked with the Ft. Worth Hospital to raise money for a new trauma wing.

Later, Dub Gillum, always on duty, was assisting a stranded motorist with a flat tire when the man said he felt very tired. The motorist was resting in the front passenger seat while Dub changed his tire when he heard the man shout out, and he ran to see that the fellow had thrown up and was unconscious. Immediately clearing his airways and calling for an ambulance, Dub was able to save the man's life. The man's fiancée told Trooper Dub that when he was shot, they had kept Dub in their prayers to heal and fully recover. Years later, Dub's recovery would lead to saving their loved ones' life.

I have enjoyed the privilege of being on the same speaking venue with Dub Gillum on several occasions and always marveled at his sense of humor and positive attitude toward life and the opportunities that lie before us. Dub's current position as Public Information & Safety Education Officer is a perfect fit for him because he has a strong passion for law enforcement and young people. He spends time talking and visiting with children and young adults about the dangers of drug abuse and has educated the public about the proper use and installation of car seats while personally inspecting over ten thousand child car seats. As a police instructor, Dub Shares his experiences on Officer Safety and Survival through a program he presents to police officers called "Mindset."

When asked about his many experiences with the Texas Highway Patrol, Trooper Dub Gillum smiles, "Life is simple—when life gives you lemons, you make lemonade."

Thank you, Trooper Dub Gillum, for all you do to keep the community safe and to making Texas and this world a better place!

State Senator Brian D. Birdwell, Texas

September 11, 2001, was a fateful day for Lt. Colonel Brian Birdwell. As military aide to the deputy assistant chief of staff for Installation Management, he arrived at his office in the Pentagon early as always and began this Tuesday morning, sorting out the day's work ahead. After a quick coffee, he took a break to visit the men's bathroom down the hall from his office. In the flash of a minute, he was thrown from the second floor of the Pentagon to ground level. He had no idea that an American Airlines 757 passenger jet, Flight 77, had been hijacked by terrorists and flown into his side of the building or that he was one of the few survivors from his office sector of the Pentagon. Nor was he to know the levels of pain and agony that would be associated with his resulting injuries and recovery. He was unconscious when rescued by another Air Force officer, Rob Maness, and taken to a local hospital, where it was determined that he had sustained burns over 60 percent of his body. He was transferred to the Brooke Army Burn Center in San Antonio where he would remain in recovery and rehabilitation for most of the next year. On his second day in the hospital, he received a surprise visit from President George W. Bush, who stood patiently in salute as Brian could barely raise and lower his wounded arm. He underwent thirty-nine operations and numerous skin grafts over the next several years. Brian credits his physical and spiritual healing to grace through Jesus Christ.

A native Texan, Brian graduated from Lamar University in Beaumont with a degree in criminal justice and a commission as a second lieutenant in the Army from the ROTC program. He entered active duty with the Army in 1984, at Fort Sill, Oklahoma. From there, he was stationed across the United States, South Korea, and Germany. In 1990, he was deployed to the Middle East as Operation Desert Shield built up and on into Operation Desert Storm. He was assigned to the 2nd Armored Cavalry Regiment in Iraq, where he was awarded the Bronze Star. For his wounds at the Pentagon, he was awarded the Purple Heart.

Brian was forced to retire due to the injuries sustained in the Pentagon attack and awarded the Legion of Merit for his service. Not one to give up on life, he decided to enter politics. He ran for the Republican State Senate, District 22, in a special election to fill the vacancy in 2010, caused by the illness and withdrawal of Senator Kip Averitt, and won.

He ran unopposed in the general election on November 2, 2010. His present State Senate District 22 is composed of Bosque, Coryell, Ellis, Falls, Hill, Hood, Johnson, McLennan, and Somervell Counties. Senator Birdwell currently serves on five state government committees: Higher Education (Vice-Chair), Veterans Affairs & Military Installations (Vice-Chair), Economic Development, and Government Organization.

I met Brian Birdwell shortly after he moved to Granbury, Texas, and began his political career. I had the privilege of serving with him in the local Military Officers Association of America (MOAA) and introduced him on numerous occasions as the keynote speaker at various events. He, in turn, introduced me when I was called to meet the State Senate Confirmation Committee following my second term appointment by Governor Rick Perry, to serve on the Board of Directors, Brazos River Authority. He and his wife, Mel, presently reside in Granbury, Texas, where he continues to serve in the Texas State Senate.

3

Notable Political Encounters

everal of the following notable encounters with political figures were, in some cases, brief, while others evolved into lengthier visits, exchanges, and lasting friendships. Each began with a salutary handshake and words of greeting. Each of those I have chosen to characterize herein was also exceptionally special and remain indelible in my memory bank. I have chosen to recall and share these memorable encounters as they surfaced in my thoughts rather than as favorites or in alphabetical or chronological order.

George H.W. Bush, President, United States

I received an invitation during the summer of 2007 to attend and participate in the centennial celebration of my hometown of Tomball, Texas, scheduled for December 2, 2007. I had grown up in Tomball since the age of three when my family moved there from North Louisiana. I was also advised that former President George H.W. Bush was being invited as the guest of honor and keynote speaker. I had been back to my hometown many times over the years, even as my parents passed on, to speak at Rotary Club events, Chamber of Commerce meetings, and the locally "famous" Oil Patch Kids Reunion.

The latter group was created decades ago to honor and bring back home those of us who grew up in the heyday oil drilling days

that made Tomball famous. Among those "notables" of the times who worked in the Tomball oil patch industry was George H.W. Bush.

The mega event took place as scheduled at the Tomball High School football field and stadium, complete with wide screens, orchestra music, and all the trimmings to honor the one hundredth birthday of our hometown. The president arrived just at dusk and was met at his limousine by a greeting party in golf carts. As I observed his arrival from the main stage, I noted that he rejected the golf cart and chose to walk the length of the stadium, shaking hands with all the lucky ones sitting on the front row. Following his greetings tour around the field, he sprightly bounced up the stairway to the stage, smiling and continuing to shake hands.

I stood up from my chair, and when President Bush spotted me "in uniform," he walked directly toward me, extended arm and hand and with a big smile, "Hello, General Adams, good to see you!"

Without attempting to describe the feeling of first meeting the former president, it was the shock of his calling me by my name. I had, of course, never met nor even seen him before, but he had obviously done his homework with regard to people's names in preparation for greeting each of those on the program. He was quite a gentleman and I was impressed by his genuine warmth and friendly manner.

I was honored to introduce him, recalling in my remarks, "The experience of the life and pride of growing up in the small town of Tomball, with very close friends, small classes, knowing every teacher and knowing them well. And, there's no greater honor than to be invited back home."

I also referred to President Bush's oil field "heritage" in Tomball as well as honoring his military service. I chided, as I have frequently, that I wore my uniform for the event for "three reasons:" First, I was invited to; second, I wore it in honor of all of our service men and women, past and present; and thirdly, "because it still fits!" He, of course, in kind, recalled the Tomball oil fields and responded that his ragged old uniform was still out in the Pacific Ocean somewhere, referring to when he bailed out during World War II and was rescued by a Navy submarine. It was truly a notable encounter to remember! And as I continue to scribe memories in this work, the coincidence of the death of his beloved wife, Barbara Bush, has occurred and the close-up visuals of the aging president on television brings back that pleasant memory of meeting him just a few years past. He has sadly lost his vigorous energy I remembered of that evening, walking spritely across the stage happily greeting everyone.

I will digress here following that incredible latter-day honor of sharing the pleasure of my encounter with President George H.W. Bush and continue in a somewhat chronological order with the meetings of other notable political figures along the way.

Edgar J. Herschler, Governor, Wyoming

I had met Ed Herschler a year or so before he was elected governor of the State of Wyoming. I arrived at F.E. Warren Air Force Base, Cheyenne, in November 1973, to be the vice wing commander, 90th Strategic Missile Wing, to a very pleasant reception by members of the wing and a number of citizens in the city. Cheyenne was one of the most military-friendly communities during our service career, equaling that of Abilene, Texas, of course. Among those I was first to meet was Ed Herschler, a rancher from Kemmerer, Wyoming, and a member of the State Legislature. He had served in the Marine Corps during World War II and returned to the University of Wyoming to secure a law degree. He was a typical small town, easygoing cowboy, known for his warm, cheerful charisma. His cheerful and gracious wife, Casey, was the same.

As time moved on and he became governor, they invited us numerous times to the Governor's Mansion for receptions and special occasions. Anytime that we might have a distinguished visitor on the Air Force Base, the governor and Casey would extend an invitation to bring them to the Mansion for a reception, tour, or just to meet and greet them to Wyoming. I can recount the many times that the governor went out of his way to express his interest in the base and our service members. After serving as commander of the 90th SMW for a year, I was promoted to brigadier general and required to move on. I was given an incredible departure reception, and among the many Cheyenne citizens that came was Governor and Mrs. Herschler. Fast forward to my retirement from the Air Force in 1983 and a letter from Governor Ed Herschler, hand delivered by a Cheyenne citizen.

It was a very gracious letter and also included his down home "cowboy sense of humor": "Chris, when we first met, you were a colonel and I was just about to be the governor of Wyoming and now, you are a major general and I'm still just the governor of Wyoming!"

A memorable encounter with a wonderful gentleman and his lady. Governor Herschler passed away in 1990 at age seventy-two following an unprecedented three terms as governor of the great state of Wyoming.

Terrence A. Todman, U.S. Ambassador to Spain

In 1980, I was pleased to be invited to accompany General Richard Ellis, Commander in Chief, Strategic Air Command on an official trip to visit U.S. Military facilities. He wanted, in particular, to visit our airborne tanker units that were stationed at three different Spanish Air Force Bases in support of our Cold War strategic operations plans. He also invited me to join him in a visit to the U.S. Embassy. There we were greeted upon entry by Ambassador Terrance Todman himself. I knew nothing of the ambassador's background until I hastily studied up about him before the visit. Born in St. Thomas, he was a native of the Virgin Islands and served in the U.S. Army for four years, mostly in Japan. He was appointed Ambassador to Spain by President Gerald Ford. Prior to this assignment, he had served as ambassador to Chad, Guinea, and Costa Rica.

He greeted us with a very warm welcome and escorted us into a posh reception room, offering coffee and snacks, which he served himself. General Ellis thanked him for the opportunity to visit and to discuss our military relations with Spain. He was particularly interested in how well our SAC air crews were conducting themselves at the three bases where we were tenants. The ambassador assured us that all was going well and that the Spanish government welcomed our presence in their country. I found him to be the most pleasant, gracious, and soft-toned person of his position that I had ever met. General Ellis and I later discussed his manner, bright intelligence, and well-informed knowledge of U.S. Military activities. This was a most pleasant encounter, and later I was to observe that Todman went on to serve as ambassador to Denmark and Argentina under Presidents Reagan and Bush. Honored as a Career Ambassador, he had served the United States in six nations.

Michael J. (Mike) Mansfield, U.S. Ambassador to Japan

In the summer of 1981, I was en route to Japan from a visit to U.S. Military operations activities in Australia with General Ellis and members of the SAC staff. As we approached Yakota Air Base outside Tokyo, the general looked across the aisle at me and said that upon landing, he had an appointment with Ambassador Mansfield, and that he wanted me to accompany him. I was completely taken aback.

I promptly replied, "Yes, sir." Thoughts raced through my mind; "If anyone might accompany him, it would be the SAC chief of staff or director of intelligence."

We landed and disembarked. I asked Jim Enney, Director of Intelligence, sitting next to me during the flight, if he would see my luggage to our quarters. He, of course, agreed. I followed General Ellis across the ramp to a waiting U.S. Embassy helicopter. We got aboard, and being used to him being a man of very few words, I didn't pursue my purpose in accompanying him on this visit. I will insert here that it was the hairiest chopper ride I had ever taken. The bird skimmed across the rooftops of Tokyo at what appeared to be no more than a few feet. TV antenna and wiring galore! They were Marine pilots, and I didn't know whether that was routine flight procedure or were they trying to impress the general? We arrived at our destination safely and landed on top of the embassy building.

Ambassador Mansfield greeted us warmly. General Ellis had met the ambassador previously and introduced me. The ambassador extended his hand and welcomed me to the embassy. The general described our visit to Australia and meetings with the Australian Military leaders and facilities. He then pursued questions about our military activities in Japan from the ambassador's perspective. General Ellis called on me to briefly address our strategic planning and weapons activities in the Far East, which seemed to please the ambassador. I was both surprised and pleased with his knowledge of ongoing strategic planning in the Far East. He asked several questions and provided informative responses to my replies. It was a most surprising and enlightening meeting, especially for me!

This encounter was an exceptionally interesting learning experience. Previous to this impromptu visit, I knew little more than the ambassador's name, and admittedly, I learned more about him following our visit and after returning home than I might have ever guessed. His was an extraordinary life's journey. For the interested reader, I will share herein my latter research. Born in 1903, and at age fourteen, Mike Mansfield dropped out of school and lied about his age in order to enlist in the U.S. Navy during World War I. He sailed on numerous overseas trips voyages aboard the USS *Minneapolis*, before his real age was discovered and he was discharged from the Navy. After his discharge from the Navy, he enlisted in the U.S. Army, serving two years from 1919 to 1920. From the Army he joined the Marine Corps, serving two more years until 1922. A tour of duty with the Asiatic Fleet took him along the coast of China, establishing a lifelong interest in Asia.

Having never attended high school, he took entrance examinations to attend the Montana School of Mines where he earned a Bachelor of Arts degree in 1933, and was offered a graduate assistantship teaching at the university. He earned a master's degree from the University of Montana in 1934 with a thesis entitled, "American Diplomatic Relations with Korea." Entering politics, he served as a U.S. Representative for ten years and as a senator for twenty-four years from Montana. He was also the longest-serving Senate Majority Leader. Following retirement from the Senate, he served as the ambassador to Japan from 1977 to 1988. With a full life behind him, he passed away in 2002 at the age of ninety-eight.

As we departed from this visit, General Ellis advised the ambassador that we would be proceeding on to Seoul, Korea, from Tokyo and thence up the Aleutian Chain to our Air Force facilities in Alaska. Our visit lasted for over an hour, which appeared to satisfy the two of them and especially me. And, you are as informed as I became thereafter this improbable encounter.

Barry M. Goldwater, U.S. Senator, Arizona

I was honored to meet Senator Goldwater on three different occasions, each memorable!" While stationed in Washington, DC, and serving at Defense Nuclear Agency, I kept up my flying proficiency at Andrews Air Force Base, flying the T-39 Sabre Liner. The usual routine included being scheduled for a local area, nominal four-hour local flight, make a few touch-and-go landings, with only an occasional requirement to take someone of importance or an emergency, etc., to someplace not far away and return.

On one such occasion, I showed up at Andrews Base Operations and met the other pilot who was there to also get in his proficiency flight time. As we were about to file a local area flight plan, the operations officer asked if we minded flying out to Phoenix that afternoon. "What's up?" I asked, and he said that Senator Goldwater was there, "looking for an opportune flight out west." Turns out, we became the "opportune," if we agreed, and it was difficult to not do so. I went out on the flight line, fired up the little jet, and taxied around to the "red carpet" in front of base ops. The other pilot escorted the senator out to the plane, he got aboard, stuck his head in the cockpit, and shook hands with me, thanking us for "the lift." Just as we were about to close the entrance door, the ops officer came running out with a paper bag along with a plastic bag of ice, "for the senator," he said, smiling. The other pilot took the "products" back to him in the cabin, making sure that there was a drinking glass in the bag with the bottle of whiskey. The flight was uneventful, and we landed at the Phoenix Airport where a car was waiting for the senator. He shook both our hands when he disembarked, thanking us for the ride. The other pilot took the yoke for the flight back, and it all made for an eventful day.

My second opportunity to meet with Senator Goldwater occurred at Davis-Monthan Air Force Base, Arizona, where I was stationed as commander, 12th Air Division. I decided to host a dinner party for the good citizens of Tucson, who were so much in support of the base and our military stationed there. I also contacted Senator Goldwater's office to invite him to come and be our speaker, if he was available. Indeed, he was and accepted my invitation. During the intervening weeks or so before the dinner, I was contacted by the commander, 15th Air Force, that my 12th Air Division Headquarters was going to be relocated to Dyess Air Force Base, Texas, near Abilene. He also advised that the planned move was to be held in confidence, pending an official formal announcement at a future time.

My first thoughts were, "Wow, moving to Texas!" I had not told my staff and sat on the information per my instructions from higher up, pending a forthcoming formal announcement. The time came for the Tucson dinner party; I met the senator when he arrived on base and escorted him to the Officers Club. I reminded him of the time "years ago" when I flew him from Washington, DC, to Phoenix.

He smiled and thanked me, as if he really remembered . . .

The dinner party reception and dinner went off very well, especially with the senator being there to meet and greet. Then the unexpected happened. During his remarks, he commented that he was very regretful that the Air Force had decided to "move the 12th Air Division, General Adams, and his people to Texas."

I sat frozen in my chair as I looked around at the audience and to many of my staff officers also sitting there. I tried to look as surprised at his statement as all of them. As soon as he finished his talk and I thanked him, I eased out of the room as fast as I could, leaving my wife, Alene, to continue to host him, as he milled around with his citizen fans.

I called General Harris at 15th Air Force Headquarters and told him about the event. He wasn't very happy, to say the least, but, "stuff happens." I returned to the Officers Club, escorted the senator back to the flight line and his waiting aircraft; not one word was said about our impending move. My mobile phone rang for most of the night, citizens of Tucson, the local newspaper, etc. I tried to be as uniformed as everyone else. What an evening to remember!

My third "notable" encounter with Senator Goldwater occurred during my duty at Headquarters, Strategic Air Command, some years later, when I along with General Davis, the CINC, were "invited" to testify before the Senate Armed Forces Committee, chaired by Senator Barry Goldwater. He summoned us to come in and provide his committee with a classified briefing on strategic nuclear war planning. I had provided him and the Committee with a detailed written outline before we were to present ourselves. The event turned out to be routine; just a few questions from him and some of the members, all easily addressed. He thanked us for responding to his invitation, addressing their questions, and, the pressure off for that one! It was a pleasant overall encounter with a very conservative and patriotic gentleman.

Secretary of State Alexander M. Haig, General, US Army (Ret)

I had the pleasure of meeting Secretary Haig at an event at Offutt Air Force Base, Nebraska, in 1981. I was introduced to him by my hero and mentor of all time, General Russell Dougherty, former CINCSAC. It was a very casual and brief introduction during which General Dougherty went out his way to provide the secretary "too much" of my Air Force background, but as all of our egos enjoy being stroked, General Dougherty was a pro at ego-building. The secretary extended his hand and was very cordial, exchanging a few words between General Dougherty and myself. I very much enjoyed the meeting encounter and chat.

A brief respite, Secretary Haig was a war-tested highly decorated Army veteran, a "faster burner," we would call such as he in the military. He also became a highly controversial political figure. He served as White House Chief of Staff to Presidents Nixon and Ford, where he requested and continued to retain his Army commission and rank. He was later appointed Secretary of State by President Ronald Reagan. There is much more to be learned about Alexander Haig, but I will leave that to the reader. I do recall one bit about his rise in rank in the Army. I was returning from a trip to the Far East with Lt. General Carroll Dunn, my boss at Defense Nuclear Agency, when we landed at Vanderberg Air Force Base to refuel. Major Tom Kelly, General Dunn's aide, went into base operations to contact our office back in Washington. When he returned, he told General Dunn that the news in Washington was that Major General Alexander Haig had just been promoted to four stars. General Dunn was in shock. He said that was impossible to be promoted from two to four stars! He said that he remembered when Haig made brigadier just a "couple years ago!"

Orrin G. Hatch, U.S. Senator, Utah

Strategic Air Command observed a policy of ensuring that all aircraft arriving at Offutt Air Force Base during normal or after hours with a VIP on board would be met by a general officer. If it was an official visitor, they would be met by the appropriate office of interest. If it was an impromptu stop by, to refuel, etc., then the general officer on call for the day or night would meet the aircraft, welcome the VIP passenger and host him or her until the aircraft was refueled and on its way. One such early two o'clock morning in the summer of 1982, my phone rang with the SAC Command Post officer advising me that they had a VIP inbound, Senator Orrin Hatch. I rubbed my eyes, put on my dress uniform, and headed to base operations. The T-39 Saberliner taxied up to a stop, the door opened, and the senator ducked his head to clear the overhead as he stepped down the steps.

He looked up with a smile and ask, "General, what on earth are you doing out here at this time of the morning?"

I saluted and held out my hand, "Welcome to Offutt and Omaha, Senator. Come on in, stretch your legs, and relax for a spell."

He patted me on the back as we walked into the VIP Lounge, asking me where I was from, etc. Once inside, he walked around for a bit, commenting on the pleasant lounge. I offered him coffee and fresh made cookies that were prepared daily for the lounge by wives on the base. The senator from Utah had been in office since 1977 and was a super gracious gentleman. He asked about what my job was, general questions about SAC, and was exceptionally complimentary about our hospitality. I had met a few other VIPs transiting Offutt, but Senator Hatch was by far the most impressive and memorable. The CINC received a pleasant letter from the senator thereafter, lauding the Command for its considerate hospitality. A memorable encounter.

Dan Quayle, Vice President, United States

In the summer of 1990, Dr. Floyd English, President, Andrew Corporation, with whom I was employed, invited me to accompany him and a Chicago Business Leaders group of twenty-five, to travel to Washington, DC, for a three-day visit to include the White House, Congress, and many other features in the city. I supposed that it was a reward for my work in China and Saudi Arabia; both countries I had visited on behalf of demonstrating Andrew communications systems. Following a superb dinner the evening before and accommodations at the Sheraton Hotel, we boarded a bus to the White House where we were expected to meet the president. After a guided tour of the beautiful facility, we were escorted into the main briefing room. As we sat waiting for the president to enter the room, in came Vice President Dan Quayle. We all stood as he walked up to each one of us, extended his hand in welcoming. I must say, I was most impressed with his gracious and polite demeanor.

In my own case, he walked up to me briskly, looking me straight in the eyes, shook my hand, "Dan Quayle," he said, smiling.

I responded with my name and—

He quickly said, "Welcome to the White House," as he moved to the next guest. He then advised the group that President Bush had

been called to attend to other business and apologized for his not meeting with us. He continued speaking in general terms about present goings on in government for twenty minutes and then walked by the group again, shaking hands with each one, and thanking us for coming. A very brief encounter, but another one in the memory book.

James A. Baker III, White House Chief of Staff

We received notice in mid-March 1981, that President Reagan was planning a visit to Headquarters, Strategic Air Command sometime in early April and that his Chief of Staff, James Baker, would be coming out for a survey pre-visit beforehand. Mr. Baker arrived a week or so later and was met by General Ellis, SAC Commander in Chief. After a series of briefings on the SAC mission, Cold War preparations worldwide, operational planning, etc., Mr. Baker was handed over to me for an orientation and tour of the secure SAC/ JSTPS underground facilities. My position at the time was deputy chief of staff, SAC, Operations Planning and the dual-hatted position of assistant vice director, Joint Strategic Target Planning Staff (JSTPS), and in that position, reporting to Vice Admiral Ken Carr. All of that said, I escorted Mr. Baker downstairs three stories to the highly secured "SAC Underground."

In doing my homework and that by other staff members in preparation for his visit, I did the traditional review regarding "who we were about to meet and entertain." James Baker had been a Houston attorney. Born in Houston, he attended the Private Hill School and Princeton University before serving in the United States Marine Corps. He later graduated from the University of Texas School of Law and pursued a legal career. He became a close friend of George H. W. Bush and worked for Bush's unsuccessful 1970 campaign for the United States Senate. After the campaign, he served in various positions for President Richard Nixon. Thereafter, Baker served as Undersecretary of Commerce under President Gerald Ford and ran unsuccessfully for election as the attorney general of Texas.

He ran George H. W. Bush's unsuccessful campaign for the 1980 Republican presidential nomination, which Ronald Reagan won. But he made a favorable impression on Reagan and was appointed as his White House Chief of Staff.

Mr. Baker was exceptionally friendly, polite, and cordial; he immediately put you at ease when speaking with you. He told me to lead the way as we entered the elevator and exited on the underground floor where my office was located. We were confronted by a SAC Elite Guardsman when we departed the elevator, and I vouched for Mr. Baker. I escorted him first into my office where I had a slide briefing prepared to describe the JSTPS organization, its purpose for being co-located with SAC Headquarters, and our mission. None of that I will go into here, but it was very important and pleasing to those of us on the SAC/JSTPS staffs to know and understand that the president of the United States was interested in US Cold War central war planning operational activities.

I briefed Mr. Baker as planned, during which he demonstrated exceptional interest and asked numerous questions that centered to the core of our operations. It was obvious that he had done his homework prior to the visit and was preparing to provide the president a detailed overview prior to his scheduled visit. After completing my presentation and responding to his questions, I offered to take him on a brief tour of the facilities.

As we departed my office and began our walking tour, he asked me where we were going. I told him that I was going to show him "where the rubber meets the road." He smiled. Then, I explained, "Sir, this is where all US nuclear war planning is conducted. I have two hundred plus bright young Air Force and Naval officers who are charged with matching anticipated target intelligence with the size of nuclear weapon that might be used to destroy that target should the Cold War descend into a 'heaven forbid' actual war." He nodded with a grim smile. I also explained that Air Force weaponry planning included bombers, nuclear bombs, and intercontinental ballistic missiles, as well as Navy submarine launched missiles.

I went on to explain that the JSTPS briefed the Joint Chiefs of Staff on the national war plan each year for their consideration and approval. Baker asked a number of questions regarding detailed planning and appeared very satisfied with our responses. He thanked me and our staff members, after which I escorted him upstairs to General Ellis's office. There, he expressed his satisfaction with all that he had been provided during the visit and had no further questions. He said that he would brief the president and keep us informed regarding his anticipated visit. The anticipated visit by President Reagan did not happen after all, due to the assassination attempt against him on March 30, 1981. President Reagan and three others were shot and wounded by John Hinckley Jr. as they were leaving a speaking engagement at the Washington Hilton Hotel. A sad day for America.

James Baker later served as Secretary of the Treasury under President Reagan and as U.S. Secretary of State and White House Chief of Staff under President George H. W. Bush. Thereafter, he became the Secretary of the Treasury. He resigned as treasury secretary to manage George H.W. Bush's successful 1988 campaign for president. After the election, Bush appointed him Secretary of State. As Secretary of State, he helped to oversee U.S. foreign policy during the end of the Cold War and dissolution of the Soviet Union, as well as the Gulf War. After the Gulf War, he served another stint as White House Chief of Staff from 1992 to 1993. A tireless political pursuant, Baker served as United Nations envoy to Western Sahara and as a consultant to Enron. The James A. Baker III Institute for Public Policy at Rice University is named in his honor. James Baker was one of the most pleasant political notable encounters I had the pleasure of enjoying and interacting with over my years at Headquarters, Strategic Air Command.

Robert S. Strauss, U.S. Ambassador to Russia

I made my initial business trip to Moscow in July 1991. It was an eye-opening experience that was difficult to absorb at first! The arrival at Sheremetyevo II Airport and the stairway down into the dungeon-like, sparsely lighted airport building was a shocking introduction of more to come over the next five years, transiting the country, working in the city and beyond. That's a whole other story about which I have written and shared. It took over a year to get my company, Andrew Corporation's joint venture operation organized and running.

Later, herein this work, I will share encounters with other new-found friends in Moscow and beyond. After getting settled in and comfortable with the social and working environment, I asked my agent/interpreter, Erika Nobel, to make an appointment for me with the U.S. ambassador. I felt it important to inform the U.S. ambassador, especially, and other American entities working within the region's local and long-distance communication systems. Virtually all of the telephone systems had either been taken over by the military, destroyed, or worn out. AT&T, among others, were also there to capitalize on a fresh market. As mentioned, the social environment, living conditions, common utilities in Moscow and beyond within Russia was indescribable. It was a war-torn city and country that had not even been bombed during the Cold War but had all appearances. It had destroyed itself. That is a whole other pitiful story of that time. Erika made the appointment with newly appointed Ambassador Robert Strauss.

The ambassador had arrived in Moscow in December 1991, following my July arrival and just four months after the "official" end of the Cold War. A lifelong Democrat, former chairman of the DNC and native Texan, Strauss was appointed by President George H.W. Bush, as the story goes, because he wanted to prove to him that Republicans can trust Democrats. I'll not delve into his incredible background and bio as a lawyer, FBI Agent, and devoted politician, except to say that his is a most interesting study, which I researched in the event the appointment was made. I was back in Dallas when Erika notified me of the embassy's confirmation. I then thought it would be a clever idea to call Ambassador Strauss's brother, Ted, who lived in Dallas, and ask if I might convey any messages or take anything to him. Ted Strauss said that his brother loved Tabasco sauce; he said that he used it on everything from his eggs to his steaks. Before departing, I loaded up a dozen large bottles of Tabasco sauce. Back in Moscow I showed up at the U.S. Embassy at the appointed time along with my company British partner, Pat Murrin. Pat and I had worked together on different company projects for several years, and I thought it to be a good idea to have him along to participate in our discussions. Erika had also advised that we had only a fifteen-minute appointment.

We were met at the embassy by a U.S. Marine sergeant who escorted us to the ambassador's office. I commented to him that we were headed toward the old embassy building entrance rather than the newly constructed towering embassy. The sergeant said that the ambassador preferred the office in the old building rather than next door in the new one. I asked him how they liked the new ambassador.

He replied, smiling, "Sir, he is the best; polite, tough, no nonsense, and we love him!"

The ambassador's secretary met us at the entrance way and guided us to his office. Ambassador Strauss stood up, moved from behind his desk, and welcomed us with warm handshakes, as I introduced myself and Pat. He escorted us to large chairs in the corner of his office, motioned us to sit down. and asked if we would like coffee or tea. We both nodded that we did not.

"I understand you are a former Air Force, General?" He looked at me asking.

"Yes, sir," I replied.

He had obviously looked us up. Looking at Pat, he said, "And, you're from London."

Pat, not one of many words, smiled and nodded. I handed him the package containing the Tabasco sauce and greetings from his brother, Ted. He smiled and began opening the package.

When he saw the Tabasco sauce bottles, he shook his head and said, "Tabasco, great! But where in the hell is the beef? The meat over here is rotten and hardly edible!"

I replied, "Next time, sir."

He asked where we were from originally. I told him that Pat was a native Brit and with our company office in London and I grew up in Tomball, Texas, near Houston. I then commented that I had once been stationed at Dyess Air Force Base, near Abilene. I was familiar with his hometowns of Hamlin and Stamford and had visited both of them.

He chuckled and said he didn't think anyone knew where "those Podunk towns are!"

I knew we were on a short visit time and began to tell him why Andrew Corporation was in Moscow. His phone rang just as I was getting started. He got up, went to his desk to answer. We heard him say, "Hello, Ron, how in the heck are you?" After a time, he continued, "Well, I want to tell you one thing, I want those planes to begin flying into Moscow ASAP. We need to show these people that America also has airlines the same as the UK and Germany!" After a bit, he concluded, "Okay, Ron, that sounds great! Thank you, bring'em on! I will be looking for 'em."

He came back and sat down, "I've been trying to get one of our American air carriers to begin flights into Moscow since I arrived here. That was Ron Hansen, President of Delta, and I believe he is going to get it done." He grumbled and mused on for a while and then asked, "You're not short of time, are you?" I told him no, that our time was his time. "Okay, good!" He smiled. "Now tell me about what you are doing for this godforsaken place."

Before I began to explain our projected work in Russia, I commented that I was surprised that he was still occupying an office in the old embassy with the new one next door. He smirked and said, "Chris, this place is wired like a bird cage, and I want these bastards to hear everything I say in here and especially from people like you, who are here trying to recover the disaster they created for themselves!"

"Wow! Okay," I thought to myself, nodding with a smile. I proceeded to explain that our mission was to create several joint venture U.S.-Russian companies to reconstruct the local and long-distance telephone systems for the people of Moscow and St. Petersburg. I told him that Andrew Corporation was putting up the initial investment, in terms of millions of dollars, as means of a good faith effort to get started. He commented that was most courageous and brave of us! I told him that our engineering concept was to work with the metropolitan underground rail authorities in order to use the subway tunnels as conduits to string fiber optic cables; also that approach would preclude excavating trenches in the city for burying communication cables, as well as not stringing wires across power poles. He was impressed as we discussed the project and asked numerous questions for another hour, which meant the fifteen-minute interview time limit was, "just in case, he became bored" with whomever. I told him that we would also be working with the governments in Belarus and Ukraine in the same manner.

Before departing, I told him about a conversation I had recently at a social gathering with the Russian Vice Minister of Railways, Dr. Boris Nikiforov, and that the minister said that on any given day in Russia, they did not know the whereabouts of upward to ten thousand rail cars. I said he told me that they had no means of tracking their railway cars, if they were placed on a siding or incurred an accident, etc., and that the cars were continuously robbed and vandalized. Then, I told the ambassador that our company had a means of tracking such cars with a bar coding system, and briefly described it to him as I had also to the railway minister. The ambassador said to contact Dr. Nikiforov and tell him that the United States might well be interested in assisting them in such a project to control their rail system if they wished. By the time we finished our conversations, Pat and I had been there for over two hours, and the ambassador displayed no rush for us to depart. He thanked us for coming and sharing our project intentions, wished us good luck, shook hands, and invited us back whenever we wished. He was a delightful gentleman, obviously tough-minded, committed to his assignment, but very easy to interact with, and indeed for us that day, a notable encounter!

Brief footnote: The next evening, back at the Olympic Hotel where Pat I were staying temporarily, we came out of the hotel restaurant and observed at least a dozen Delta Airlines flight crew personnel milling around in the hotel lobby. I walked over to one of the captains and introduced myself; then told him of our visit with Ambassador Strauss and his conversation with their president, Ron Hanson, earlier in the day. The captain said that this was their "virgin" flight into Moscow and they had two flight crews on board for orientation. The ambassador's mission was accomplished! This super patriot passed away in 2014 at the age of ninety-five.

Raymond S. Cline, PhD, CIA

We are privileged to meet many special and unique people along life's pathway. Perhaps the most interestingly unique and broad-based encounter I ever experienced was Dr. Ray Cline. I was introduced to Ray by a mutual CIA friend shortly after I returned from a visit to Beijing, China, in 1988. My friend thought that I would enjoy exchanging stories about my visit and Ray Cline's vast experiences in China and the Far East. By the time I met Ray and his wife, Marjorie, he had long since left his position in the CIA and was operating a private think tank in Arlington, Virginia. I was just slightly overwhelmed when I first met Ray and entered his small office on the second floor of the nondescript office building where he and his wife managed his research activities. He was very gracious when we were introduced and offered me a chair at his work table, where he sat at the end facing me at an angle. I couldn't help but scan the walls surrounding his desk, file cabinets, and work space. The walls were literally covered in individual photographs: large and small, of some of the most notable people in the world. Virtually, if not all, were personally autographed photos: Queen Elizabeth, Winston Churchill, Chiang Kai-shek, Presidents Eisenhower, Truman, Kennedy, Johnson, and senior U.S. generals and admirals by the dozens. I regretted much later that I didn't record or at least jot down all of the major noteworthy people that he had met over his career.

We had a good introductory meeting. Ray asked about my background, which I shared both my Air Force, Strategic Air Command, Los Alamos, and onward to Andrew Corporation, where I was at that time. He asked me dozens of questions about all three of my past experiences, people I had met, known, etc. He was acquainted with several I mentioned, commenting opinions about some of them. We discussed my recent company trip to Beijing, and I explained that I took strictly unclassified communications equipment with me in the form of pulse analyzers, frequency discrimination devices, etc. He shook his head, commenting that "nothing" was unclassified in China. I told him that I had enjoyed an unexpected pleasant meeting and exchange with the Minister of the Navy, Admiral An. The admiral had made a surprise visit to our company trade show display. He was accompanied by two Chinese admirals and his English-speaking lieutenant aide. All of their questions were of a general inquisitive nature, and they didn't stay very long. I added that I had also invited the admiral to attend a social reception that evening for our trade show guests and he, of course, declined. Then to my surprise, that evening a large black limousine drives up and out steps the admiral with his aide!

"They are all unpredictable," Ray commented soberly.

I then told him that our next stop with our mini-communications display was Adelaide, Australia, and their military representatives. But, to our surprise and shock, when we arrived, we found that all of equipment crates and boxes had been vandalized, the electronics dismantled and essentially destroyed.

Ray snickered, "You learned a lesson about the Chinese, didn't you?"

I acknowledged that we had and that our mini-trade show ended. He mused further and shared with me some of his own experiences in China, Taiwan, Korea, etc. Ray Cline was, without a doubt, one of the most brilliant and thoughtful people that I had ever had the privilege of meeting, and I had met many, before and after him! Three degrees, including a PhD, he joined the Office of Strategic Services during World War II and quickly became chief of current intelligence. He later traveled to China where he continued to work with the OSS. In 1946, he was assigned to the Operations Division of the General Staff of the Department of War. He joined the Central Intelligence Agency in 1949. He was initially responsible for intelligence on Korea, but he said that he failed to predict North Korea's 1950 invasion of South Korea and the Korean War. In 1958 he became chief of the CIA station in Taiwan, with undercover title as chief of the United States Naval Auxiliary Communications Center. In 1962, as head of the CIA's Directorate of Intelligence, Ray Cline played a pivotal role in the Cuban Missile Crisis when he concluded that the Soviet Union had shipped nuclear warheads to Cuba and was among those who personally informed President John F. Kennedy. He left government service in 1973, becoming executive director, Center for Strategic and International Studies at Georgetown University. While there, he became a prolific author on American intelligence and foreign policy, and a fiery defender of the CIA in testimony before the United States Congress and public releases to the media. He was best known as a thinker, a "ruminator," and a worrier.

I was privileged to visit and work with Ray Cline for several years, seeking his advice and counsel as I traveled on company business to Saudi Arabia during Desert Storm and the former Soviet Union following the Cold War. He was of exceptional help with advice and counsel as I dealt with issues in both countries. He was always gracious, but direct as well, when it came to asking his opinion or advice on issues. Socially, he was equally open, direct, and very pleasant.

I was having lunch with him at a restaurant in Washington once when he looked up and said, "That's Zbigniew Brzeziński sitting over there. I'm sure you remember him; he was Carter's National Security Adviser. I would like for you to meet him."

He kept an eye on him and when Brzeziński got up to leave, Ray called out to him, "Hey Zbig, how are you doing?"

Brzeziński waved to Ray and strolled over to our table. We both got up; they gave each other bear hugs and Ray introduced me as a "good friend" of his. We shook hands and that was sufficient for me. They chatted for a few minutes and said their goodbyes. I didn't consider this particular meeting a notable encounter.

Another Ray Cline gratuitous surprise occurred when I was visiting in his office one day. He was quizzing about my venture into writing and documenting some of my experiences ongoing in Russia at the time. I shared with him that I had the urge to write about my impressions of Russia in contrast or comparison with what many of us perceived about them as our Cold War enemy. Suddenly, he asked if I had ever met Tom Clancy. Of course, I said that I hadn't.

"Well," he said, "you're considering doing some writing and you're still in town tomorrow, right?" I acknowledged that I was going to be in Washington for another couple of days. "Good," he replied. "Let's do dinner tomorrow evening at the Quinn's Irish Pub here in Rosslyn and you'll enjoy meeting Tom Clancy. Marjorie and I will meet you there at seven."

That was the way with Ray. He was always coming up with impromptu notions and carrying them out. I will delve into that dinner meeting sequel later in this treatise.

I last visited with Ray Cline in his Arlington office in early 1995, which turned out to be a strange meeting. A good friend of mine, Lt. General Lincoln Faurer, former Director, National Security Agency, whom I introduced earlier in this work, was with me. After we concluded our visit with Ray, we chatted about our mutual conclusions that he was having minor delusional problems. Linc and I both detected from the just concluded discussion that while he spoke clearly, he frequently drifted from the subjects at hand and wandered off into unrelated, unconnected topics. This was totally out of character for this astute scholar that I had known for several years.

Several months after that last visit with Ray, I wrote him a brief note, not knowing that he was seriously ill, asking if he would consider providing a blog endorsement for a book I was working on regarding Russia.

I received a brief note shortly afterward from his wife, Marjorie, in which she said, "Chris, unfortunately, Ray can't help you, he can't remember a damn thing. I'm sorry."

That was it, sadly, an extraordinary and notable encounter that I had enjoyed and absorbed for several memorable years.

Ray Cline published ten bestseller nonfiction books, writing up until months before he died in 1996 of Alzheimer's at age seventy-seven. His several publications described the evolution and history of the CIA, its operations under various presidents, revelation of spies, and much more that many in some parts of government wished that he hadn't revealed.

James Richard "Rick" Perry, Governor, Texas

Over the years, I enjoyed several opportunities to be in the company of Governor Rick Perry, either at social dinner events or other special occasions. My last brief encounter occurred in Farmersville,

Texas, where he presented posthumously the Texas Medal of Honor to World War II hero, Audie Murphy. Audie's sister accepted the presentation on behalf of her brother. This special recognition is typical of Rick Perry's attention to veterans and others within Texas who have excelled in service and life. This was also a special event for me, as I have been invited twice before to speak at the Audie Murphy Memorial Museum at Greenville, Texas.

A graduate of Texas A&M University, where he was one of their notable "Yell Leaders," Rick Perry remains a "dyed in the wool" Aggie! He graduated with a degree in Animal Science in 1972, and received a commission in the United States Air Force. Thereafter, he completed pilot training in 1974. He served as a C-130 pilot with the 772nd Tactical Airlift Squadron at Dyess Air Force Base, Texas, where his unit made frequent two-month overseas rotations to RAF Mildenhall in England and Rhein-Main Air Base in Germany. I chided the governor once in later life, reminding him that I was the commander, 12th Air Division at Dyess, while he was stationed there. He responded, "Yes, sir, General, I remember your name, but I was a lowly lieutenant, and we didn't reach that high up to you."

We had a good laugh. His unit was assigned to Dyess, but not under my command, so I told him that he was safe from me.

At that particularly time of Governor Perry's service, his squadron was heavily involved in the 1974 State Department drought relief effort in Mali, Mauritania, and Chad. Two years later they provided earthquake relief in Guatemala. After five years' service, with agriculture in his heart, he decided to leave the Air Force in 1977 with the rank of captain and returned to his West Texas hometown of Haskell and into farming cotton with his father.

In 1984, he successfully ran and was elected to the Texas House of Representatives as a Democrat, which put him on a fast track political career. He served on the House Appropriations and Calendars committees during his three two-year terms in office. Perry became a part of the "Pit Bulls," a group of Appropriations Members who sat during the 1980s. The *Dallas Morning News* named him one of the ten most effective members of the legislature. He announced that he was switching political parties and becoming a Republican in

1989. His political career is a matter of current history, eight years as Texas Commissioner of Agriculture, thence to winning the election to become lieutenant governor under Governor George W. Bush in 1999. He moved into the governor's chair in 2000 following George W. Bush's election as president. He was elected on his own as governor in 2002 and continued to serve for three terms, inclusive of his interim service, to become the longest serving governor of Texas in history. President Trump appointed him Secretary of Energy in 2017, where he continues to serve.

On a personal note, I was honored to be appointed by Governor Perry to serve on the Brazos River Authority Board of Directors in 2005 and reappointed to a second term by him in 2011. This gubernatorial appointment also conferred on me, the title of "The Honorable," which I have preferred to not embrace in favor of my more distinctly earned, military service title.

He and his childhood sweetheart, Anita, a graduate nurse of West Texas State University, have been married since 1982 and have two grown children. If I were to predict the future, I would say, "Look out for more from Rick Perry!"

Kenneth Michael "Mike" Conaway, U.S. Congressman, Texas

I met Congressman Mike Conaway shortly after the realignment of the 11th Congressional District of Texas, which included the City of Granbury where I resided at the time. I was previously aware that he was also an alumnus and graduate of my alma mater, Texas A&M University-Commerce. He had graduated with a Business Administration degree in accounting in 1970, after also enjoying a successful college football stint. He elected to not attempt to play professional football, instead joining the Army.

I was exceptionally impressed, meeting him for the first time. He was full of Texas cordial charm and, as we call it, "down home" humor. We chatted about our respective experiences at A&M-Commerce; both of us agreed it was a most pleasant small college experience and provided us both a considerable kick start into our respective careers.

Mike Conaway is originally from Odessa, Texas, where he also played high school football and was a member of Permian High School's first state championship. Following graduation from A&M-Commerce and his Army service tour, he returned to the Permian Basin, became CPA with Price Waterhouse, and settled in Midland. He joined Arbusto Energy, Inc., owned and operated by George W. Bush, as the Chief Financial Officer. He developed a lasting friendship with President Bush. As he says, "We learned together what it takes to run a business."

After George Bush was elected governor of Texas, he appointed Mike Conaway to the Texas State Board of Public Accountancy, which regulates accountancy in Texas. He served on the board as a volunteer for seven years, the last five as chairman. With Governor Bush's encouragement, he ran for Congress in 2002 but lost. He ran again in 2004 and won with almost 75 percent of the votes. Thereafter, into his seventh term, he has handily won each reelection with an overwhelming majority. With the redistricting of Congressional Districts in Texas in 2010, he became the representative of the 11th District with its twenty-nine counties, reaching three hundred miles across the state, including the cities of Midland, Odessa, San Angelo, Llano, and Granbury.

As a member of the Brazos River Authority Board of Directors, I have invited the congressman to attend an occasional ad hoc committee meeting in Granbury when his schedule permitted. In doing so, he has been very supportive of the Authority's management and initiatives relative to Brazos River which traces far across his district.

A notable political leader, patriot, and friend, it was my pleasure to nominate Congressman Mike Conaway as a Distinguished Alumus of Texas A&M University-Commerce in 2012, which he received at the university's annual gala in 2013.

Congressman Conaway presently serves as chairman, House Committee on Agriculture, member of the Armed Services Committee and the House Permanent Select Committee on Intelligence, as well as Deputy Whip of the Republican Congressional Delegation. In

2017, he was asked by the Speaker of the House to lead the investigation into Russian interference in the 2016 United States elections, with legal assistance from Republican Colleagues, Trey Gowdy and Tom Rooney. The appointment has given him considerable public attention and visibility, all of which he has managed professionally.

As of this writing, Congressman Conaway released the findings of Select Committee on Intelligence: The report, which had undergone the Intelligence Community's (IC) classification review process, followed the March 2018 release of findings and recommendations. Congressman Conaway led the probe since April 2017, released the following statement:

> Last January, we set out to investigate Russian active measures during the 2016 election. Today, we are one step closer to delivering answers to the questions the American people have been asking for over a year.
>
> The findings and recommendations that we are releasing today show a pattern of Russian active measures in the United States, both through cyberattacks and their use of social media to sow discord. This poses a serious threat to future U.S. elections, including the primary elections that are already underway. It's critical to release this information now, to protect our country and our elections from foreign interference. I'm incredibly grateful to the Members and staff who worked tirelessly on this investigation, and this report. It's now time for us to share what we've found, and move forward as one country, united against foreign aggression.

I had the pleasure of enjoying a visit and dinner with Congressman Conaway in the home of Texas A&M University-Commerce, Dr. Ray Keck, as I was wrapping up this treatise. Truly an American Patriot, notable encounter and friend.

An ordained deacon in the Baptist church, Congressman Conaway and his wife, Suzanne, maintain their permanent home in Midland, Texas. They have four children and seven grandchildren.

4

Notable Professional Leaders

My Air Force career and beyond opened a mecca of unexpected encounter opportunities with people I would have never expected to meet within normal circumstances. As portrayed in the previous memorable political meeting ventures, my encounter experiences were virtually unlimited, ranging across a broad spectrum of business and professional leaders, from education to industry to science. Herein, it my distinct pleasure to recall and share many of those memorable meeting adventure encounters.

Thomas K. Kim, PhD, President/ Chancellor, McMurry University

I met Tom Kim shortly after arriving at Dyess Air Force Base near Abilene, Texas, in 1976, when I was reassigned there to become commander of the 12th Air Division. Abilene was an exceptionally friendly city, and especially so to Air Force personnel stationed at Dyess. Dr. Kim and his wife, Martha, were among many at a reception hosted by the Military Affairs Committee of the Chamber of Commerce in honor of the arrival of the 12th Air Division to their city. All three of the local university presidents were present at the reception with, it seemed, "most" of the city. Tom Kim was president of McMurry University, a small private liberal arts Methodist sponsored college of about two thousand students.

Thomas K. Kim (née Kim Kun Hyuk), of Korean heritage, had a natural interest in the military due to the historical nature of his own country, which had been ridden with war throughout its history. We hit it off at the very beginning and became good friends during our assignment there. Over time, he shared with me many stories about his roller-coaster life, growing up within his home country. Although he was born in Shanghai, China, of Korean parents, Tom's early life was spent as a refugee from the Japanese occupiers of the Korean peninsula. Following the end of World War II, his family was able to return to their home in the northern tier of Korea. His life and that of his family was little better due to the growing dissention between the northern segment of Korea, under communist influence and eventual control, and the southern provinces. He once shared with me the pivotal event that literally saved life. His mother has passed away and his father, determined to find a better way of life for Tom and his older brother, took them late one night to the eastern seashore of North Korea where he earlier spotted a motorized fishing boat. His father broke the boat away from its mooring, put Tom and his brother on board, and the three of them set sail out to sea and south. They arrived safely in South Korea and were taken ashore and given safe haven by friendly Koreans. When Tom turned eighteen, he was able to immigrate with his brother, to the United States. With the support of relatives already in the U.S., he was able to attend Berea College in Kentucky. From there he attended Indiana University where he obtained an MBA. After some considerable time, he became an American citizen as a result of a special act of Congress and signed by President Eisenhower.

He returned to Berea College to teach and met Martha Zoellers whom he married in 1958. The couple moved to New Orleans where Tom obtained his PhD in Economics at Tulane University. He immediately began an academic career. Following brief appointments in Ohio and Kansas, he moved on to teach at Texas Tech University in Lubbock, Texas. In 1970, he became president of McMurry College in Abilene, a position he held for twenty-three years. As president of McMurry, he saw the completion of several major construction projects including the Fine Arts building, the Athletic Center, and Student Center. In 1990 McMurry College was renamed McMurry University.

Tom Kim received numerous professional and civic honors along the way, including Citizen of the Year of Abilene in 1986. He retired as president of McMurry in 1993 and resumed his first professional love: classroom teaching. He taught Economics at Abilene Christian University and Hardin-Simmons University, both located in Abilene. He finally concluded a magnificent teaching and administration career in 2011 when his health began to fail.

I will digress to share a particularly memorable story about Tom. He came to Omaha on a recruiting tour in the summer of 1979 after which we had been reassigned there and called me to say hello. I promptly invited him to stay with us on the base at Offutt while he was there. He agreed, and we shared two pleasant evenings chatting about our friendship and Abilene experiences. On his last evening, I thought it would be a fun opportunity for him to attend dinner at a genuine Korean restaurant that we had discovered and enjoyed many times.

The A-Ri-Rang Club was owned and personally managed by Helen Ben, a native Korean, and her restaurant was *native* in every sense: from the decor, to the menu, to the Korean chef and wait staff. I called Helen and told her that we were bringing a very important Korean friend for dinner that evening. When we arrived, we were greeted graciously by the maître d' and escorted to our table. Shortly after we were seated, Helen came strolling in, dressed in the most elegant formal Korean attire I had ever seen. As she approached our table, Tom was awestruck. He stood, bowed, and greeted her in their native Korean; they bowed to one another again and she joined us for dinner. Needless to say, everything was beyond any expectations, from the service to the food and beyond.

The two of them chatted throughout the dinner, mostly in their native language, exchanging backgrounds, etc. And then, I suddenly noticed that Helen had tears streaming down her face, and Tom laid his hand on hers. I asked Tom if anything was wrong.

He looked at me and said, "Chris, would you believe that Helen and her husband came to the United States on the same ship as my brother and I did back in 1948?" He continued, "I don't believe I ever mentioned it to you, but 'Tokyo Rose' was also on that ship. She was a prisoner of war, being brought back to the United States for interrogation. And now, Helen says that she and her husband, a lieutenant in the Korean Army, were also on board; he was coming to the States for training with the American Army."

As I listened to the excitement of the two of them as they exchanged their stories, I thought to myself, "This is one of those events that happens once in a lifetime, if ever!"

My wife and I were in mild shock as we marveled with their story as they both continued to reunite and recall the incredible coincidence within their lives and of that evening. After a lengthy and incredible evening, we said our goodbyes. Tom was exuberant; he smiled and chatted about the evening's experience all the way back to our quarters. He and I enjoyed recalling that special evening several times thereafter over the years.

I learned later from Tom and my own research that the notorious Tokyo Rose, Iva Toguri Aquino, Japanese radio propagandist, was arrested in Tokyo after the war and later transported under military control to the United States. Indeed, she was aboard the same ship that Tom, Helen Ben, and her husband were aboard. They arrived in San Francisco on September 25, 1948, and Tokyo Rose was turned over to the FBI. She was tried for treason and spent six years in federal prison before being released and eventually pardoned by President Gerald Ford in 1977. She passed away in Chicago in 2006. A little more history to add to this special encounter.

My notable encounter and dear friend, Dr. Thomas Kim, passed away sadly after a brief illness on March 12, 2012. His wife, Martha, followed him to heaven on September 17, 2017, leaving behind a son and daughter and six grandchildren.

Robert R. Brownlee, PhD, Astrophysicist, Los Alamos National Laboratory

Bob Brownlee was among the first true scientists I met when I was assigned to Joint Task Force Eight (JTF-8) at Sandia Base, New Mexico, near Albuquerque. As previously stated, to this day, I do not have a *clue* as to why the Air Force chose to send me to this nuclear weapons scientific assignment: a nonscientist, non-engineer, state teachers college business major, and Air Force pilot? Also previously discussed, JTF-8 was a subordinate unit of the Defense Atomic Support Agency (DASA), Washington, DC, where I was eventually to be assigned, and worked closely with the Department of Energy scientific laboratories. These included Sandia Laboratory, co-located on Sandia Base, Los Alamos National Laboratory, Los Alamos, New Mexico, and Livermore National Laboratory, Livermore, California. JTF-8 was responsible for coordinating weapons and associated testing with the various laboratories.

Accordingly, Johnston Atoll, a small island located in the South Pacific, belonged to JTF-8 and was the operating location for numerous scientific testing and exercise activities. I spent many a week and month at Johnston Atoll over the next few years with such work. Bob Brownlee was an esteemed Los Alamos scientist working principally with astronomy and astrophysics, which were his principal degree majors from the University of Kansas and Indiana University. Bob and I hit it off at the very beginning of our introduction, I believe because he has served in the Army Air Corps in WWII and held great respect for the military. Our friendship grew as we worked together at JTF-8 and during the various trips to Johnston Atoll. To digress, when Bob heard that I was retiring from the Air Force and accepting an appointment to Los Alamos, he traveled to Omaha and Offutt Air Force Base to attend my retirement ceremony.

He and his lovely late wife, Addie Leaha, were to become the closest of our friends during my assignment to the Laboratory. It is also important to briefly summarize this great and wonderful man's history and contributions to science and the world. Bob spent virtually his entire career at the Los Alamos National Laboratory, retiring in 1992 to Loveland, Colorado. In his early life, he was an Air Corps B-29 navigator during WWII and was on the island of Tinian in the Marianas at the end of the war from where the B-29s launched to drop the atomic bombs on Japan. He joined Los Alamos after the war where he was Alternate Division Leader of the Nuclear Test Division and Division Leader of the Geosciences Division. He had many direct duties associated with JTF-8, including responsibility for nuclear atmospheric testing in the Pacific and was the Scientific Deputy Commander of Joint Task Force Eight at the time of its inactivation in 1972. Bob was a principal participant in more than three hundred underground nuclear tests. He was also a member of the US Delegation to the United Nations for the Geothermal Energy Program. He spent a year as Visiting Assistant Professor of Astronomy at UCLA. He participated in solar eclipse expeditions to Mexico, Canada, South America, and Africa. He was a participant and sometimes the test director of research rocket launches in Kauai and Poker Flat, Alaska.

Two memorable experiences with Bob Brownlee had to do with my son, Christopher, whom Bob found considerable favor with during our Los Alamos tour of duty. He was to be involved in an experiment to track the reentry of the rocket booster engine following the launch of a NASA shuttle from Cape Canaveral. The reentry tracking was to take place on the north end of the island of Hawaii, and he thought it would be a great experience to invite my son, Christopher, to accompany him and the scientific team to witness the event. We agreed, and excitedly the high school freshman flew off with the team to Hawaii. When he returned, he said that Dr. Brownlee had kept him busy with a clipboard and documenting various activities during the exercise. Great adventure and another memorable experience for this young high schooler.

The second experience that our son had with Bob occurred after I left Los Alamos and was living in Dallas. Christopher was a senior in high school then and a member of the academic decathlon team. When the team began a study of astronomy, he ventured to invite Dr. Brownlee to come to Dallas and provide a presentation to the decathlon team members on his experiences in the world astronomy and astrophysics. Bob readily agreed and flew to Dallas to the delight of the students and the high school.

Dr. Robert Brownlee's honors and awards include being named a National Foundation Fellow, a University Fellow, and having an Honorary Doctor of Science Degree from Sterling College. In March 2015, an active space asteroid was named in his honor, "Asteroid 15970 Robertbrownlee." The Department of Energy had previously named Robert Brownlee, Distinguished Associate of the Department of Energy in 1993. He was a member of the American Astronomical Society. He has been listed in American Men of Science, Dictionary of International Biography, Leaders in American Science, and in Marquis, Who's Who in the West.

Sadly, as I urged to complete and share this published work, I was informed that Dr. Robert R. Brownlee, a notable friend for life, passed away on May 2, 2018.

Dr. Donald M. Kerr, Director, Los Alamos National Laboratory

My unexpected and surprising assignment by the Air Force to the nuclear testing unit, Joint Task Force-Eight, at Sandia Base, New Mexico, in 1967, brought an equally number of unexpected encounters. Among those just introduced, Dr. Bob Brownlee. JTF-8 interacted with each of the National Laboratories, including Los Alamos, Sandia, and Livermore Labs. Due to the mission of JTF-8 and weapons testing, we worked more closely and interacted with the personnel, engineers, and scientists at Los Alamos than the other two labs. In addition to Bob Brownlee, I bonded a friendship with a young Cornell University nuclear physicist, Donald Kerr, PhD. We interacted and worked on numerous programs and projects, much as I did with Dr. Brownlee. It became apparent to me early on that Don Kerr was headed for greater heights in science, executive administration, and beyond.

Dr. Kerr received his bachelor's degree in electrical engineering in 1963 and went on to earn an MS in microwave electronics and a PhD in plasma physics and microwave electronics, all at Cornell University. He joined Los Alamos in 1966, becoming an early leader in conducting and directing research in high altitude weapons effects, nuclear test detection and analysis, weapons diagnostics, ionospheric physics, and alternative energy programs. He left Los Alamos briefly to work with the Department of Energy (DOE), from 1976 through 1979, first as deputy manager of Nevada Operations, and then in Washington, DC, as the deputy assistant secretary and acting assistant secretary for Defense Programs and later for Energy Technology. He was chosen as the fourth director of the Los Alamos National Laboratory in 1979.

I had little contact with Don after I departed JTF-8 in 1970 for Washington, DC, and the Defense Nuclear Agency, although his activities and professional successes with the DOE and at the Laboratory were well-known and easily followed.

In the fall of 1982, while serving as chief of staff, Strategic Air Command, Offutt Air Force Base, I was caught by complete surprise when who would walk into my office but Don Kerr. We enjoyed a pleasant reunion, chat, and catching up visit. I was then caught by further surprise when just before departing, he asked, "What are you going to do when you retire from the Air Force?"

Taken aback, I replied, "Don, I have another five years of active duty before I need to even think about retiring."

He smiled and said, "If you should change your mind before then, give me a call."

His question left me thinking for the rest of that day, pondering what he meant, and then I got back to the business at hand. Almost a week to the day of his impromptu visit, I received a letter from him. Thinking it was a thank-you note from his visit, I laid it aside with the other mail to be opened later in the day when I had time. When I got around to opening the mail for the day, including his, I sat down in mild shock. The "Thank you" words were therein and then the bombshell offering within; "If you should consider departing the Air Force before your mandatory date, give me a call and let's talk."

I called Don the following day and asked about his comment in the note, and he invited me to come out to Los Alamos and chat if it was convenient for me to get away. I took his invitation with much interest and not a clue with regarding what he wished to discuss, so I planned an "official" visit to Kirtland Air Force Base, near Albuquerque. I rented a car and drove up to Los Alamos. He graciously greeted me, and after lunch with several lab colleagues, we went to his office. He motioned me to a chair and proceeded to turn back the large sheets on the tripod before me. The opening page was entitled, Associate Director, Technical Operations. He cut straight to the point by telling me that the incumbent, Dr. Brown, was retiring and he was in great need for a replacement. "Are you interested?"

I must admit that I was dumbfounded. I let his question buzz around within my brain and then asked a stupid question like, "Are you serious?" I knew him well enough to know that he was. He finished the overview of the directorate and all of its both broad and finite details of responsibilities. I was just slightly dumbfounded. We concluded the meeting with an hour of back-and-forth questions on my part and his responses. In the end, he said that he just wanted to test my reaction and looked forward to further discussion. I thanked him for the visit and the consideration and departed with my brain overflowing.

I received a letter two days after returning home, tendering an official offer for the position to become an associate director. My wife and I discussed it for the next twenty-four hours, weighing all the pros, cons, and what the future might hold, either by remaining in the Air Force or retiring and accepting the very lucrative offer to go to the Laboratory. I must admit that beyond the financial considerations and even the possibility of further promotions in the Air Force, the incredible lofting to such a position at the prestigious Los Alamos National Laboratory was overwhelming. First off, I held only a bachelor's degree from a state teachers college, having been called back to the cockpit out of graduate school and only tacit experience while serving with the Defense Nuclear Agency. But, as Don explained, he was looking for a "manager and leader" and not a scientist. So, we made the decision to accept his offer. I did not go directly to my boss, General Davis, Commander in Chief, SAC; there was one more hurdle to be crossed. I had to be accepted into the position at the Laboratory by the Board of Regents, University of California, Berkley, the overall contract manager of Los Alamos.

Don advised me a few days later that I had been accepted by the university; then came the worst part of all, advising General Davis that I wished to retire from active duty to accept the offer made by Los Alamos. That meeting became the most agonizing of any meeting I had ever endured during my career! Not to belabor that lengthy "discussion," in the end, he congratulated me, asked my opinion regarding whom I thought should be considered to replace me as chief of staff, which I was sincerely honored to suggest the name of an officer to succeed me and made plans to move onward.

I reported to Los Alamos in January 1983, as associate director, Technical Operations. There were three other associate directors, each responsible for their respective places within the operation of the laboratory. Each of the other three, of course, held doctoral degrees in their respective disciplines. I was accepted not only by my new colleagues but by the five division leaders within my area of responsibility. I was assigned two deputies to assist in managing the duties of the directorate; the highlight was Bob Bradshaw, a crusty old engineer who had been at the lab for many years and knew all of the ins and outs. He became my "right hand" in management. My other deputy was a PhD "psychologist," which I never quite understood her initial, nor her present roll, within my organization or the Laboratory, but she was there. We worked well together, but also mostly "independent" on her part.

I'll not go further into the details of my extraordinary journey with the esteemed Los Alamos National Laboratory that I have documented in other writings, except to say once again, it was an exceptional and unique opportunity experienced and enjoyed by few! I worked well and with considerable ease with Director Kerr. He called on me frequently to act in his absence during his off-site journeys. That was not always favored by the other associate directors since they felt more "senior" to me. But since my office was upstairs above Kerr's, it was convenient for both him and me. The other associate offices were located in buildings across the Laboratory. I remained at the Lab for almost four years and only decided to depart when

Director Don Kerr made a career decision to depart the Lab and move onward. I also entered an uncomfortable zone with his newly appointed successor, who, for the most part, was a pure scientist and did not understand organization management. Several of his initial operational decisions made it clear that the path ahead would likely become difficult. Virtually at the same time, I received an opportunity to return to Texas to accept an unexpected opportunity with industry. That is another story with many more notable encounters to be shared!

Dr. Donald Kerr's career continued to accelerate as he became president and director of EG&G, Incorporation, thence to assistant director of the Federal Bureau of Investigation in charge of the Laboratory Division, deputy director for Science and Technology at the Central Intelligence Agency, and principal deputy director of National Intelligence. He presently remains consistently hard at work as principal adviser to numerous national government agencies, a valued friend, and Christmas card correspondent.

RADM Eugene A. Barham, USN (Ret) Chairman, Board of Directors, Scientific Communications, Inc.

Coincident with Don Kerr's decision to depart Los Alamos to accept another position, I received an appointment offer that brought about another surprise in the road of life. Two years prior, I had been invited to join the board of directors of a small communications electronics company, Scientific Communications, Inc. (SciComm), in Garland, Texas. The board appointment had been brought about by Dr. Larry Blackwell, one of my laboratory staff members. Larry had served on the SciComm board for several years. One day he popped into my office, described the company and his board roll. He suggested that perhaps as a "diversion" from laboratory life, I might be interested in serving on the SciComm board of directors. He said that they were looking to fill a board vacancy, and with my military background and SciComm's military systems business, I might fulfill their requirement. He further told me that he had already told the board chairman and company president about me and my background. It all sounded interesting, so I asked Don Kerr, Director, Los Alamos, if it was permissible for me in my lab position to serve on an outside company board. He assured me that it was, so I was accepted and began serving on the SciComm board in 1985.

The chairman of the SciComm Board was retired Rear Admiral Eugene Barham, a Louisiana native and resident. It was never clear how he became connected with Garland, Texas based Scientific Communications, but he was clearly in charge of the board of directors and SciComm business ventures. I enjoyed the respite of flying over to Dallas quarterly for board meetings as well as participating in the business operations discussions. In addition to the Chair, Admiral Barham, the board consisted of nine members, including SciComm President, Joe Halpain. Joe had founded the company some ten years prior and had developed a thirty-million-dollar business, primarily in military communications and electronics.

The admiral was a relatively quiet and pleasant, easygoing chap, and as I learned along the way, had served a distinguished career and became a naval hero in World War II. He was a graduate of the Naval Academy and was a young naval engineering officer aboard the USS *Laffey* during the battle of Guadalcanal when it was sunk by a Japanese submarine. He became the senior surviving officer from his ship and took charge of the 1,100 survivors from his and others on the Island of Guadalcanal until they were rescued. He then became commanding officer of the USS *Dashiell* and participated in the battles at Tarawa, Kwajalein, Saipan, and Guam. Thereafter, he returned to the Naval Academy training cadets. When the war broke out in Korea, he went to Tokyo to serve on the staff of the Far East Naval Forces. Thereafter, he served in the Mediterranean, retiring as commander, Naval Air Defense Center in Virginia.

The admiral's decorations included the Bronze Star with Combat V with a Gold Star, the Navy Commendation Medal with Combat V, a Presidential Citation, the Presidential Ribbon, American Defense Service Medal with Fleet clasp, American Campaign Medal, Asiatic

Campaign Medal, World War II Victory Medal, Korean Service Medal, and National Defense Service Medal.

With that background summary, needless to say, I got along well and enjoyed interacting with the admiral in board meetings and our social events. Thence, out of the blue one evening, I received a phone call from him asking if could meet with him and SciComm President, Joe Halpain, in Albuquerque to discuss some company issues. The call surprised me, causing me to wonder what I might offer in the way of "company issues." I agreed to meet and drove down to Albuquerque and met the two of them at the hotel where they were staying. Long story short, the admiral got to the purpose of their visit quickly with Joe Halpain remaining relatively quiet. The admiral asked if I would be willing to come to Garland and serve as executive vice president, SciComm. I looked at Joe to see his reaction, and he nodded with a smile. Up until that time, the SciComm organization consisted of the president, Joe Halpain, and two vice presidents: one for operations and the other administration. The offer took me by surprise, more like shock, but I had already become uneasy with the new director appointee for Los Alamos, which is another story and previously discussed in another of my books. I readily agreed to his position offer and the accompanying economics. I engaged Joe in the conversation, and he seemed to agree, but I felt Joe reluctantly agreed. I was to determine later that he preferred to operate and manage the company single-handed, and likely felt that I might be an intrusion.

I relocated the family to the Dallas area, moved into the position, and began to work well with Joe and the staff. He gave me the latitude to broaden our marketing area overseas, which brought forth numerous additional notable encounters to be discussed within this work. Admiral Barham continued on as Chairman of the Board, until a day came when a major communications entity, Chicago based Andrew Corporation, showed up on the business scene and purchased Scientific Communications. The abrupt acquisition by Andrew brought changes to many lives within SciComm.

Admiral Eugene Barham, a special notable encounter in my life, retired from his position at SciComm, returned to his home in

Ozark, Louisiana, and passed away peacefully in November 1999, at age eighty-seven.

Floyd L. English, PhD, President and CEO, Andrew Corporation, Inc.

As the acquisition of SciComm process by Andrew Corporation took place, I was privileged to spend considerable time, both business and social, with Andrew President, Dr. Floyd English. He was a very friendly and affable business executive and listened intently to both Joe Halpain and myself as the transition took place. Many SciComm employees chose to retire while others accepted positions offered them by the new corporation. Joe Halpain profited greatly from the sale of the company he created and retired shortly afterward. Dr. English offered me a newly created position as vice president, Government Systems, principally to continue the ongoing contractual activities of SciComm. More importantly, I was permitted to remain in my office in Texas and not relocate to Chicago, which was a considerable relief in itself!

Floyd English received his PhD in physics from Arizona State University. He became widely recognized for his business acumen and foresight, as senior executive with Andrew Corporation, a world leader and international supplier of telecommunications systems, equipment and services, including cellular technology, fiber optics, and satellite communications as well as sophisticated navigation systems. During his tenure with Andrew and its manufacturing facilities around the world, Floyd was named one of the top ten "high impact" CEOs in the country. The author of several technical publications, he has been listed in Who's Who in America and Who's Who in Science and Engineering. Dr. English retired as chief executive officer of Andrew in February 2003, after twenty-three years where he had concurrently served as a director, Executives Club of Chicago and the Illinois Math and Science Academy.

My company appointment by Floyd took me to places and adventures throughout the world of which I would have never dreamed; among those were China, Korea, Australia, Ukraine, Belarus, Russia, and beyond. As this work continues herein, it is a special pleasure to share the many inconceivable notable encounters that both SciComm and Andrew Corporation brought into my life's journey.

With considerable loss, Floyd English died unexpectedly on May 25, 2017, at his home on South Padre Island, Texas, leaving behind his beloved wife, Elaine, three children, four grandchildren, and two great-grandchildren, along with many special friends. I am honored to count myself among the latter.

H. Ross Perot, The Perot Group

This notable encounter requires no introduction. I first met Ross Perot at Texas A&M University, College Station, Texas, in early 2000. He was there to address a special gathering invited by Chancellor Barry B. Thompson, and I was there as a member of the Chancellor's Advisory Council at the time. I enjoyed a brief discussion with him regarding the ongoing Clinton Administration's approach to national security and our defense posture. He was rabid about the perceived weak military strategy that we had endured during the past eight Clinton years!

During a lull in our conversation, I smugly commented, "You know, we have several things in common. We're both the same age, we are both listed in the 1951–1952 edition of Who's Who Among Students in American Colleges and Universities, and we are both listed in Who's Who in America." Then I said that I didn't know what happened to me between the first publication and the last.

He chuckled, slapped me on the shoulder, and said, "We both did okay!"

Ross Perot was the son of an Arkansas cotton broker. He attended Texarkana Junior College for two years before entering the United States Naval Academy in 1949 and was commissioned in the U.S. Navy in 1953, where he served until 1957. Following his tour of duty in the Navy, he worked as a salesman for International Business Machines

Corporation (IBM). In 1962, he left IBM and formed his own company, Electronic Data Systems (EDS). He developed EDS to design, install, and operate computer data-processing systems for clients on a contractual basis. The company grew by processing medical claims for Blue Cross and other large insurance companies, and in 1968, he took the firm public in a skillfully managed share offering process that yielded him several hundred million dollars. EDS continued to prosper under his leadership, and in 1984, he sold the company to General Motors for $2.5 billion worth of special-issue stock and a seat on GM's board of directors. Perot's criticism of GM's management prompted them to buy back his seat for $700 million in 1986.

A persistent patriot, back in 1969, Ross Perot mounted an unsuccessful campaign to free American POWs being held in North Vietnam. In 1979, he further attempted to rescue two EDS employees being held prisoner in Iran. In 1992, he announced that he would enter the U.S. presidential election. With Bill Clinton suffering from personal scandals and the incumbent President, George H.W. Bush, weakened by a faltering economy, support for Perot initially earned considerable popularity among voters who were dissatisfied with traditional party politics. He reached out to both Democrats and Republicans, hiring former operatives from each party to advise his campaign. He led both Clinton and Bush in the polls. He chose former Vietnam POW, Admiral James Stockdale, as his vice presidential running mate. After spending $65 million of his own money, he won 19 percent of the popular vote in the November election. After the election he organized the nonpartisan political pressure group United We Stand America.

In September 1995, he established the Reform Party, which he had hoped to create into major political party. The party's platform called for campaign reform, congressional term limits, balancing the federal budget, overhauling the health care and income tax systems, and placing restrictions on lobbying. He ran as the Reform Party nominee in the presidential campaign, receiving only 8 percent of the popular vote, and Bill Clinton was reelected.

I have had the opportunity to visit with Ross Perot on a few occasions over the years. I recall being in his office once, and upon entering the outer foyer, I strolled around a mega Remington bronze work, *Coming Through the Rye*, mounted on a large table in the center of the room. I told him that I also had a replica of the piece and that mine weighed only about thirty pounds and that his must weigh eight hundred! He just smiled.

My last encounter occurred a couple years ago, when pulling into a shopping center parking spot, my cell phone rang, "Is this Chris Adams?" the pleasant voice asked.

I replied, "Yes, it is."

"Sir, do you have a moment to speak with Ross Perot?" she asked.

Of course, you know my response; I pulled into a parking spot as quickly as I could!

"Hello, Chris," he began. "I finished your book on Texas; damn good story! Too bad we can't carry out everything in there that you suggested."

"It was my pleasure," I responded, "I'm happy you enjoyed the tale."

"Thanks, again," he replied, "and keep up your good works; send me your next one!"

I replied, "Yes, sir!" And, that was it.

The book he was referring to, was, *Texas: A Free Nation Under God*, a novel I co-authored with my friend, Manny English, in which we shredded the political on-goings in America and suggested that Texas, with our independent nature, resources, and wealth, should secede and become our own nation!

Ross Perot was a most pleasant encounter, and he continues today to enjoy his independent nature and business successes.

Judge Andrew Napolitano
Noted Attorney, Judge,
and Television News Analyst

I met the judge briefly at an event in Dallas where he spoke. We exchanged brief backgrounds during which he told me about his brother having served in the Air Force. The conversation went on

NOTABLE PROFESSIONAL LEADERS

from there about ongoing politics and the chaos our country seems to cycle in and out of. I found him exceptionally friendly and easy to converse with. He by no means carried an ego or halo above his head. I was struck by the fact that, while there were dozens, perhaps a hundred, people roaming around with many seeking an opportunity to get his attention to speak with them, he was quite comfortable with our conversation. A cameraman finally came up close and nodded for him to move on for photographs. My wife and I were privileged to have him direct the cameraman to take our photographs with him first, which we did, shook hands, and he moved on to the calling of others.

As many are aware, he has been a legal correspondent with FOX News for several years. Prior to that, he was the youngest ever member of the New Jersey Supreme Court where he served for eight years. He resigned and entered private law practice briefly before being lured into the television media business where he is now principally employed.

Meeting and visiting with the judge was an interesting impromptu encounter that frequently happens in our lives, each to be enjoyed and remembered.

Barry B. Thompson, PhD, Chancellor, Texas A&M University System

Barry Thompson, native-born Texan from the West Texas town of Pecos, was a true Texan, through and through. Like many small-town high school graduates of the '50s, including yours truly, Barry sought out a small college to begin his formal education. He chose John Tarleton Agricultural College (JTAC) in Stephenville. I learned after meeting Barry Thompson, then President, West Texas State University, that I had preceded him at Tarleton by four years. I was to also learn further that he spent several years at my other alma mater, East Texas State University. Meeting him for the first time was a "chance" encounter at West Texas State College, Canyon, Texas, where he was serving as president at the time. I was there visiting with a small contingent from East Texas State, to discuss mutual alumni and foundation activities. Barry graciously welcomed us with a reception and offered his support in any way. I was immediately impressed with his genuine "down home" mannerisms and humor.

Therein this notable encounter began and grew beyond anything I might have ever expected. As mentioned, Barry attended Tarleton State College, then a two-year school that had operated under the Texas A&M University System since 1917, and as an independent college since its founding by John Tarleton in 1899. He was an exceptionally bright and progressive student and joined in developing a student contingent that went to the State Capital to lobby the Tarleton Bill, to make Tarleton a four-year college. He earned his associate's degree at Tarleton and on to Texas Tech University to obtain a bachelor's degree in secondary education.

The more I learned about Barry's background and our distant-related connections, the more impressed and fond of him I became. Following graduation from Texas Tech, he became an instant success in the teaching and education profession. In his second year, teaching in the public schools, Barry received "Texas Junior High Teacher of the Year" while at Andrews, Texas. He moved on to become high school principal at Dalhart, Texas, at the age of twenty-five. Concurrently, he earned his master's degree in administration from Texas Tech while serving as high school superintendent at Post, Texas, and assistant superintendent at Waco. He married his high school sweetheart, Sandra Sue Davidson, in 1955. He also found time to serve as president, Tarleton Alumni Association, 1968–1969; coincidentally, I also served two terms in this position in the nineties.

Barry Thompson moved on from public school system administration, earning his doctorate degree from Texas A&M University while serving as a department head at Pan American University. From there, he became professor and head of the Department of Secondary and Higher Education at my old alma mater, East Texas State University. Barry was brought to Tarleton by then President W.O. Trogden, who created the position of executive vice president, just to get Thompson there. Trogden left office shortly thereafter, and Barry was appointed to the presidency. The executive vice president position was abandoned after he was inaugurated; "creative politics" are even in the education world.

Changes in higher education within Texas also changed the relationships with several universities. West Texas State University joined the Texas A&M University System, and Tarleton became a four-year university. The A&M Regents moved Barry Thompson from president of Tarleton State University to West Texas A&M University, where he served from 1991 to 1994. He was appointed chancellor, Texas A&M University System by the regents in 1994. A year later, he convinced East Texas State to become a part of the Texas A&M System.

I received a surprising phone call from Chancellor Barry Thompson in 1996, asking me if I would consider serving on the Texas A&M System Chancellors' Advisory Council. He told me that with my respective backgrounds at Tarleton and East Texas State, I would be a welcome member and resource to the Council. I was shocked by the invitation, which, of course, I readily accepted! The Chancellor's Advisory Council appointment honor was one of the, if not *the*, most special honor that I cherish today. The next three years serving with chancellor and friend, Barry Thompson, on his Council was an exceptional learning experience. I remained on after his retirement for two more years with Chancellor Howard Graves, whom I also thoroughly enjoyed his presence and my honor to serve.

I remained in contact with Barry Thompson for several years after his retirement, mainly working interactive projects with Tarleton. He had retired to his love for the country lifestyle on his ranch near West, Texas, where he raised competition race horses. He also renamed the back country road leading up to his ranch, Bugtussel Road. At his invitation, I visited his ranch with him and his wife, Sandra, several times, to discuss one notion or the other, mostly regarding his first education love, Tarleton, regarding the alumni association, fund-raising, or whatever he had on his mind. He was a deep thinker and always alert to issues that he might support.

We lost this special notable encounter and great friend with his passing in March 2014, after a struggle for life illness. Dr. Barry B. Thompson left a tremendous legacy of service and influence on public and university education in Texas! I hope that this brief portrait of a truly great man was of informational value to those of you who either knew Barry Thompson or wished you had.

Amil Imani, American Patriot

I met Amil Imani several years ago at one of Allen Clark's Combat Faith Luncheons, also referred to within this work. My first meeting with Amil led me to share with him that I had attended U.S. Air Force flight training, back in the '50s, with ten young Iranian officers, and that one of my Iranian classmates, Lt. A.H. Rabeii, eventually became General Rabeii and Chief of Staff, Iranian Air Force. I also shared with Amil that on one ominous morning, a few days after the 1979 coup in Iran, following the demise of the Shah and takeover of the U.S. Embassy, I sat in an intelligence briefing at Headquarters, Strategic Air Command, where I was shocked to view a photograph of the just executed Iranian military chiefs of staff. Among them was my former classmate, Rabeii, his bullet-ridden body still tied to a large wooden pole. I also shared with him that my flight mate during training was another Iranian Lieutenant Amil Azarbarzin, who also rose to the grade of general in the Shah's Air Force, but he allegedly escaped capture by the militants, never to be heard from again. That not so pleasant introductory story became a bonding friendship with Amil Imani.

Amil was born in Tehran, Iran, into what he describes as a loving and intellectual family. He tells of growing up in a Muslim society and witnessing firsthand the horrors and indignities that Islamic ideology imposes on the people it subjugates. From a very young age, Amil took it upon himself to do the best he could in defeating this supremacist doctrine of oppression, hate, and violence. Defeating Islamic ideology has become the focal point of his life and career by not allowing Islamic doctrine to devour other cultures and especially his adopted home, the United States of America.

Amil was able to come to the United States at the end of 1978 as the Islamic Revolution of Iran began. Notably, this untimely revolution installed one of the most oppressive theocratic Islamic systems known as Sharia Law. With the Ayatollah Khomeini at the helm, it renewed an era of Islamic terrorism. Amil says that he left Iran to continue his education abroad, but never envisioned that radical Islamic ideology would overrun such a modern and prosperous country as his Iran. Amil is almost sure that he would likely not be alive today had he remained in his home country.

After completing his initial college education, Amil was determined to work for the FBI, an agency that he had gained tremendous respect, but he was denied the opportunity since he had not become a U.S. citizen at the time. He began working in the hospitality management industry to support himself while continuing to read, study, write, and research about the threat of encroaching Islam in his native Iran.

Amil initially earned a triple bachelor's degree in Communications, English Literature, and Speech and Hearing. He then completed a master's degree in Political Science and more recently earned another MS degree in Homeland Security. He says that the Homeland Security and Terrorism Program provided him the opportunity to better understand homeland security issues and challenges in the context of an ever-evolving political environment, in the United States and around the world. He also began to understand terrorism as the key emphasis to be addressed in homeland security. Amil says that the program provided him the opportunity to study, view, and better assess real-world situations within our multi-layered local, state, and federal organizations.

Over the past thirty years, Amil has written countless articles focused on his native Iran, Islam, and the Middle East. He also actively participates in lectures, talk shows, and interviews, focused on educating Americans on the threat of the spreading of Islam, and attesting his determination, he says to do what he can to safeguard his adopted America from an Islamic invasion.

Amil's work has appeared on numerous websites, including the American Thinker, Family Security Matters, Israel National News, and thousands of other Internet websites and magazines. He has authored two books, *Operation Persian Gulf* and *Obama Meets*

Ahmadinejad, and has completed the manuscripts on three additional books, which he hopes to have published this year.

Amil has been interviewed on several radio shows, including BBC International. In each of his interviews, he attempts to emphasize the grave importance of every terror attack around the globe and their potential impact on the United States.

Amil Imani was a 2010 honoree of the "Rays of Light in the Darkness" award from the Endowment for Middle East Truth (EMET) on Capitol Hill in Washington, along with Ambassador, former Congressman, Sam Brownback, and US Congressmen Doug Lamborn and Brad Sherman.

This true American and international patriot, a man of faith, special notable encounter, and friend, Amil Imani, with his many talents and skills, speaks and writes in several languages, is currently active with his own company, Amil Imani National Security Initiative, and spends much of his time with public speaking engagements, touting American democracy and patriotism. I encourage each of you to learn more about this incredible man: www.amilimani.com

Thank you, Amil, for your service to our great nation!

Air Medal awarded by Lt. General Benjamin O. Davis

Greeting President Bush

President George H.W. Bush

Greeting Gen. Russ Dougherty and Secretary of State Al Haig

Honoring General Edgar Harris

General Robert R. Scott

Lt. Karl Richter, USAF, Memorial

Honoring Lacy Breckenridge and Family

Congressman Mike Conaway

Robert R. Brownlee, PhD

Texas State Trooper Dub Gillum

Chief Master Sergeant of the Air Force, Jim McCoy

Pat Halloran Still Flying

Mackye Evans

Donna Seebo

Dorene Sherman

Notable Ladies!

Alene Adams Enjoying Barry Goldwater Humor

Honoring Judge Napolitano

Wyoming Governor Ed Herschler

Greeting Admiral An, PRC Navy

Curious Dr. Ho and Admiral An

Games with Mr. Dubchenko and Irena

Toasting with Mikola Balatskiy, Erica and Sergiy

General Phil Ford and Russian Comrades

Paul and Susie Pearce

Manny and Jeanette English

Toasting General Jimmie Doolittle

Amil Amani American Patriot

Chatting with Hamouid Al Hamoud
and my Deputy Charlie Clark

Honorable Allen Clark and Linda

5

Notable International Encounters

Joining Scientific Communications (SciComm) and thereafter, Andrew Corporation opened unexpected doors to an international world to which I had not been exposed. Virtually all of my travel adventures in the Air Force had been interacting with United States military and political contacts here and in friendly nations abroad. Both SciComm and Andrew business interests extended around the world and developed many surprising personal encounters with additional international military and business leaders. Venturing into Russia became the eye-opener of a lifetime! After serving the majority of my active duty career in strategic operations deterring the Soviet Union during the Cold War, I then found myself "on the ground" in our former enemy's territory, which became an extraordinary adventure. Following in more or less chronological order are several of those memorable encounters, beginning while I was still on Air Force active duty and with a stopover visit to Tokyo with Strategic Air Command, Commander in Chief, General Richard Ellis.

General Yamada, Chief of Staff, Japanese Air Self Defense Force

As I described earlier, returning from a visit to Australia with General Ellis and the SAC staff, we made a stopover in Tokyo. Following that meeting earlier in the day with Ambassador Mansfield, General Ellis, and several members of the staff were invited to join the Japan Self Defense Force commanders and staff for dinner. We were driven to an exclusive *ochaya* (tea house) and escorted into an equally so *tatami* (dining room). I had been to Tokyo several times previously but never to visit such an ambient facility and setting! Our escort told us that we were being hosted to a geisha dinner. He said that the *ochaya* are highly exclusive due to their traditional way of hosting only special and trusted customers.

General Ellis instructed us to wear civilian attire that evening so as to not arouse attention if we were in U.S. Military uniforms. Our escort guided us into the elaborate dining room where the tables were traditionally low (very low) in height; so much so, that I knew that we would have to sit cross-legged. They were also arranged in a large rectangle, with everyone facing the center.

General Ellis was greeted by the Chairman of the Joint Chiefs of Staff, Japanese Defense Force. There were a dozen or so Japanese officers in attendance, all in dress uniforms. Each of us were escorted to a place at the table where our name tags were positioned. We all stood waiting to be joined by a host who would be seated next to us. I was then joined by a very smartly dressed Japanese officer, whom I noticed immediately wore four stars, or the equivalent symbols, on his uniform epaulets. His interpreter introduced him to me as "General Yamada, Chief of Staff, Air Self Defense Force." The general bowed and then held out his hand. We shook hands warmly and he bowed again, offering me to please sit down. Sit down we did, cross-legged, facing the beautifully set table before us. The general's interpreter squatted down behind and centered between the two of us.

General Yamada was very gracious, speaking some words in English, but mostly in Japanese, which his interpreter simultaneously translated for both him and me. Our conversation was considerably truncated, but nevertheless interesting and informative. As the many and various courses of food began to be placed before us, the cultural highlight of the evening began with the geisha's performing a traditional *onal* dance. The music was provided by another geisha playing the *shamisen*, a string instrument similar to a small guitar. The dinner, entertainment, and conversation was and *is* one to remember always.

Herein, I wish to share the *onal* dance and music with you on YouTube: https://youtu.be/n6CwzULoJdc, with hopes that you may copy and paste it to Google or otherwise, and enjoy it as we did back then. Memories . . .

As the evening began to come to a close, I noticed General Yamada fiddling with his shirt sleeve cuff links. I tried not to notice and then, suddenly, he reached over with his clasped right hand and bumped my left hand, nodding for me to open my palm. I looked at him, thinking this was another tradition and opened my palm where he placed his two cuff links and tie clasp. I was shocked when I looked at them. They were his personal military cuff links and tie clasp, each reflecting his four-star rank. I was speechless and looked back at the interpreter, who was smiling and nodding approval. I did not know what to do at first! "What did I have of any equivalence?" Nothing! And then, I remembered that I was wearing a B-1 Bomber tie clasp that was given to me when I visited the Boeing Aircraft Company some time in the past. I immediately removed it and handed it to him. He took it in his hand with a big smile and studied it for a long moment. He then held out his hand and shook mine, thanking me profusely, as if I had given him a diamond! What a gracious gentleman. This impromptu encounter became another of the most notable along my pathway!

Dr. Ho ('Hoo')

Andrew Corp was invited to participate in a communication electronics trade show in Beijing in January 1988. We were highly suspicious of the invitation, although it came via a respected business agent in Taiwan with whom the company had conducted business in electronics for several years. We were asked to bring whatever commercial equipment we wished to display. Still wary, we decided that it would be an adventure of perhaps a lifetime for our engineers. Upper management approved the journey, so we accepted the invitation and took several of our unclassified general purpose electronic systems to the show. These included pulse analyzers, frequency management instruments, etc. I was asked to head up the trip and chose three engineers who helped to develop the systems and could describe them to interested patrons. These included Dr. Hershel Murray, our senior engineer, and two of his assistants. The planned trip was also a special opportunity for our wives who also accompanied us. Since I still retained a sensitive security clearance, I advised the appropriate office in Washington that I was going to make the trip and would be dealing with strictly commercial interests.

Our Taiwan agent, Johnny Wong, met us on arrival at the Beijing Airport terminal along with a Chinese gentleman and lady. The greeting party accompanied us to the Sheraton Great Wall Hotel. The hotel was first class and surprised us all with its upscale quality and amenities. The greeters said that they would be with us and available throughout our stay and all that we needed to do, to contact them, was to ask the Front Desk to do so. We were impressed with our first introduction to China and Beijing.

Shortly after I checked into our room, the phone rang. I was just "slightly" surprised when the caller identified himself the United States Defense Attaché, Brigadier General Jon Reynolds. He welcomed me to Beijing, then asked if I would meet him downstairs in the hotel coffee shop. I countered by inviting him to come up to our room, which he declined and said that he would prefer to meet downstairs. I left promptly and went downstairs to the coffee shop, looked around, and spotted a fellow who appeared to be American in casual civilian clothes, standing near the entrance to the coffee shop. Reynolds smiled as I approached, held out his hand, and introduced himself. He was exceptionally cordial and apologized for the noisy atmosphere in the coffee shop but explained that it was a good place to talk in privacy. We found a table, and when I asked how he knew we were in Beijing, he replied that they are generally aware of all Americans who come into the country, especially retired military officers!

He apologized for the impromptu contact and then dropped the news on me that my room, number 812, was "hot." I understood what he meant; the room was wired with surveillance equipment.

I asked how much so, and he replied, "Audio and visual, at least three TV cameras; make sure that your wife changes in the bathroom!" He went on to tell me that the Chinese intelligence agencies are well aware of everyone who comes in the country, especially U.S. Military, active or retired. They are paranoid, he said, and there are special rooms in the hotel designated for just such as us. That was our introduction to Beijing!

As we continued to chat about his attaché position, the city of Beijing, and so on, I learned to my complete surprise that he was a former Vietnam POW, having spent over seven years in the Hanoi prison. A notable encounter indeed and an American hero!

I told him about the nonsensitive commercial equipment we brought with us to display and invited him to drop by the trade show if he wished to do so. He said that he likely would not. I asked if there was anything in particular besides, of course, my wired tapped hotel room that we should be sensitive to or concerned about otherwise during our visit.

He said that the city was relatively safe, but that we should be cautious about suspicious strangers during our stay. "Your people will have encounters; just advise them to be careful and remain where there are other people around. Try not to find yourselves alone on the street or in otherwise vulnerable places."

In parting, I thanked him for his service and sacrifice as a prisoner of war. He invited me to come by the embassy and to meet the ambassador, if I had an opportunity while we were there. I told him that I would if the opportunity presented itself.

The trade show was to be located upstairs on the fifth floor of a very modern and clean building. We were provided a private room to set up our equipment displays and given keys to "secure" the room after hours. The show was scheduled to last for five days and we would take turns meeting with visitors and describing the systems. As we were setting up our display in the trade show building, General Reynolds proved to be accurate with regard to intrusive strangers.

The door to our display room opened suddenly and in walked a young forty-something Chinese fellow, dressed in an "almost Mao" suit: baggy black wool trousers, matching hip-length jacket, and a white shirt. The shirt collar and sleeve cuffs were well-worn and tattered. He introduced himself with a big toothy smile, and in perfect English, "Greetings, welcome to Beijing, I'm Doctor Ho ('Hoo')," he said.

I introduced myself and our engineers and asked how we might help him. He smiled and said that he would be accompanying us throughout our visit and to call on him for any of our needs. I asked about the greeting party lady and gentleman, and he said they would also be in our company during our stay. There was *no doubt* that he was "in charge." As we continued to visit, he said that he had spent many years in the United States and that he had attended Notre Dame University and acquired a master's and doctoral degree. As it turned out, he was an entertaining character; nonstop chatting and from that day, he was everywhere we were! Our greeting hosts arranged for pleasant dinner gatherings, a day trip to the Great Wall, and made the visit an overall pleasant journey.

Dr. Ho became a mystery of sorts, also everywhere we were! If a photograph was to be taken, he was in the center with his big toothy smile. It also became obvious that he just might be interested in more than a social interchange. From the first day, he began to ask if we might go up to my hotel room for business discussions. If it were in the morning during breakfast, at the trade show display area or after dinner, for the entire ten-day visit, he pestered me to go to my room for "discussions."

I could only think that he was solely interested in having me situated where there were cameras and recording devices in order to ask questions of interest to the Chinese intelligence agencies. My response was always that I was either busy or my wife was in the room, and we couldn't go up there. He would smile and move on to some other subject, but *always* in our company. I attempted to ask him about his personal life, job, etc., to which he would smile and tell me that he stayed busy and worked very hard. I determined that he was a persistent intelligence agent and we were his targets for the period.

Regrettably, timing did not permit me to accept General Reynolds's invitation to visit the U.S. Embassy, which was a missed opportunity to be in Beijing perhaps for the first and last time.

Admiral An, Minister, PRC Navy

On the morning of the last day of our trade show display, Dr. Ho came in and told me that Admiral An, the Minister of the Chinese Navy, wished to come by and view our systems displays. That took us by surprise, but we quickly agreed and told Dr. Ho that we would be delighted to have the senior Chinese Naval official to visit us. I also suggested that we would close our display room door at noon-time and permit no more visitors after that time. Shortly after 1:00 p.m., I looked down on the street to see a large black limousine pull up to the curb with another smaller vehicle park behind it. I asked all of our people to be present. The door opened and leading in the minister was Dr. Ho.

The minister was dressed in a Mao-type suit and accompanied by two Navy admirals and the minister's aide. Dr. Ho introduced each of us to the minister, the admirals, and the aide with handshakes and warm smiles all around. The minister was a short stocky fellow, very pleasant, gracious, and constantly smiling. The two admirals were more stoic and stood back, mostly observing the activities. The young aide was a giant of a fellow for Chinese and at least six feet, four inches tall. He spoke good English.

Dr. Ho proceeded to act as translator for Dr. Murray as he described each of our types of equipment and their purpose. The minister mostly nodded, smiling with approval and had little to say. I had noticed the admiral's uniforms when they came in and that of the aide who was introduced as a lieutenant.

I asked the aide why were his and the admirals' uniforms, insignia, etc., all the same? "How do you tell one's rank from the other?" I said, "Your uniform insignia is the same as the admirals and you are a lieutenant?"

He smiled and pointed to himself and said, "It's in the face; we recognize each other and their rank by who we are."

I wasn't convinced that was entirely correct but accepted his response. I then told the aide that I was hosting an evening in the garden of the hotel to express appreciation to everyone who had visited us and others who had been so gracious during our visit I told him I would like to invite the minister, the admirals, and him to attend. As they were preparing to depart, I noticed that he whispered something to the minister. He then turned to me and said that the minister was very grateful for the invitation but must decline.

As we gathered at the Sheraton Hotel garden that evening to express our appreciation to our new Beijing friends for their gracious hospitality, the minister's black limousine pulls up and out he and his aide stepped. I walked over and greeted him, with Dr. Ho close behind smiling broadly. Dr. Ho was also surprised by the sudden change of plans on the part of the minister as he escorted him to a comfortable chair. The evening ended pleasantly as did our visit to China.

The next day we said our goodbyes and expressed our appreciation to our hosts. With fond memories, as well a big sigh of relief, it had been a very pleasant experience. On a final note, Dr. Murray and I said goodbye to our wives and colleagues as they departed for the States, while he and I headed to Adelaide, Australia, to visit our Andrew office there. We had also made arrangements to ship our electronics equipment display to Australia as well for a mini-trade show there. The day after our arrival at the Adelaide office, Murray told me that while our equipment had arrived, it had obviously been thoroughly "investigated" before it left Beijing. Since the shipping crates had all been securely sealed, apparently our Chinese "friends" took the opportunity to fully inspect and analyze everything!

Patrick Murin, Andrew Corporation, London

I must briefly introduce Pat Murin, Andrew Corporation office manager. Pat was a notable encounter and interesting character to recall! Short and stubby, red face complexion and gray hair, Brit, through and through. He was abrupt and frequently tactless and rude, or both, in meeting people and conversations. I'll not belabor too much about my encounters with Pat, except to recall that he kept most of us entertained, so to speak, with his mannerisms and frequent unusual behavioral antics. He came to Dallas on one occasion to coordinate some business activities. He arrived unannounced on that visit, rented a car at the airport, and drove to our office. I had my secretary book him a room at the local hotel that we used for guests. We had a good visit during his stay, showed him around the city of Dallas, etc. He didn't come into the office one morning; I was busy and didn't think too much of it. Later that afternoon, my secretary said that the car rental company had called and inquired about the car Pat had rented, that it was due to have been turned in that morning. That worried me, thinking something had happened to him. I drove to the hotel and spotted his rental car in the parking lot with the driver's door opened about halfway.

I rushed into the hotel and asked for this room number. The clerk said, "Oh, Mr. Murin checked out early this morning and took a taxi to the airport."

Duh! The opened door on the car was not an unusual stunt of Pat's. He would frequently open door of a car before the vehicle came to a stop.

On another occasion in Moscow, Pat and I were being driven in a van to a meeting. As he gazed out the window of the van, he said, "You know that you Americans are responsible for all of this abject humiliation and rot in Russia."

I looked at him and asked, "What do you mean by that statement?"

He smirked and said, "You let that Cold War go on for almost half a century and you could have made peace with these people anytime along the way."

I said, "Pat, you don't have a clue. Your Great Britain was also a sworn enemy of the Soviets and a heck of a lot closer to their continent than the U.S. If you check the record, the U.S. provided you protection all along that you couldn't afford." He just smiled. He knew that he had hit a nerve and that was that. Neither did I pursue the empty discussion.

My last encounter with Pat occurred in Moscow as I was preparing to depart for the last time. He was sent in, so he said, to upgrade the leased apartment we had rented for several years and to rent a second one for company visitors. I accompanied him one day to do some *shopping*. After observing him spending money on overly expensive furniture, unnecessary cookware, and an overabundance of outrageous bedding, I cautioned him, but to no avail and departed the shopping tour. I also departed Moscow a few days later never to return and also never inquired about the revised upscale living in Moscow. I never saw Pat again as time moved on and as I departed the corporate world scene. A noteworthy memorable encounter along the way.

Sir John Richards, Lt. General, British Royal Marines

Pat Murin introduced me to Sir John Richards during one of my stopovers en route to Moscow. I found him to be a delightful and cordial fellow; he greeted me warmly and welcomed me to London. When I first met Sir John, he was serving as aide to Prince Charles. As you would expect, he was very polite and polished. Educated at Worksop College, he had joined the Royal Marines in 1945. During his active duty career, he served in various positions as he moved up the chain, eventually becoming commandant general, Royal Marines, retiring from active duty in 1981. He was then knighted by the Queen and began to serve the Royal Household as Marshall of the Diplomatic Corps. He retired from that position in 1991 and became special aide to Prince Charles and took up residence in his assigned portion of St. James Castle, where the prince also lived.

Pat shared with me later that he had enlisted support from Sir John under a consulting contract to assist with contacts and business interests. I thought it odd that an individual of Sir John's position would even consider working outside his royal duties. I had the opportunity to visit with him numerous times thereafter when passing through London to Moscow along with Pat at Andrew office.

On one memorable occasion, Pat arranged for us to have dinner with Sir John, who, in turn, invited us to come to his home for wine before we departed for the restaurant. Pat, with his wife, drove my wife and me to St. James Palace where he boldly pulled his car right up to the curb and entrance to Sir John Richards's palace apartment. Two uniformed guards with tall fur hats, standing at attention with rifles at their sides, had to step back out of his way. That was Pat Murin! The two guards regained their positions and saluted with their rifles when we got out of the car. I would have approached the place differently, but Pat was a bit of a show-off and frequently demonstrated as much. Pat rang the doorbell, and a servant in full formal tuxedo dress opened the door and welcomed us.

The introduction to the royal quarters was an interesting adventure. We entered a small foyer and then was guided up a long flight of stairs. At the top of the stairs, we came to the kitchen; thence up another shorter flight of stairs to the dining room area. We were then led up a third flight of stairs to the reception and living room. We were shocked at how small and compact each of the rooms were including the dining room. Sir John and his wife greeted us warmly and guided each of us to large overstuffed chairs. A well-groomed and dressed servant took our wine orders. Sir John and his wife were a delightful, pleasant, and cordial couple, certainly living up to their chosen positions. We presumed that the bedroom(s) must have been further up another flight of stairs. It was an introduction to an unforgettable evening!

We chatted and sipped our wine for the better part of an hour, and Pat announced that we must move on to dinner. Once downstairs, we walked out into a beautiful, for London anyway, evening and Sir John suggested that we stroll to the St. James Hotel restaurant, the same name as the Palace, which was a short distance away.

Our dinner was something to remember! In typical British high life-style, course after course were served, followed by decorative desserts, never to forget. I should mention also that the tab the waiter handed me at the conclusion met all the expectations and was also something to remember!

The highlight of the evening was being driven back to St. James Palace by way of Number 10 Downing Street where the prime minister of England resides. Dumb me, I had no camera with me that evening, and those were the days before iPhones! Missed opportunities, but an incredible encounter!

Barry Houlihan, Andrew Corp, Australia

I was privileged to make several trips to Adelaide, Australia, to work with our Andrew Corp office there. Director of Andrew Australia operations was a class Aussie gentleman, Barry Houlihan. Equally so were his engineers and staff members. Much of our work with the Australia group was focused on supporting that continent's communications requirements and interacting with projects in the U.S. and Europe. Needless to say, if you ever had the opportunity to meet and spend some time with the Aussies, you will understand and appreciate their native hospitality and humor! I had visited the country previously while still in the Air Force and once enjoyed accompanying the commander in chief, SAC at a meeting with the Australian Joint Chiefs of Staff. They, likewise, were not only professionals, but enjoyed humor and chiding us as Americans for our over abundant serious natures.

Barry Houlihan and his guys and ladies were wonderful to visit and to work with. He had only one engineer, PhD, head floating "well above himself," individual that more than once interjected himself into areas not of his calling. On that one note, he once passed along some bogus information to Andrew President Floyd English, regarding a project I was working on that prompted the president to call me aside to a private luncheon, bordering on my being terminated, had the erroneous information been true. When Dr. English challenged me with that which had been passed on to him, I was taken aback. I then provided him with the facts which he then showed relief and smiled nodding. He thanked me, shook my hand, and the issue went away. I later called Barry Houlihan and passed on the challenge I had received from Dr. English via his engineer, to which he promptly apologized and said to *worry not further*. I knew what he meant. Jealousy within all environments unfortunately exists.

More than once, when visiting the Adelaide office, I gave Barry a chuckle when I strolled to the right side door of his vehicle to get in and he would comment, "You wish to drive, Chris?" Australians drive on the left side of the roadways. Barry's daughter, Laura, wanted to visit the United States once during my tenure, and we invited her to come and stay in our home for a month, which was a most enjoyable experience. She fell in love with Texas and especially, Texans. I recall many wonderful and humorous experiences visiting and interacting with my Aussie friends; great allies to America!

Hamoud Al Hamoud, Business Agent, Saudi Arabia

Scientific Communications had developed a high frequency direction finding, (HF-DF), system back in the early 1980s in response to a competitive bid offering by the Department of Defense. They had successfully tested it in the Nevada desert to meet the specified requirements for a communications detection system that could identify and locate the direction and origin of voice and electronic high frequency emissions. Operation Desert Shield was initiated in August 1990, by the U.S. Army in response to the invasion and annexation of Kuwait by Iraq and the defense of Saudi Arabia. Andrew Corporation, by then, had absorbed SciComm, offered to lend the U.S. Army a prototype HF-DF system to tryout in the Sahara Desert. The Army promptly agreed and requested three systems. Andrew responded and assembled three HF-DF systems, code-named, Dakota, and shipped them to the U.S. Army forces in Saudi Arabia. Desert Shield became Desert Storm when combat and open warfare broke out between the U.S. coalition forces consisting of thirty-five other nations against the Iraq Army.

I was asked by Andrew President, Floyd English, if I would go to Riyadh, Saudi Arabia, to coordinate and evaluate the effectiveness of the Dakota systems in use by the Army. I chose Charlie Clark, a former SciComm international market manager to accompany me. Charlie knew the mid-East desert area well; he had been in Iran in 1979, when the Shah was overthrown and barely escaped being captured and held hostage along with the Americans trapped in the U.S. Embassy at the time. He had also been an agent with the CIA, which gave me some comfort support, traveling into a totally unknown environment.

Charlie and I flew to Riyadh via London and Jedda on Saudi Air. That became an interesting experience in itself to be discussed later herein. Charlie had made contact with a Saudi government marketing individual that had been recommended to him. We checked into the Al Khozama Hotel which had been arranged by Charlie's contact. This was to be an experience of a lifetime! The environment, the culture, and the observations were a mild shock to me personally. Riyadh appeared to be the busiest city in the world, and I thought Beijing was a clutter of people and activity! Of course, the dress of the people was the most interesting of all; virtually all the men were dressed in traditional white thobes, or long loose-fitting gowns that reach to below their knees. They all wore a headdress, the ghutra. The ghutra was usually made of cotton and worn folded into a triangle, centered on the head. Saudi women were usually dressed in voluminous black cloaks, called abayah, with a scarf covering her entire head and a full-face veil. Very few men acknowledged foreigners and the women on the streets shied far away from strangers.

The hotel clerks and servers were all male, in traditional dress, and all were very cordial and respectful. We had no sooner checked into our room, when the phone rang. Sound familiar: China! Charlie answered and it was our local contact, Hamoud Al Hamoud, to work with us while in the country. Charlie invited him to come up to our room.

Hamoud arrived in "full dress" attire; by that, he was in exceptionally prim and neatly tailored Muslim apparel. He was a slight built fellow, five feet, four inches or so. I guessed him to be in his early

forties, dark complexioned, well-groomed with a trimmed mustache. He spoke excellent English, very polite, friendly, and verbal. He said that he had worked with Americans, British, French, and many others, in assisting them around the city and countryside as needed. I asked about his background, and he said that he was in the "lineage" to the Crown Prince; likely 1300 or so? That was never verified . . . nor, could we. He left little doubt that he was well-educated.

I explained that we were there to work with the U.S. Military command regarding communications equipment that our company had provided to support the ongoing conflict. I said that we did not have a time table and would be there until we had completed our coordination with the military. Hamoud, in turn, offered to provide transportation and a driver anytime, day or night, while we were there.

We called on the U.S. Army command office the next day, explaining that we were there to provide any coordination and support necessary to the success of the Dakota systems. We were told that the three systems were deployed across the country, and they were working as designed in detecting, identifying, and pinpointing communications from the deployed Iraqi forces. Since the Dakota systems were effectively "on loan" to the Army and had not been approved for formal acquisition, I asked what they intended to do with them once the conflict was over. I was advised that decision couldn't be made at the field level there in Riyadh, which is what I guessed. I asked the commander to provide me with a full critique of the Dakota systems' operation features, successes, and any recommendations they had for improvement and so forth.

Saudi Arabia Culture Experience

Charlie and I had considerable time to move about Riyadh, observe and learn considerably about the culture while we waited on call for whatever might be needed from the Army. One of the most uncomfortable situations for the people of Riyadh were the U.S. female soldiers in uniform casually walking about the city. The natives would turn their backs on them and move away as fast as they could. Our military did not endear us to the Saudis in any way; although we were there to protect and defend the country and its people. It's the world we live within.

We learned even more about the severity of the Saudi culture one evening, sitting in the hotel lounge. The double doors to the lounge suddenly burst open with two men in uniforms, holding rifles. Then a gross-looking, shaggy-headed, filthy-clothed giant of a man stepped in. He stood for a minute looking over all the people seated in the lounge which included Saudis and probably a hundred others from all over the world. Everyone was caught by surprise and several crawled under their tables. Charlie and I sat, ready as well to make a fast move if necessary. The man finally eyed his target and headed across the room to a terrified couple, who had sat, not moving. The man grabbed the young woman by the hair and literally dragged her, screaming bloody murder, out of the lounge.

I looked over at a man at the next table and shrugged my shoulders as if to ask, "What was that all about?"

He looked back at me and whispered, "*Mutaween*, the religious police. She is obviously not married and with someone she shouldn't be, or she is married and shouldn't be in here."

I had heard about the religious police who are always on the lookout or searching for women who break Muslim morality laws. I had previously asked Hamoud about the *mutaween*, whom I had heard horrific stories about. He told me that the stories were all likely true. The "police" were authorized to take custody of any female whom they believed, or had been accused of abusing Sharia Law. That extended into minor dress apparel codes and a multitude of immoral behaviors. The police frequently beat the abusers with whips or straps, with some suffering lasting injuries, even death. That episode is a memory we could have well not experienced!

As it turned out, the Saudis began to observe Ramadan while we were there. Ramadan is observed by Muslims around the world as a month of fasting. The religious period is set aside in the ninth month of the Islamic calendar to commemorate the first revelation of the Quran to Muhammad according to Islamic beliefs. The annual observance is regarded as one of the Five Pillars of Islam. The month lasts twenty-nine or thirty days based on the visual sightings of the crescent moon, according to numerous biographical accounts compiled in the hadiths. Muslim worshipers fast from dawn to sunset and refrain from consuming any food, liquids, or smoking. They are also required to refrain from any misconduct and bad behavior, such as telling falsehoods, insulting, backbiting, cursing, and fighting except in self-defense. Fasting for Muslims during Ramadan also includes the increased offering of prayers, reciting scriptures from the Quran and doing good deeds and charity.

In that regard, a Saudi businessman whom we had met early in our visit and expressed interest in our company's communications activities, called one evening during the Ramadan period and invited Charlie and me to come to his office to discuss some potential communications business interests with him. Late in the day and night meetings were not uncommon due to the oppressive heat during the day with temperatures commonly reaching 120 degrees or more. When we first met him, he appeared to be sufficiently professional to trust, so I agreed to come and visit with him. He said that he would send a car to pick us up around 9:00 p.m. The car arrived at the entrance of our hotel with a Filipino driver. When we arrived at man's office building, the driver escorted us upstairs and to his office. He met us in the elaborate reception room, in full Saudi dress; welcomed us with a bow and firm handshakes. He excused the driver and his secretary sitting at her desk, telling her to go home for the day. He then escorted us into his private office, closed the door, walked over to a huge wall cabinet, and opened it to reveal virtually every alcoholic beverage in the world. "What is your pleasure, gentlemen?" he offered with a smile and bow.

Charlie and I were both in mild shock. I looked at our host and responded, "Sir, I thought your people were celebrating Ramadan?"

He took the ghutra off his head and swirled it over to the top of his desk. "Ramadan is for those of the old school," he smiled. "We, of the new Arabia, live in the modern world as do you non-believers. Please join me and tell me what is going on with your business."

Charlie, unabashed by the religious concerns, mixed a drink for himself, and I proceeded to pour a glass of wine. I told our host that it appeared that the war was coming to a close, that our business was done and we might be departing soon. I then pursued his interest in our company's communication system area. As we enjoyed his pleasant company, he said that he would like to come to the United States and to visit Andrew Corporation. He had researched the company's capabilities and perhaps he could be of further use to us in Saudi Arabia beyond military support. I told him that while I might be the only one departing shortly, that Charlie would likely stay on for a period to close out our activities with the military.

I said that we would keep him informed of our plans and that if were interested in coming to visit us in the United States, I would be pleased to coordinate such a visit. We enjoyed the remainder of the late evening. He called his driver to meet us downstairs, and we returned "better informed" about the Muslim religion practices, but little about his business interests.

As we know, the Gulf War was short-lived. The military forces, under the command of General Schwarzkopf, successfully pushed the Iraqis out of Kuwait and back within their own borders. The Army advised me that we could reclaim the Dakota systems and return them to the company. I contacted Andrew Corp and suggested that we might offer them to the Saudi Army with temporary technical support for training and their use in the future. This gesture would avoid the handling and expense of shipping the heavily used equipment back to the States. Andrew agreed that it would be a goodwill gesture that might pay dividends for business in the future. That turned out to not be the case!

I made an appointment with the Saudi Ground Forces commander to discuss future "business opportunities . . ."

Lt. General Ahmad Ameri, Saudi Arabian Army

I requested my Saudi business agent, Hamoud, to an appointment for me to meet with a Saudi Army Officer to discuss possible disposition of the Dakota systems. Hamoud was successful in

arranging for a meeting with Lt. General Ahmad Ameri. Charlie accompanied me to the general's office where we were escorted in and introduced a man whom I immediately recognized to be an arrogant, disheveled military officer, who was not a fan of the Americans in his country. We took our seats in front of his desk as he lighted a cigarette and blew smoke across the room. I thanked him for the opportunity to meet with him, explained who we were, and wished to discuss the possibility of providing some valuable communications equipment to the Saudi Army. All the while I was talking, he stared out the window or looked otherwise bored. I told him that we, our American company, with the permission of the U.S. Army, would like to convey to the Saudi Army the Dakota communications systems for their future use. I asked if he was familiar with the capabilities of the Dakota, which he shrugged with a nod. I told him that the net worth of the systems was about one million dollars each. I also told him that the U.S. Army had agreed to provide training for his people on the equipment. There was little doubt that this meeting was not going well, nor should we even be there.

I finished the one-way discussion and then asked if he had any questions or was his government interested in my company's proposition.

He looked directly at me, exhaled tobacco smoke, and said, "No, I do not want your gifts. We have no use for them."

I responded, "General, they could be of considerable use by your military for communications training as well as," and continued, "should another conflict occur."

He looked at me after an orchestrated period of long silence, and finally blurted, "We have no use for your equipment for our people, and if another war happens, you will be back here to fight again. For now, we just want you to leave our country and take all your soldiers and equipment with you!"

I sat for a minute, looked at Charlie, shaking his head slowly, and then I slammed my fist down on his desk, "General, the United States Army just saved your ass from being run over by Saddam Hussein and destroying your country, and that is your way of showing your appreciation? Let's go, Charlie."

He didn't budge from his chair behind the desk as we walked out. Another "notable encounter," not easily forgotten. I had made preparations to fly out the next day, while Charlie was to stay and negotiate the transfer of the Dakota systems to the U.S. Army. We had previously agreed that he would remain with the Army's permission and the equipment, and with Hamoud's support, he would prepare for the shipment of the Dakota communications equipment back home.

I departed as planned, bade goodbye to Charlie, wishing him good fortune with dispatching the equipment; to which, he smilingly responded, "You sure left me here in a 'mell of a hess'!"

We both chuckled. I boarded the PanAm Clipper for London and soon experienced another cultural encounter. Once I got seated, I noticed several Saudi couples also on board. They were all attired in their traditional Muslim dress and seated in pairs, in adjoining rows. They were chatting cheerfully and obviously looking forward to their departure. My next societal surprise came after we were airborne and the captain turned off the "Remain Seated" signs.

The three young ladies were the first to get out of their seats, pulled down their carry-on bags, and headed to the rear of the airliner. Meanwhile, the flight attendants began to take refreshment orders, which the three Saudi men cheerfully placed. It became more obvious that their fun was about to begin.

After about fifteen minutes or so, three totally unrecognizable young women returned to where the men were sitting. All three were dressed in obviously expensive flashy mini-skirts with all the trimmings. The guys welcomed them back, handing them their drink orders. They all toasted one another after which the guys departed, taking their carry-on bags with them. You can imagine the rest of the story . . . three young dandily-dressed young men returned to greet their ladies and the party continued until we landed in London. So much for Ramadan and Muslim virtue.

Saudi Arabia became one of the most disconcerting experiences of all my travels, including Vietnam! Hence, 9/11 brought a grim reminder when it was revealed that eighteen of the nineteen hijackers of the four doomed airliners were Saudis. Notable encounters, indeed!

Yevgeny Grigoryevich Dubchenko
Director General, Moscow
Underground Railway

As the Cold War began to come to its inevitable end, Andrew Corporation was alerted to an opportunity by our State Department that basic communications across Russia was marginally operating and virtually destroyed in most metropolitan areas. Over the years of growing control and dominance by the central government, commercial communications had been mostly confiscated by the military. I was invited to accompany Andrew President, Floyd English, and several engineers to Moscow to assess the communication situation and to determine if our company might assist in recovering basic local and commercial telephone system operations.

Not knowing what to expect, we were greeted in the city by a couple of Moscow representatives who welcomed us to Russia and the city. President Reagan had opened the door with Mikhael Gorbachev to lend assistance by U.S. companies to assist in restoring basic industries within the war-torn country.

The old adage, "Losing a war to the United States can be a blessing," was true of Japan and Germany at the end of World War II and to become so as well, in Russia. The opportunity benefited many U.S. industries to come into the country and reestablish lost services. We were provided hotel accommodations in the Olympic Hotel, given guided tours of the city, and treated as special guests by our hosts. I was personally shocked by the cordial treatment after serving most of my Air Force career in strategic operations developing war plans to defeat the Soviet Union. I then found myself in the heart of our "enemy's" territory! Although suspicious of our cordial greeting, I soon realized that the Russian people were no different than people all over the world, including our own America. It was the Soviet government that had subjugated their lives with theoretical beliefs of superiority over the rest of the world.

Meanwhile, the masses witnessed their leaders' promises and their country and their lives gradually disintegrate to economic and social impoverishment. I witnessed events and situations that one could only see with their own eyes to believe . . . vendors in horse-drawn wagons and carts loaded with spoiled vegetables moving down the streets of Moscow, trying to sell their goods. Trucks and vans were pulling up to the street curb with milk bottled in jars, cans, etc., and were being sold for whatever people had to spend. I witnessed men on the streets attempting to sell or barter alcohol in corked bottles. We heard horror stories of people being poisoned and dying from consuming the distributed milk and alcohol products. I have frequently commented that neither Moscow nor Russia were subjected to being bombed during the forty-five-year Cold War, yet the city and countryside were devastated with neglect, deterioration, and ruin.

With that introduction, we also met business and industry people from all over the world, coming in to Russia to assist as well as to benefit from the potential opportunities to assist in recovering the country's basic needs. Our engineers assessed the telecommunication failures and determined that the most efficient and cost effective way to restore city-wide telephone systems would be with fiber optics. They also suggested that an ideal and economic way to distribute fiber optic cables across the city of Moscow would be to utilize the existing underground rail, or subway. Tunnels would greatly reduce the requirement for telephone poles and trenches.

The Moscow underground rail system is the largest in the world with over two hundred miles of tunnels. Another social feature we discovered in Moscow that was unknown to us was that there were virtually no single homes within the city; everyone, no matter their status, lived in apartment buildings. Apartment telephones were nonexistent. Only the government elite had such a convenience, and they were limited, if they even worked.

That introduction brings us to meet Yevgeny Grigoryevich Dubchenko, Director General of the Moscow Underground Railway. Dr. English, our senior engineer, myself, and an interpreter paid a call on Mr. Dubchenko. He graciously welcomed us into his office where he was accompanied by several of his staff members, as well as his own interpreter. Dubchenko was a tall, heavyset Russian with a cheerful nature. Dr. English described the concept of utilizing the underground train tunnels to string fiber optic cable throughout the

city with outcroppings at desired locations to distribute telephone lines to apartment buildings, offices, etc. Dubchenko listened, as did his staff members to the proposal. Dr. English anticipated that economic reward would be at the forefront of the minds of his audience. He then proposed a joint venture agreement that was rapidly becoming the operating norm for outside businesses to do business in Russia. Andrew would fund the operation in return for the metro system providing the tunnel resources; in the end, it was hoped that the U.S. and other nations funding the recovery of the defeated Soviet Union would benefit from such projects. It was a gamble, but Andrew was willing to take the risk.

Dubchenko promptly expressed interest, as did his staff members, agreed to consider the proposal and welcomed us to meet again in a few days. We did meet again, and all agreed that it appeared to be a worthwhile venture. It was at that point that Dr. English asked me if I would be willing to take on the responsibility to work with the metro, create the joint venture agreement, and manage the program. The offer he made to me to remain and work in Moscow was sufficient for me to accept. That decision began a five-year sojourn in Moscow and across the other major cities in the former Soviet Union . . .

Dubchenko and I became good friends as we progressed with the project. He jokingly began to call me "Kristobal," and I called him "Evgenie." He would smile and say with broken English, "Comrade Kristobal, tell me this or tell me that . . . . I want your opinion."

We organized a joint venture company, consisting of our engineers and project managers as well as Russian counterparts in communication skills, planning, and coordination with city administrators. As with any such bi-national organization, there were issues, but Dubchenko managed his people as did I. We forged into the project, made new friends along the way, and importantly, restored local telephone communications within the city of Moscow. I shuttled back and forth to home in Dallas as well as to our home office in Chicago whenever I found an opportunity. After a time, I invited Mr. Dubchenko to come to Dallas, along with several of his key personnel.

Their visit was a time to remember for them as well as for us as their hosts. A memorable highlight of their visit was their introduction to Wal-Mart. They couldn't believe their eyes when they saw the array of merchandise. I provided each of our visitors with one hundred dollars to spend as they wished in the shopping outing. It was a day to remember as were many others during their visit. I recall strolling through North Park Mall in Dallas, with Dubchenko, when he looked at me, shook his head, and said, "Kristobal, just too many things to look at; too much wealth in America!"

That gave me pause to think that he was right and that we probably overdid their visit, exposing them to such apparent wealth. I hired a van one day and took them for a tour of the city of Dallas and the surrounding communities where another exposure to America occurred. As we drove along the outskirts of the city and came upon one large apartment complex after the other, one of our guests asked, "Are those buildings where all the workers live?"

I replied, "Yes, many people who work in the city live in those apartments."

I also escorted Dubchenko and several members of his party to Chicago and Andrew Corp offices to become more acquainted with the company and our people. I'll not forget the ride from the Chicago airport, cruising in our limousine along Riverside Drive, above which are located mega-sized mansions.

Mr. Dubchenko's personal assistant and interpreter looked up at the sight of the huge homes and asked me, "Chris, how many families live in those incredible large apartments?"

I was surprised by the question and then realized that she was comparing the mansions to the traditional apartments back in Russia and Moscow. I smiled and said, "Galina, usually just one family with maybe some children." She was likely reminded of the similar referral to the workers homes in the large apartment complexes back in Dallas. She just slowly shook her head as if in disbelief.

Their visit to the United States was no doubt a culture shock. After observing their cities deteriorate and literally crumble over the years, they couldn't imagine that most of the rest of the world was in relatively good order. The upbeat atmosphere, modernization, and

ambiance they were witnessing in Dallas and Chicago was almost too much for them to absorb. But, we all became even closer friends following their visit to America and created memories never forgotten.

Colonel Dmitri Sodolov, Soviet Army, Retired

My Moscow joint venture manager, Vasily, came to me one day, a year or so into the project, and said that he had a good friend, a retired Soviet Army Colonel, whom he would like to hire on to his staff. He said that they believed the colonel could assist him immeasurably with staff management and planning. I told him that it was fine with me: If he had the means within his budget, to go right ahead. I met retired Colonel Dmitri Sodolov shortly afterward. He was a well-groomed and very polite fellow and spoke English very well. I seldom saw him for a while after our first meeting until I arrived back in Moscow from a trip and Dmitri met me at the airport. I asked him why he was there to meet me.

He replied, "Comrade Vasily has assigned me to be a driver for a while; I suppose that I didn't please him well in my office duties?"

I didn't bring up the subject with Vasily. He and I were on a strictly business relationship and neither was he very friendly. Thereafter, Dmitri drove me wherever I went around the city to monitor our work, to the airport and so on. We became very good conversant friends. Each time I departed Moscow for the States, he would always stop by one of the small street kiosks, jump out of the car, and purchase a small inexpensive gift.

"Take this back home to your wife," he would smile. On my return, I would always bring him a thank-you gift.

Fast forward a few years. As my time in Russia came to a close, I met with a gathering of our Moscow Joint Venture Team to wish them all goodbye and wished them continued good luck with our project. I moved around the circle, shaking hands with each and when I came to Dmitri, we shook hands, he gave me a big hug and handed me a large envelope package. He then drove me to the airport as usual. We shook hands and bear hugged again, and I was on my way.

Along the way during the flight to Frankfort, I opened my briefcase to go over some paperwork and spotted the envelope Dmitri had given me. When I opened the soft, puffy envelope, I could have shed a bowl of tears. Therein, carefully wrapped in soft paper, was Dmitri's Soviet Uniform Colonel's shoulder boards. There was a handwritten note folded between the two shoulder boards that read, "Thank You, Comrade General Adams. God Bless America, Dmitri."

I sat there for I don't know how long, reflecting on the past five years working with so many people from among our former Cold War enemy. I lamented as I had often during my time working, interacting, and becoming friends with the Russian, Ukrainian, and Belorussians, that they are no different than Americans. We are all born free, grow up and become adults to carry out that which is before us. It is the ideology, culture, and influence of the ruling government's umbrella that directs and rules our behavior. The people of the former Soviet Union were now able to restart their lives and to hopefully live them free of an obsessed government.

Anatoly Sobchak, Mayor, St. Petersburg, Russia

Soon after we initiated and organized our Moscow Joint Venture operation, I went to St. Petersburg, along with two of our engineers and our interpreter, to meet with the governing officials there and to offer our support in rehabilitating their local telecommunication systems. I made an appointment with Petersburg Mayor Anatoly Sobchak. I had little background information on the mayor except that he had been a professor at St. Petersburg University, and as the Cold War began to diminish, he left the university and ran for mayor. It was a very uncomfortable meeting at the outset.

Our welcome by his staff was abrupt and cold. We sat for a half hour or so before we were invited into his office. During our waiting time, I took note of the number of telephones on his secretary's desk.

I counted twelve telephones distributed across her desk. I pointed to the telephones and asked her how she managed all the phones at the same time: She just looked at me and said that she just . . . "used them one at time."

I told her that we have call directory telephone systems in the United States that connect several telephones together, and when one rings, you just push a button on the instrument on the desk to answer. She just looked at me and shrugged.

We were finally ushered into the mayor's office. Sobchak was seated behind his desk and did not get up to welcome us. There were no handshakes offered. He nodded with a dry, "*Dobre utra* (Good morning)."

I responded in turn. Behind him, standing against the back of his office were a half-dozen or more men, staffers, I suppose. I thanked him for the opportunity to visit with him, and noticing his apparent uneasiness or boredom, I cut to the subject. I told him about our ongoing project in Moscow, the installation of fiber optic cables in the underground rail tunnels and the rapid successes we were having with reconstituting local telephone service. He listened without comment. After I completed my twenty minutes or so, over-view, he nodded to one of the men behind him, instructing him in Russian to go with us and to get the details.

We departed the mayor's office, no goodbyes or handshakes. His appointed staffer guided us to another office where we again described the communications project. After an hour or so, we came to an agreement that we had permission to meet with the director of the St. Petersburg Underground Railway to coordinate a possible joint venture operation similar to that in Moscow. This was bureau-cratic arrogance at its worst, but only the beginning! Thereafter, we met with a half dozen Petersburg railway "administrators." The "depth" of senior officials with whom we had to meet to discuss our proposal made it almost time to pull out, but we persisted; meeting with each one, in turn, we finally were successful in attempting to "help" them!

The highlight of the zigzagging course of coordination was a young and very bright interpreter assigned to our party, Tatyanna

Selitskaya. Tatyanna understood our frustration well, having to work with the conglomerate of bureaucrats on a daily basis. She patiently guided us through the process of coordination until the joint venture agreement was completed and the work began, recovering the St. Petersburg local telecommunications network. In the end, it was difficult to understand how two Russian city administrations, Moscow and St. Petersburg, could be so different, as well as complex!

I was to learn years later that when Mayor Anatoly Sobchak departed his professorship at the University of St. Petersburg and successfully campaigned to become mayor of the city, he recruited a former KGB lieutenant colonel by the name of Vladimir Putin, to come serve on his staff. Putin had been a KGB recruiter at the university, and when the Cold War came to a close in the summer of 1991, he found himself essentially without a job and accepted Sobchak's offer. As we know, Putin eventually moved on to Moscow, and that becomes history.

An afterthought that has bugged me for years, "Was Vladimir Putin among those standing behind Mayor Sobchak on that day we briefed him on our joint venture proposal?"

Aleksey Bolshakov, General Manager, High Speed Railways, Russia

The only means of communications between Moscow and St. Petersburg for decades had been radio, either high frequency (HF) or various other military connections. Our joint venture staff in Moscow in cooperation with the Petersburg joint venture concluded that it was imperative to "reconnect" these two major cities with basic telephone communication capabilities. We also decided that the best manner with which to directly connect the two cities would be via a major fiber optic cable, and the railroad right of way between Moscow and Petersburg would provide the most direct routing. It was suggested that I contact Mr. Aleksey Bolshakov, General Manager, Railways for all of Russia, who would be the most logical one with whom to coordinate the project. An appointment was made for me with Mr. Bolshakov, whose office was in St. Petersburg.

I took along Sasha Katsanov as my interpreter. Sasha, I had presumed from my first meeting with him to be a former KGB officer/agent. He was pure Russian, heavy stock build, rough appearance, but spoke fluent English. I also enjoyed Sasha's sense of humor as well as his insight to reading personalities, of whom I met many in that bedraggled post-war country.

The initial and subsequent meeting with Bolshakov was to be more of a memorable than notable encounter. We were ushered into his office by a cool and not very cordial secretary on an even colder drizzly morning. In the traditional manner of haughty greetings to which I became use to over time in Russia, Bolshakov was seated behind a huge wooden desk and did not make an initial move to stand up.

I greeted him with *"Dobre utra* (Good morning), Comrade Bolshakov."

He sat for a moment, sizing us up, and then finally rose, moved around, and held out his hand. We shook hands, and as I introduced myself, Sasha began to translate for me. Bolshakov nodded us toward chairs, and we sat down without his speaking. There were no further words of greeting, and I began to explain the purpose of our visit as Sasha translated for me. Over the years I spent in Russia, I could seldom determine if those with whom I met could understand or speak English, unless they indicated that they did. I told him about our joint venture developments in Moscow and St. Petersburg to assist in restoring normal telephone service to the residents and businesses within the cities. As I spoke and Sasha translated, my host maintained a sober, impassive demeanor, mostly just staring at us. After explaining our mission, I asked if he had any questions. He said that he did not and that he was aware of our work. He then asked what we wanted of him and that we must have a purpose in calling on him. He was coy.

I then began to explain the desires of the two cities to directly connect them with basic telephone communications and that our imported fiber optic technology was the best and most efficient way to accomplish the objective. Further, I stated the railroad right of way was the most direct route to place a cable between the two cities; the right of way was sufficiently wide, and there would be no interference with the railroad tracks.

He sat staring for a while and then asked, "How much are you willing to pay for use of the right of way?"

I attempted to explain to him that this was a joint venture project between the two largest cities in Russia, that it was a nation-wide project to serve the people of Russia. I told him that we had already partially surveyed the railroad right of way and that the property was sufficient to accommodate a buried cable without any interference with normal operations.

He shook his head, "Nyet!" Someone has to pay for use of state property! The back-and-forth conversation continued for a while longer and I finally excused us and asked if he might consult his superiors and reconsider. Upon departing, I also asked if we might visit on the subject again the next day. He shrugged, nodding.

That evening in the hotel, Sasha and I discussed the disappointing meeting. I asked Sasha, as I had others on the joint venture staff in Moscow, "Why should I meet with the general manager of High Speed Railways? Isn't there someone in charge of the Russian railway system?"

Sasha said, "You were directed to Bolshakov because he has strong political influence and he remains a part of the old establishment. He also has deep pockets and wants more to share with his cohorts."

I asked, "Can he make the decision or influence the right people in the system to approve our right of way request?"

Sasha replied, "Likely, he can influence the right people, or just tell you to go ahead and do it, if you can put some rubles in his pocket."

I told Sasha that I had a plan. I would go into our meeting tomorrow and tell Bolshakov that we no longer need his help, that we have contacted other property owners outside the railroad right of way and they have agreed to our proposal.

Sasha looked at me and said, "Chris, that dog won't hunt! He knows that you cannot cross seven hundred kilometers of Russian land without it costing a fortune, no matter who you talk to."

That was Sasha! He not only could speak our language but had learned our quipish culture as well. He was aware of the "system." I had him to cancel our next meeting and we returned to Moscow. It was there, working through the complex network of old Russia world bureaucrats, that I located the proper "authority" to speak with, Mr. Boris Nikiforov.

Boris Nikiforov, Minister of Railways, Russia

I had wondered why I wasn't directed to the minister of the Russian Railways in the first place. The obvious answer was that there was kickback money to be shared at many levels if we negotiated with a designated contact. I learned much more about the former Soviet culture from the Bolshakov experience! During my meeting with Ambassador Strauss, I asked his advice regarding our initiative to connect Moscow and St. Petersburg with telephone service, via fiber optic cable along the railroad right of way.

He applauded the idea and his response was prompt. "Try to make an appointment with the Minister of Railways, Boris Nikiforov. I have not met him yet, but my staff tells me that Nikiforov is an amiable fellow and most 'un-Soviet'!"

I took the suggestion from the Ambassador to my joint venture Russian counterpart, and he just shrugged. Another learning experience in a convoluted society. Who could we trust? I promptly hosted a small dinner party with my company people and invited Mr. Nikiforov. He agreed to attend and brought his own interpreter. He turned out to be the complete opposite of Bolshokov. He was a slight built fellow, along in years, with a very soft and quiet demeanor.

He greeted me warmly and seemed very much at ease surrounded by a half dozen Americans. He may have been of old school Soviet Union, but it was also obvious that he held his position due to his railroad operational knowledge and management skills. We enjoyed a pleasant getting acquainted hour, dinner, and then I invited him to chat with me privately for a few minutes. I invited his interpreter and Sasha to join us.

Once again, I described the initiative to connect the two major cities with telephone service and Nikiforov responded with, "Great idea, what may I do from the railroad?"

I explained our concept involving the railroad right of way and again he enthusiastically agreed. He said that he would develop the necessary clearances and get them coordinated and approved. All knowing where and who to contact! Following that brief exchange and successful outcome, he said that he would like to discuss another railway issue with me and get my perspective from an American perspective.

Nikiforov told me that on any given day in Russia, that an estimated forty to fifty thousand rail cars couldn't be accounted for due to the long distances between cities, particularly in the Siberian Region and between Moscow and Vladivostok, far down on the Pacific Ocean, near Japan. He said that virtually every day, rail cars loaded with produce, supplies, machinery, equipment, and so on were broken into and the goods stolen. He said there is often distances of hundreds of miles between sub-stations and rail cars. They were often placed on a side track overnight or even for days, if an engine suffered mechanical problems. He also said that they did breakdown frequently! The Cold War had taken its toll in many ways in Russia and this was another.

I told him that there were various bar coding systems in the United States that were used to track products, and it might even be feasible to place bar code placards on the rail cars, and then to install bar code readers at designated places along the railway to transmit the rail car identification and location back to a central location. I suggested that the bar code reader could transmit the information via satellite signal or even HF radio.

He was impressed and said, "How much does such a system cost?"

I said that I had no idea, but that I would attempt to get that information for him and perhaps even the U.S. government might be interested in such a project.

During a later meeting with Ambassador Strauss, I told him about the conversation with Mr. Nikiforov, including our fiber optic cabling to St. Petersburg and the bar code initiative. He was delighted with the success of my meeting and the rail car bar code notion and told me to relay to Nikiforov that the United States might be most interested in supporting the bar code project. "Just get us the information and a proposal," he said.

As mentioned previously, the ambassador was a refreshing pleasure during my Russian experiences!

Mikola Balatskiy, Chief, Kiev, Ukraine Subway System

Another novel meeting experience was that with Mikola Balatskiy. He and his deputy, Sergiy Zurik, came to Moscow to attend a presentation I was presenting to a group of businessmen and bankers regarding our joint venture initiative in restoring local and long-distance telephone services in Moscow and St. Petersburg, and the particular details of utilizing the underground railway tunnels to distribute the fiber optic cabling. He was an exceptionally pleasant, smiling, and easygoing fellow, an abrupt contrast to some Muscovites and those in St. Petersburg, with whom I had come to be suspicious and leery of their motives. Mikola invited me to come to Kiev, meet his people, and survey their underground railway system for a similar project.

Within a few weeks, one of my engineers and I flew to Kiev for a visit. I will inject here that was also my first, and *last*, experience flying with Russian Aeroflot Airlines! The check-in at the Moscow airport was normal. Bill and I received our boarding pass and seat assignments as usual. When we boarded the aircraft, a hefty rude flight attendant looked at our tickets and pointed to the rear compartment.

I protested, pointed to my ticket, "Nyet, first class."

She shook her head and again, pointed to the rear of the aircraft and pushed me to move on. So, we shrugged, obeyed, and followed the line of passengers before us although there were vacant seats up front and all along the way. When we got to the rear compartment, another ill-mannered, frowning flight attendant was standing, blocking the aisle, and directing passengers where to sit, row by row.

She pointed, "Dah, dah, dah!" as we approached a row of seats. That included the two of us. We took our seats without any further argument. The procedure simply meant that no matter what your boarding pass reflected, including passenger class or seat assignment, you sat where the flight attendants directed.

Once we got seated, I began to look around the cabin and first noticed that the oxygen ports above some seats were open and the interiors were bare. Bill then nudged my arm and showed me that one end of his seat belt straps was missing. I waved at the flight attendant to come to our aisle. I motioned to the missing seat belt connection and she shrugged and walked away. To top off the beginning of this flight adventure, a young couple with two young kids sat down in their seats in the row across the aisle from us. They each placed one of the youngsters in their laps and pulled the seat belts across the two of them. At least they had seat belts, even though one of the oxygen ports above them was empty. That was an airline flight to remember and never to board Aeroflot again!

Thereafter, I visited Kiev many times, traveling either by train—ten arduous hours!—or, I would fly from Moscow via Swissair or some other carrier, to Zurich, and then back into Kiev—at considerable expense, I might add!

Mikola became a great friend and colleague, and a considerable relief from so much of the other "post-Cold War Soviet Union" experiences. During my visits, we would meet frequently at a cafe owned and operated by his sister where they served the best ever beef and potato stew. I suggested to him once that the stew was excellent, but perhaps it would even be better with a few drops of Tabasco sauce, to which I surprised him with, pulling a bottle out of my briefcase. He was delighted and had his sister come out and sample her new stew flavor. They both seemed pleased and on the next trip back to the States, I brought him a case of Tabasco as I had previously brought a sample package to Ambassador Strauss.

I learned quickly that the Ukrainians *did not* like the Russians, especially Muscovites. I was riding across Kiev in a van with Mikola one day shortly after I arrived in the city when I noticed two uniformed military officers who appeared to be Russians, strolling casually down a sidewalk with briefcases in hand. I asked Mikola if those were Russian officers here in Kiev.

Before he could respond, the woman van driver blurted, "Dah, they are Russian! They have no business here in our country; we don't want them here. They have no place to go, no job, not anything anymore. They get up every day, put on their fancy uniforms, and walk the streets trying to look important. Their briefcases are empty except for maybe food to eat."

It was obvious that she was angry. Mikola shrugged with a smile and said, "It is true; they are left over from occupying our country and likely have no means to go back to Russia. There are hundreds, maybe thousands of Russians who are still in Ukraine; some have found jobs, but many are beggars and living off our cities and land."

Two other memorable experiences with Mikola which once included "someone" on my staff informing him that I had a birthday forthcoming during one of the summers of my five-year Russia trek. My wife came to Russia once during my stay and traveled to Kiev with me. Mikola said that he wished to have us come to his home for dinner during that visit. I had not previously visited him in his home, nor met his wife, Maria.

He sent a driver and drove us to an ancient-looking, worn, white, five-story building. I was surprised at the appearance of the building and surrounding area, but it was not much different than most all of the cities across the continent. Mikola met us downstairs and guided us up two flights of stairs to his apartment home. We met Maria, who was exceptionally gracious and welcomed us. Their apartment home consisted of two bedrooms, which within one was Maria's bedridden mother, whom we did not meet. There was an incredibly small kitchen, no more than 8'×10' in size. The living room and dining area were combined, with a large table against one wall, which Mikola pulled out to the center of the room. I am describing these modest conditions while reminding myself that Mikola Balatskiy was the chief operating officer of the Kiev Subway, a major transportation system the size of those of New York and

Chicago subways. We can seriously doubt that the CEOs of those systems live in such crowded two-bedroom apartments!

Maria served a delightful dinner topped off with a huge colorfully decorated birthday cake! The highlight of that special evening came when Mikola got up an turned on a reel-to-reel tape player that filled the small room with soft music. Mikola then shocked us when he began to sing in a deep baritone voice, joined in shortly by Maria! The two of them sang a melodiously love song to one another sufficiently to bring tears to our eyes. An evening and experience never to be forgotten!

Later, I invited Mikola, his deputy Sergiy, and three of his Kiev Subway staff members to come to the United States and Dallas, as we had previously, Mr. Dubchenko and members of his Moscow staff. We housed them in first-class hotel accommodations and as we had with our Moscow associates, took them shopping and toured the city. The highlight of their visit was hosting them at dinner one evening at the Trail Dust Steakhouse. A well-known stunt at the Trail Dust was for the waiters to come to the table, take drink orders, return with the drinks, and then promptly take out a pair of scissors and methodically cut off the neckties of the men. I made sure that each of our guests wore a necktie that evening, and we shall never forget their shock when the waiters did their deed! After they caught on to the joke and the hooting settled, one of my office guys went around the table handing each of our guests a gift box with a new necktie.

I continued to communicate with my friend Mikola for years after I completed my time in Russia and Ukraine, especially at Christmas, and I always received a response. And, then suddenly the communication ceased and some of my notes and cards began to be returned. It was impossible to determine what might have happened to Mikola and/or his family. Another wonderful encounter and friendship!

General Alexandr I. Tushinskiy, Minister of Defense, Belarus

We made initial contact with Mr. Pavel Mitasov, Deputy of the Minsk City Counsel and Chief of Minsk Metro, to discuss the poten-

tial of creating a joint venture agreement similar to that of Moscow and the other cities to address their degraded telecommunications systems. We were immediately summoned to first have a meeting with the Minister of Defense, Belarus, to describe our proposal. Along with two of my Andrew Corp engineers and my Moscow interpreter, Sasha Katsanov, we traveled by train to Minsk to meet with Belarus General Alexander Tushinskiy. We didn't have a clue as to the purpose of the meeting with the Minister of Defense, since we had not encountered any military interest in our projects in Moscow or the other two joint venture communications recovery efforts.

We arrived at the National Defense Headquarters in Minsk and were escorted into a posh briefing room. There were at least two dozen men in military and civilian dress already seated around a large oblong table. We were guided to three chairs on one side, near the end of the table. I also noted that Mr. Mitasov was not present in the room. There was not a place for Sasha at the table, so he sat down in a cushy chair in the back corner of the room. No one spoke to us. Everyone remained silent, not even talking among themselves. It gave us a pretty eerie feeling. A side door opened and the general, in full uniform, walked in without speaking. Everyone promptly stood up. He took his place at the center head of the table, eyeing all of us who were seated. He homed in on us and nodded to his interpreter seated at the opposite end. The interpreter then asked me to introduce myself and those with me. I did so, briefly, stating my name and my company and then began to introduce my two American engineers. The general suddenly held up his hand for me to stop talking, pointed to Sasha seated in the corner, in Russian, gruffly asked in Russian, "Who is he?"

The interpreter repeated in English and I replied, "He is my interpreter."

The general then asked, again in Russian, "Moscow?"

I recognized the question and replied, "Dah."

He then said again, in Russian, waving his hand, "Out, out!"

I nodded to Sasha to leave the room, and once the door was closed, I took a deep breath and continued to introduce my associates.

When I finished, he said to his interpreter, "Tell me why you are here."

I caught the gist of his direction and proceeded to brief our joint venture work in Moscow, Petersburg, and Kiev . . . that Andrew is a highly recognized and credible international telecommunications company, and we have been invited by the Russian government to assist in recovering their degraded and depleted local and long-distance telephone systems. I described our initiative in utilizing the underground metro tunnels to accomplish the tasks. I was not at all pleased with our welcome, much less being there, and my presentation lasted less than fifteen minutes, mainly providing an overview. When I came to the end, Tushinskiy sat for a few seconds, scanned the room, didn't speak, and departed the room. No one in the room spoke to us as we departed.

Sasha was waiting outside in the adjacent room. I apologized to him for his being dismissed by the general.

In typical Sasha humor, he said, "It was an honor to not have to interpret for that gangster." No love lost with that event, just arrogance at its best demonstrated by the general and many I encountered during my journey.

Pavel Mitasov, Deputy, Minsk City Counsel and Chief of Minsk Metro

Following the meeting with General Tushenskiy, and while still in Minsk, I asked Sasha to contact Mr. Mitasov and to determine if he was interested in our meeting with him. He said that he was and we arranged to meet with him the following day. Mitasov was a very mild-mannered, soft-spoken fellow, much to the opposite of our previous day's encounter. I was to learn that the Belarus's disdain for Moscow and Russia in general was mixed, as opposed to that of the Ukrainians. I mention that, in spite of General Tushenskiy's dismissal of Sasha from the previous day's meeting. Belarus leaned heavily on Moscow for financial support and virtually everything else.

To support our work in Russia, Andrew acquired the services of a Washington, DC, based resource company to further provide interpreter/translation support. Erica Nobel, president of ASET

(American Services for European Trade), arrived in Moscow and promptly flew over to Minsk to join me and become involved in the process. She became a welcome asset! Her presence also provided an opportunity to relieve Sasha from some of the stress he had endured.

I brought Erica up to date on our business venture concept and our progress in the various city operations. She attended my second meeting with Mr. Mitasov, his people, and our engineers. Mitasov brought into the meeting Vassili Voloshuchuk, Deputy Minister, Telecommunications and Informatics, Belarus. Voloshuchuk clearly understood the need and our purpose for being in Belarus. He confessed that their local and country-wide telecommunication systems were near nonexistent and welcomed our services. He factually explained that the Soviet military had taken over all of the telephone systems in their country and that the city of Minsk had virtually no telephone operations, except the local police and military.

We became aware of that in the hotel where we were staying, just as we had in Moscow and the other cities. If you wished to make a phone call, you would go to the hotel communications office, place a call with the on-duty operator and then sit and wait, maybe even hours, if it happened to be a call back to the United States. The real shock came when the operator handed you the bill for the call, which if to the States, it could easily range into thousands of dollars. The former Soviet States may have lost the war, but they had learned quickly how to make money off the "foreigners," Americans, Germans, French, Swiss and others, who were coming in to help them recover.

Our progress with Mitasov and Voloshuchuk went fairly smooth. Voloshuchuk clearly understood the need for restoring telephone communications, and Mitasov agreed to the use of the railway tunnels for cable distribution. One small "hitch" occurred when it came time to sign the contract releasing to us access and use of the tunnels. Erica and I showed up at his office on the morning to sign the documents, and for some reason we never figured out, he was very pensive.

He suggested that we take a drive around Minsk. "I want to show you our city before you depart," he said.

I shrugged and agreed, but asked Erica to advise him that we had a train to catch early that afternoon. We got into his automobile. I sat in the front passenger's seat and Erica sat in the back and performed her translation duties between Mitasov and myself. He casually drove and drove around the city, pointing out one building, statue, park and so on, for almost two hours. Finally, I told Erica to advise him that we had a train to catch and should get back to his office to sign the contract. As it turned out, when we arrived back to his office, he advised me, via Erica, that this was to be an interim contract, and that he wished to send two of his staff members, including an attorney back to the United States and Andrew Corporation, to negotiate the final contract agreement. I was taken by surprise, but I had no choice but to agree to his terms. His interim agreement did permit us to begin work on the project. With that small alteration agreed to, we signed the interim contract with his attorney present to certify the document.

That wasn't the end of our day. One of Mitasov's staff came into his office and advised that the train to Moscow had been canceled. There would not be another one until the next morning. I took the opportunity of the extra time to send a fax message back to Andrew to advise my point of contact that we had signed an interim agreement, pending Mitasov's representatives coming to the States for a more formal signing.

Another disconcerting, but somewhat humorous event occurred after I had carefully penned the fax message on a lined pad and asked one of Mitasov's staff members, Sergiy, to please send it for me. After a while, Igor, who spoke relatively good English, returned and said, "Mr. Adams, I cannot send the fax because we have no paper."

I said, "Sergiy, you don't need paper to send a fax; the paper is on the other end and it will be printed out there."

He looked at me and replied, "But, how does the message get through the wire?"

Another of the many fond, frequently fun and all too often, serious encounters in the former Soviet States.

Later, during my work with the Belarus entities, we negotiated a contract with the Gorizont Telecommunications Company for future

satellite operations. That was to be an interesting experience. If your history recalls, Lee Harvey Oswald was employed by Gorizont during his three years living in Minsk prior to returning to the United States and committing the assassination of President Kennedy. In working with Gorizont, I was tempted, but did not ever refer to Oswald, although the temptation was great. Neither did I refer to Oswald with my Minsk friends, which historical research also revealed that when he first arrived in Minsk, escorted by the KGB, he was met by the mayor of the city at the time, provided lodging well above that of the average citizen at the time and a fairly substantial-paying job. More history . . .

6

Notable Exceptional Encounters

As we travel down the road of life, we encounter many who are more exceptional than others. Most encounters happen via an introduction, others by accident or a twist of fate. My exceptional encounters were, more often than not, the most unique, with many becoming friends for life. Herein, I want to highlight just a few of the most exceptional encounters with those that have endured in my thoughts and memories. I recognize that I take a great risk in choosing these few to recognize while there are multitudes of others whom also deserve equal recognition and remain so with pleasant memories of the past.

In highlighting these exceptional encounters, I will address them in order of my chronological recall.

Paul L. Pearce, DDS

Paul Pearce and I each transferred to East Texas State Teachers College as we entered our junior year. Paul transferred from Tyler Junior College and I transferred from Tarleton State College. Our coincidental meeting occurred in the dining hall shortly after the semester began, and we hit it off right away relating to one another

that we were both from South Texas, Paul from Houston and I was from nearby Tomball. Paul became instantly interested in the fact that I had transferred to East Texas for the purpose of continuing my ROTC military training, which I had completed the first two years at Tarleton. I told him that my interest was also in pursuing an Air Force commission, offered by the ROTC program at East Texas. My principal purpose also included avoiding potentially being drafted by the Army, since the Korean War was ongoing and military service drafting was in high order. Paul had not had the opportunity to acquire the first two initial years necessary to enroll in the final two years required to receive a commission as an officer. I encouraged him that if he was seriously interested in seeking a commission in the Air Force, to go and discuss opportunity options with the ROTC military staff.

Paul did just that and was promptly enrolled in dual ROTC courses, freshman and junior, concurrently. This meant that at the end of his senior year, he would earn a commission in the Air Force when he graduated from college. We became good friends after our first meeting and Paul travelled with me to our respective homes in my sturdy 1935 Chevy Coupe during breaks in school.

While at Tarleton, I had been a member of the Wainwright Rifles military demonstration drill team, which took us all to most all of the football games and around the state for special event parades. I took the idea of my experience at Tarleton and proposed that we develop a similar precision drill team at East Texas. The professor of Air Science agreed and we did. Some forty cadets joined us in creating the Mitchell Grenadiers, which we named ourselves after World War II General Billy Mitchell. The Air Staff purchased special uniform attire for us, including white leggings, combat helmets, M-1 rifles, etc. Paul joined in with us, having never had any military training, as many others didn't. He became our guidon bearer and performed as if he had marched and carried a guidon flag always.

Over the two remaining years in college, Paul and I became the best of good friends. I applied for pilot training to succeed graduation and Air Force commissioning and so did Paul. We both passed the aptitude tests and physicals and became fully qualified for pilot training. Following graduation from college, we were assigned pilot training classes, but at different locations. I was assigned to go to Spence Air Base, Moultrie, Georgia, and Paul's orders sent him to Greenville Air Force Base, Mississippi.

As it turned out, neither of us had to report until August after graduation in May, which meant an opportunity to get a job and acquire a few dollars to carry us through the summer and onto active duty in the Air Force. After arriving home to Tomball, I heard that Production Service Corporation had an oil drilling rig operating north of town, across Spring Creek. I drove out to the rig and, as luck would have it, the Tool Pusher (oil rig supervisor) happened to be on site. I introduced myself and told him of my situation and my previous "roughneck" experience with two different drilling companies over the past three summers in the Panhandle and West Texas. He promptly told me that the swing shift drilling crew had an opening for the back tong operator. I told him that I would take it! After all, $1.75 an hour was a good wage in those days. I went to work that evening with the swing shift crew (3:00 p.m. to 11:00 p.m.). Two days later, I was told that the day shift had lost a crew member and had an opening.

I drove to Houston early the next morning, looked up Paul, and asked if he would like to have a go at "roughnecking." He promptly said that he would and drove out to the rig that afternoon. I introduced him to the day shift driller, who was just going off duty as my shift crew was coming on. Paul was upfront and told the driller that he had no drilling rig experience but was willing to learn. He was hired on the spot and went to work the next morning, driving thirty miles from his home in Houston. As it all turned out, he took to the job well, learned the operating system and happy days thereafter!

We both had orders to report to our respective pilot training classes on September 1, 1952. We both gave notice to the drilling company well in advance of our departure times and prepared to leave for our respective pilot training bases to enter active duty with the Air Force. Paul took off to Greenville, Mississippi, and I went to Moultrie, Georgia. For the next eight months we were both too busy to communicate very much except by brief written note, exchanging our experiences in learning how to fly airplanes. We did receive a week off at Christmastime and joined up for a brief day visit back in Texas. When we graduated from our respective primary pilot training classes in May 1953, we each departed for basic flight training. I was sent to Reese Air Force Base, near Lubbock, Texas, and Paul was assigned to Columbus Air Force Base, Mississippi. We each began training in the vintage World War II B-25 "Billy Mitchell" bomber. I contacted Paul in late July and told him that I was going to get married in late August, and that I would like to have him serve as my best man. He said that he would desert the Air Force to be there, if he couldn't get away legally. He did, and he was my best man!

We graduated from our respective basic pilot training programs, and I was assigned to Biggs Air Force Base, near El Paso. Paul was assigned to Goodfellow Air Force Base to become a pilot training instructor. That was quite a feather in his cap, to transition from student to instructor in one quick step! We were proud of him! And then, the worst of worst happened. I received a letter from him that he had been in an accident. It seems that he was taking off in one of the ancient B-25 bomber trainers with two student pilots, when right after takeoff, both engines failed, and they made a "dead stick" crash landing. All three survived, except that Paul's back was shattered, and he was to be in the hospital for weeks, or possibly months. By that time, I had been assigned to a combat crew at Biggs and couldn't get away to go visit him. It would be almost a year later before we saw Paul; he was still in a heavy back brace and had been discharged from the Air Force. In the meantime, he had fallen in love with a school teacher in San Angelo and decided to get married. He summoned me to be his best man and so I did when they were married in her hometown of Vernon, Texas.

To fast forward, Paul's new wife's father was a prominent dentist in Vernon, and he convinced Paul that he should pursue dentistry as a profession. Pursue he did and graduated after due time from the University of Texas Dental School. He initially began practice with his father-in-law in Vernon then later began his own practice in Ft. Stockton, Texas. We did not see one another for several years, both being busy in our respective careers, exchanging notes and cards along the way. Paul then advised me a dozen or so years later that he was getting a divorce from his wife and moving to Austin to accept a teaching position at the University of Texas Dental School. His wife, with two sons and daughter, would be remaining in Ft. Stockton. That was a sad time for all and very little was ever discussed about the circumstances that prevailed. Time moved on and we remained in contact via letters and cards over the years.

Paul then called me one day and announced that he was getting married again, to Susie, a dental hygienist professor at the university. He also asked if I would again serve as his best man. After brief consideration and the difficulty of getting away from my Air Force job to attend, I jokingly advised him that "I failed the first time and I didn't want to be held accountable a second time."

Paul and Susie were married and not long after, they accepted an opportunity to go to Saudi Arabia to teach, assist, and supervise the establishment of numerous dental facilities across the country. They lived comfortably, they said, within an American compound where they did not have to abide by the stringent Saudi Arabian habits and rules of religious conduct. Their tour of duty lasted for five long years but benefitted them greatly when they returned. They were able to open their own dental practice facility and move into an upscale country club environment at Horseshoe Bay, near Marble Falls, Texas. By this time, I had retired from the Air Force to Texas, and we began to visit over the years, as well as Paul becoming my personal dentist! Never thought that I would permit my best friend to mess around in my mouth!

Over the succeeding years, we visited and traveled together considerably: Alaska, Hawaii, and mostly to my condo in New Mexico. Paul and Susie had also taken up golf along the way, becoming virtually "semi-pros," playing in tournaments around the country and enjoying the good life! They decided in the mid-2000s to sell their practice and retire to Sun City, near Georgetown, Texas. We visited our best friends as often as we could, and then in 2013, we were told that Susie had been diagnosed with severe cancer cells, virtually throughout her body. Sadly, she tragically passed away within a short year. It was a sad time of trauma for all, especially Paul. After a time, his daughter, Pam, convinced him to leave Sun City and move to be near by her and her family at Marble Falls.

That is where Paul now resides, not in the best of health, mainly due to recurring back and bone structure issues dating back to his aircraft accident, perhaps too much golfing and likely anxiety over the sadness in his life. We continue to correspond and visit frequently. Dr. Paul Pearce, friend for life!

Dorene Elsberry Sherman

"Farm girl mingled with princes and generals," as she was described in a special tribute article in the Omaha World Herald. I first met Dorene Sherman in the summer of 1976. I had been selected for promotion to brigadier general and given command of the 12th Air Division located at Davis-Monthan Air Force Base, Arizona. As a general officer within Strategic Air Command (SAC), I was required to fly missions aboard the Airborne Command Post, Looking Glass.

Accordingly, I flew to SAC Headquarters at Offutt Air Force Base, Omaha, Nebraska, and checked in for orientation in preparation for flying the Looking Glass missions. Arriving at SAC Headquarters, I went upstairs to the chief of staff's office to obtain my instructions. Looking up and down the hallway for his office, I spotted Ms. Dorene Sherman, Secretary to the Commander in Chief, SAC (CINCSAC) sitting behind a desk. I cautiously walked into the hallowed office complex, as she rose from her desk and walked right over to me, asking if she might help me.

I introduced myself and my purpose in being there. She promptly greeted me warmly and welcomed me to SAC Headquarters. Her first suggestion was, "Let me show you around the Headquarters Command Section." This was where the offices of the CINC, vice CINC, and chief of staff were located. She proceeded to introduce me to the various staff members and officers that were there. We spent a couple of hours going from office to office and meeting those within each one. She provided me the most gracious and personable reception I could have ever expected. I had actually thought that I would first meet some grumbling general officer who would wave me off to a staff officer to provide me the orientation I was there to receive. Not so.

That was my introduction to a special and memorable encounter with a special lady, who remains a very dear friend to this very day of memories. I am admittedly going to plagiarize a few descriptions from the Omaha World Herald newspaper tribute to her and from my own story about Dorene in my published 2008 work, *Deterrence: An Enduring Strategy.*

Dorene Sherman (nee Elsberry) is a Nebraska farm girl, born and raised in the remote village of Wasau in northeast Nebraska, bumped right up against the border with South Dakota. Swedish on her mother's side, English on her father's, she was born in the same room as her mother, milked cows, slopped hogs, planted and harvested crops, walked miles to and from her one-room schoolhouse, slipped cardboard into the soles of her worn out shoes, wore dresses made from feed sacks, and delivered a pretty good impression of a Willa Cather character.

At age twenty, after teaching for a year in Wasau's one-room schoolhouse, she moved to Omaha where the great flood of 1952 and a polio epidemic combined to write one of the city's worst disasters. She started to work for the Red Cross and at Children's Hospital. In 1954, she met and married Harold Sherman and settled in adjacent Bellevue. After losing her husband in 1993, she remained in their same Bellevue home, concurrently becoming one of the most visible and notable volunteers in the Bellevue-Omaha metro area.

The beginning of the exceptional life story of Dorene Sherman unfolded with her applying for a civil service job at Offutt Air Force Base in 1960 as a receptionist. This simple farm girl's life immediately began transforming from an ordinary to an extraordinary world. She began meeting and making lasting friends with every mogul in Omaha and Nebraska that transited Offutt Air Force Base, but also presidents of the United States, movie stars, world leaders, and an unending succession of military generals and admirals, visiting and passing through Strategic Air Command.

She is quoted as saying, "I was so grateful to get that job. My husband had just lost his, and we needed an income. I just worked hard, and they kept promoting me." After her first ten years of working diligently at a succession of Civil Service administrative jobs in the Headquarters, in 1970, she stepped onto a path that would make her a legend in Strategic Air Command and to provide her with remarkable memories, a library of photographs and albums of written tributes from luminaries such as Bob Hope, President Jimmy Carter and Gerald Ford, Jimmy Doolittle, Margaret Thatcher, and Saudi Arabia Ambassador Prince Bandar bin Sultan. Her "modest" list continues with the Osmond Brothers, comedian Bob Newhart, Academy Award-winning actress Rita Moreno, author Tom Clancy, and an unending parade of generals, admirals, including the chairmen of the Joint Chiefs of Staff.

In the mid-1970s, Dorene became secretary to SAC Commander in Chief, which took her onward to being appointed deputy director of protocol. There she carried the responsibility for arranging the arrivals, accommodations, and itineraries of many of the VIPs already listed, including Queen Elizabeth II, whose airplane once stopped at Offutt Air Force Base for refueling and whom she met and escorted to a reception room. During her many years of service, she traveled extensively with SAC commanders and staff virtually all over the world, once attending a White House luncheon.

After almost four decades of service to the Air Force and Offutt Air Force Base, Dorene's career came to close with her retirement in 1999. Her service took her to many parts of the world and drew lengthy tributes from many journalists, including yours truly in my published work. She recounts that she "was entrusted with the most sensitive of national security information in order to understand the requirements necessary to coordinate visits of special dignitaries." I personally witnessed and can attest that while she did not wear an Air Force uniform, she was "just as committed and loyal to the Air Force and the Cold War mission as those in command who sat at the controls of nuclear bombers or the ICBMs. It has been, she says with her own shy humility, 'a blessed life.'"

From finding the Mormon Church, where she said she discovered answers to perplexing theological questions, to finding purpose and significance in the service of her country, Dorene Sherman frequently ponders about her journey. "I was just a farm girl, milking cows," she said, "but I ended up around presidents and princes and generals. How could this be me?"

If a journey ever takes you to Omaha, you might want to stop in the Omaha Visitors Center at the corner of 10th and Farnam streets. The chances are good that you just might encounter Dorene Sherman there on any given day, volunteering as usual and greeting visitors warmly as she did me upon that first meeting, with her gracious manner, smiling and welcoming you. She also volunteers at an Omaha special place, the Lauritzen Gardens and the Omaha Community Playhouse, and you will be greeted by this same special lady, offering a gentle touch on the arm as she ushers you to your seat. Not one to just retire, she frequently is on stage at the Bellevue Little Theatre, performing in some starring role.

A forty-two-year convert to the Church of Jesus Christ of Latter-day Saints, Dorene is just as involved or more so, in her church, hosting visitors and welcoming missionaries, while providing worshipers with her talented and skilled organ music. This, while concurrently serving at the Fred and Pamela Buffet Cancer Center and on the Board of Directors of the Bellevue Chamber of Commerce and so on . . .

During my twenty-five years serving in various places and positions within Strategic Air Command, including my final four years in Headquarters SAC, in three different positions, including chief of staff, I marveled at this lady warrior who had earned her "stripes" as a competent professional. Dorene Sherman was well-grounded, self-confident, and exuded animated energy and enthusiasm in every position she was assigned over the years. She was also the first to retreat into the background when the situation dictated, permitting the colonel or the general, in charge, to step into the limelight and take credit for a successful event. Within the SAC Headquarters staff of eight thousand officers, non-commissioned officers, airmen, and civilians, she was known to all for her personal enthusiasm, "can do" spirit, exceptional competence, and trust.

Upon her retirement from Civil Service in 1999, Dorene was honored in numerous ways, but the recognition by her community is held most deeply within her heart. The Distinguished Service Award is awarded to an individual for outstanding contributions to the Bellevue-Offutt Air Force Base Community and has been given annually since 1964. Each year the Bellevue Chamber of Commerce honors someone whose career and commitment to the community fully embodies the elements of "Distinguished Service."

Her citation was read as follows:

> Tonight we honor a woman who dedicated over forty years of her life working at Offutt Air Force Base and continues to be active today as a volunteer. She is seen daily volunteering and giving of herself throughout the Bellevue-Offutt Community and the Omaha Metro area. You might run into to her at the Bellevue Little Theatre, the Durham Museum, the Rose Theater, the Mormon Trail Center, or maybe Lauritzen Gardens. She has been recognized as Volunteer of the Year, Ambassador of the Year, and is a lifetime member of the Bellevue Chamber of Commerce. She always wears a smile on her face and is there to offer a helping hand. On behalf of the Bellevue Chamber of Commerce Board of Directors it is my distinct pleasure to present Dorene Sherman with this year's Distinguished Service Award as an outstanding community leader with passion, integrity, and vision who continues to serve the community with conviction, determination, and insight.

Dorene Sherman, one of my most exceptional encounters, whom I was privileged to visit with at a Strategic Air Command reunion in 2016 and to once again refresh my memories of this incredible lady.

Joe B. Hinton

I could have singled out and profiled good friend of the ages, Joe Bob Hinton, as a notable business and professional leader, notable political leader, or here as an exceptional encounter. He more than excelled in each category concurrently.

I first met Joe in 1991 at an Annual Alumni Gala event at Texas A&M University-Commerce. At that time, Joe was president, A&M-Commerce Foundation Board. We chatted for some time during the evening, getting to know one another. Joe did not reveal much more to me than he had worked for the most part of his post-college years for Mobil Oil Corporation. It was later that I learned he not only worked for Mobil Oil but that he retired from the corporation as president and CEO of Mobil Oil Corporation, Europe. Also that he spent forty years with Mobil, working from the bottom-up; oil rig roughneck to vice president, Marketing and Refining, as well as, executive vice president, Montgomery Ward, a subsidiary of Mobil Oil, an onward to operating the corporation's European business.

Joe was born in Valley Mills, Texas, and went off to college to East Texas State, ol' ET, as I mentioned earlier. He played football on the college team as well as excelling academically. He returned home each summer and worked in the oil fields. His dad, he said, had worked for Humble Oil and Refining Company for forty years. So, for him to work in oil fields during summer college breaks was a natural thing to do, besides, he said, "I made good spending money." He and I both related to the Texas oil field culture, and spending money too!

He said that his kick start into life occurred one day on the platform of a Humble Oil Company drilling rig following his junior year of college. A Humble Oil executive had dropped by the rig, struck up a conversation with Joe, asking him about what he was going to do when he graduated from college, etc. Joe said that he shrugged and said he didn't quite know what he would do after college. The Humble Oil exec told him that when he finished school to drop down to Houston and look him up. Joe did just that after he graduated the following summer. From there, Joe said that his life became skyrocket. He went back with Humble Oil's support, to college, obtained his master's degree, and promptly to work for the company that eventually became Mobil Oil Corporation. By the time he graduated from East Texas State, with two degrees, he had already worked five summers with Mobil and they put him to work.

Joe and I continued to find a number of things in common as we became better acquainted. We both agreed that graduating from our small Texas teacher's college, made us every bit as qualified take on the challenges of the big working world as an Ivy Leaguer.

Joe said that when he first went to work for Mobil, "Someone told me once that as a graduate from a Texas 'cow college,' I was going to have a big disadvantage in the corporate world of New York compared to my Ivy League counterparts. That really captured my attention; it lit a fire under me. I realized quickly that your worth in the corporate world was measured by what you produced and how you impacted the bottom line, so I did everything I could to be successful, working twenty-five hours a day, eight days a week. After the first year, I fit into the crowd."

I told him that I had experienced the same admonishments when I departed East Texas for the Air Force and arrived in Georgia for pilot training. As I met other brand-new Air Force officers, like myself, many from Ivy League universities, West Point, and so on, I took a lot of kidding and chiding, being from Texas and a small-town college. We agreed that neither of us did too badly with our commerce, Texas, college education. Joe was also a patriot and found time along his busy pathway to serve eight years with the Army National Guard's 14th Armored Infantry Battalion.

Joe met and married Betty A. Goelzer of Chilton, Texas, who readily joined him in his rapid climb to success. She provided him with the calm steady home life along with two beautiful daughters, which served to balance his otherwise fast-paced daily challenges and pursuits, as he moved rapidly up the staff to management to executive chain. He became a quick study of the activities and those surrounding him, observing everything within sight and reason.

He was rewarded accordingly. "I was the first American to serve in London as president of Mobil Europe," Joe said. "Thankfully, my boss in New York had carefully coached me about cultural differences and sensitivities, and I diligently passed that knowledge on to my team. When I saw someone fall out of line due to a cultural faux pas, I confronted them immediately. There's an education process, and if you don't want to learn proper etiquette, you won't last long working overseas."

After forty years with Mobil Oil, Joe *technically* retired. As reported in an interview article in the Texas A&M University-Commerce *Pride* Alumni Magazine, Joe said that the acquired energy and enthusiasm from his professional career steered him to continue to be actively involved. He enjoyed being with people and to participate in worthwhile projects and activities.

As his post-professional life has demonstrated, his influence and expertise was in demand by state and local leaders. In addition to serving as chairman, A&M-Commerce Foundation, he was appointed by then Governor George W. Bush to serve as chairman of the executive board of the Brazos River Authority. Also invited to serve on the Texas Rangers Museum Board of Directors, Joe said, "I grew up hearing my grandfather's stories about the Texas Rangers, and about his father who was a Ranger. Rangers are known to be fearless. They always pay careful attention to detail, work hard, and almost always get the desired result. When I had the opportunity to serve as chairman of the Executive Committee Advisory Board, I jumped at the chance."

Following his tenure with the Brazos River Authority Board of Directors, Joe was appointed by Governor Rick Perry to serve on the Texas Higher Education Coordinating Board. In a thoughtful gesture as he departed the Brazos River Board, he nominated me to the governor, to serve on the board, a position that I am currently serving my thirteenth year. Concurrent with all the other duties, he also served as a member of the Baylor University Steering Committee for the George W. Bush Library project. Being involved and actively participating in politics also became a high interest priority. Recognized for his depth of knowledge, judgment, and influence, he was elected chairman of the McLennan County Republican Party. In every endeavor and challenge, Joe was known to maintain a fearless approach, never afraid to make the right choice, even when it was unpopular.

Joe was quoted in the previously mentioned *Pride* Alumni Magazine article, "If you see a need for positive change, act on it. It's a hard road at times, but always worthwhile. It will lead you down the path to a not-so-average life."

Shortly after that first meeting with Joe I mentioned, he called and asked if I would join him on the university foundation board. He had a vacancy, he said, and would be delighted to add, as he described it, "some broader-based background and knowledge of the outside real world, beyond the mostly locals that he had currently serving on the board."

I agreed to serve on the board, although as I told him, I was then shuttling back and forth to Europe and Russia with the company I was still attached to. He said that he still wanted me on the Foundation Board and that I could attend as often as I was available. After several years and Joe completing some eleven years as chairman, he called me aside at one of our meetings and said that he was stepping down and would like to nominate me to replace him. Of course, I was honored and agreed to his offer, since my European travels were also coming to a close. His were large but enjoyable shoes to fill; he had brought the foundation to unprecedented heights in student scholarships and capital funding.

Among Joe Hinton's many contributions back to his university and through his own personal generosity, he also founded and funded the Texas A&M University-Commerce School of International Studies. Joe's spoken philosophy when he offered to create the school within the university, "If you see a need for positive change, act on it. It's a hard road at times, but always worthwhile. It will lead you down the path to a not-so-average life. Students can learn so much from these programs, and they return far better prepared for careers in our global environment. It's a worthy investment that confirms that the key to success lies in a good education."

With considerable sadness and grief, I must close this portrait and memory of an exceptional notable encounter and special friend of a lifetime, Joe B. Hinton, born in Valley Mills, Texas, on February

17, 1935, passed away unexpectedly, on Thursday, December 29, 2016, in Waco, Texas.

Mackye Evans

I first met Mackye Evans at a social event in Ft. Worth, hosted by mutual friends. She is a very personable but quietly reserved lady, whom one would never detect the breadth and depth of her extraordinary background, life's experiences, and highly successful professional business career. Mackye was, and continues to be, an exceptionally private person, with the exception of her two grandsons, whom she proudly dotes, worships, and encourages them onward in her footsteps. Many interactive encounters and visits thereafter that first meeting have bonded a special friendship with this lady.

An entrepreneur and business professional, Mackye is a native Texan, grew up in Ft. Worth, and followed in the footsteps provided by her father and mother. She says that there were no funds to pursue college when she graduated from high school, so instead, she attended a small business school for two years to learn the fundamentals of managing a business such as that which was her father's to become so successful. She began at an early age, working part-time for her father, observing and learning his business and management skills for which, she says, to this day she is eternally grateful "for all that I learned from my dad about life and business, and making wise choices in life."

Out of business school, Mackye also took on another additional job, working for a law firm to make extra money. The law firm, it turned out, had close ties with both Presidents Kennedy and Johnson, as well as other widely known politicians and she frequently took their phone calls. She recalls the fascination of being so close to activities associated with such well-known personalities of the time.

Following World War II, Mackye's father began developing a business of small Army-Navy surplus stores, which eventually grew to a chain of thirteen outlets. "I worked at each store when it opened," she said, recalling their best seller was Red Snap Jeans. "In considerable competition with the major department stores, and at much lower price, we sold thousands of Jeans!"

Her dad eventually opened a tool store in downtown Fort Worth that also became successful. Mackye says that her dad sent the husbands of his beloved six sisters out of town in small pickup trucks, selling tool sets. His business success was attributed to selling the same name product tools at considerable less price than the major stores in Ft. Worth. Numerous other small business owners would visit her dad seeking advice on marketing and selling products.

Mackye's father soon moved into leasing warehouse space in rented buildings which grew into another successful venture. "It was my dad from whom I learned the most about business and more importantly about relationships with people. I set up the computers in our office, replacing the manual and electric typewriters. I sat in all the meetings with customers and legal advisers, typed our contracts into and edited each one as we began to grow. I learned much about business management from my dad!"

Mackye's mother's family were also entrepreneurs, creating the largest florist business operation in Fort Worth. "They didn't believe in advertising," she says. "They didn't need to. They did personal marketing, door to door, successfully supporting most of the debutante parties and weddings in the local social community. My mother and dad both worked at Christmas and on all holidays to accommodate the demands of their businesses and to support their family."

Her father's and mother's individual and collective successes from virtual "shoe strings," provided Mackye a pathway, although challenging and rocky at times, but guidance, direction, and experience which now she has become one of the, if not *the*, most successful woman business leaders in Ft. Worth, Texas. Her vast warehousing empire is the largest in the Dallas-Ft. Worth area, if not the state. She attributes it to her parents' leadership by example, coupled with her deep and abiding faith in God. She clearly expresses the latter by her commitment and dedication to her church and those to whom she ministers, spiritually and benevolently. On a personal note, Mackye has also graciously hosted several book reviews and signings in her home for my modest publications.

It may appear from these success stories that Mackye enjoys talking about her family's business successes. That is the farthest from the factual truth. I learned about Mackye Evans and her family over several years of visiting and sharing backgrounds and family stories. She, on the other hand, is an exceptionally quiet and private lady about her personal life, but she also confesses in private, that "the past is fun to reminisce about one's past, especially our families . . . with special gratitude for the leadership examples of my parents! My life has been full and wonderful, and I am grateful for all whom I have met along the way."

We encounter many notable people in life, as I have commented along the way. Mackye Evans is another of those chance meeting encounters that becomes a friend for life.

Tom Clancy, Author

My good friend and former Central Intelligence Agency (CIA) Senior Analyst, Ray Cline, discussed and described earlier, was an "off the top of his head" thinker. He caught me by surprise one day in the summer of 1994 when I was in his Washington office, discussing various issues related to my work with Andrew Corporation and my notion to document or write about some of my observations in Russia. He asked, "Chris, have you ever met Tom Clancy?"

I told him that I had not, and promptly invited me to join him, his wife, Majorie and Tom Clancy, the following evening. I arrived at O'Brian's Irish Pub in Rossyln, a little before 7:00 p.m. and asked the receptionist if Dr. Cline had arrived; she escorted me to the table where he and Marjorie were seated. Ray asked me if I happened to see Tom Clancy waiting in the foyer. I told him that I didn't see anyone that appeared to be waiting there, but I would go and make sure. Back at the entrance, I spotted whom I believed to be Clancy. He was wearing dark glasses and had just sat down. I introduced myself, and we proceeded to where Ray and his wife were seated.

Ray stood up, greeted Clancy warmly and motioned for us to all sit down. "I see you two have met," Ray smiled.

We enjoyed a pleasant dinner with Ray conducting most of the conversation, providing Clancy with my background, having traveled to Beijing and now working in Russia. Tom Clancy listened attentively, nodding occasionally. It was apparent that the two of them knew each other quite well and communicated back and forth with ease. Ray told Clancy that I had indicated some interest in writing about my experiences in Russia and asked if he had any suggestions.

I interrupted Ray and said that I had more of an interest in describing the now ended Cold War, my experience in strategic operations during the period as well as my impressions of our once enemy, the former Soviet Union, Russia, etc. Clancy seemed interested and asked a few questions about my background, where I served, and what I did. I was impressed with his depth of knowledge about military operations, Russia, and so on. He was also an excellent and articulate communicator.

Clancy said that if I had a genuine interest in writing, he would suggest that I first outline that which I had experienced in my various professional experiences, both in the military and now in Russia. Clancy said that he would heartily recommend I consider first writing a novel; create a character or characters, he said, and through them, develop scenarios that conveyed my impressions.

Clancy then changed the subject to politics and didn't hesitate to express his opinions regarding conservative values and leadership in America. He was also critical of U.S. intelligence failures, especially that led up to the 9/11 aircraft hijacking and suicide attacks on New York City and the Pentagon. "Ronald Reagan would have never allowed that to happen under his leadership," he said. Ray didn't comment and remained quiet.

I was most impressed with the opportunity to meet Clancy and found him to be exceptionally knowledgeable and well-informed on national and international issues. He spoke openly about many issues that one wouldn't expect a non-military or government individual to have insight into. Then again, Clancy's own novels dealt deeply into many sensitive activities that caused some to wonder about his sources of information. The respect and close friendship enjoyed between these two brilliant men was obvious.

It turned out to be an exceptional evening: at least three hours of conversation with two very distinguished men. Marjorie Cline, also a very bright and informed lady, openly participated in the discussions as well. We concluded with pleasant goodbyes and Clancy wished me well with my writing endeavors. In the following years of my attempts to describe the many observations, suspicions, and opinions I encountered in Russia, I reflected on that chance meeting, took Tom Clancy's suggestions, and created my own principal character and friend, Sasha, to carry out various created fictional deeds in my published works.

Tom Clancy was an exceptionally notable encounter, and I will leave it to the reader to pursue and review further the depths of this well-known author. His incredible writing and publication successes began in 1984 and ended with his untimely death in 2013.

Donna Seebo, Author, Radio Entertainer, Award-Winning Author

Donna Seebo is the single notable encounter within my memory book that I have not yet had the pleasure of meeting and greeting face-to-face. We have met numerous times, however, over the telephone, cybernet, and the radio airways. I was first introduced to this remarkable lady a few years ago during a conference call merged together by some to discuss national security issues, America at risk, etc. As a result of that telecom meeting, the subject of my having published a few books drawn from my Air Force and later working in Russia experiences surfaced. Thereafter, I received a call from Donna Seebo, to further discuss some of my works and subsequently, her inviting me to participate in an interview in her *Warriors for Peace* radio program. She conducted an initial radio interview with me and thence invited me to participate in two more. Each interview focused on one of my published works. In the past, I have participated in a few magazine and newspaper interviews, radio and brief television spots, as well as a couple of Congressional Hearing interrogations, but, I have never experienced an interviewer as professionally and detailed prepared as Donna Seebo was for those which she conducted with me.

I am especially pleased and honored to introduce to you and share herein, the background and depth of this extraordinary and talented lady, which as you will discover, whose talents extend far beyond that which might be expected.

Donna Seebo and her husband reside in the South Sound area of the Evergreen State of Washington. She says that on a clear day she can see Mt. Rainier, which enables her to enjoy the richness of the environment that supports an invigorating, refreshing energy that she applies to her work.

An internationally recognized award-winning author/publisher, keynote speaker, renowned mental practitioner, counselor, teacher, broadcasting personality, and host of international talk show, her schedule is a busy one. A woman of many talents, little did she realize that innate psychic mind skills would take her on a journey of discovery, travel, and interacting with thousands of people from around the world.

Her paranormal world became normal in Donna's life due to a series of experiences she had when she was in her twenties. She learned to accept this intriguing, fascinating environment of new knowledge by taking classes and becoming involved in activities that developed her mind skills. After years of public work, teaching classes and working as an assistant minister, she was ordained as a spiritualist minister, and her family moved to the Pacific Northwest in the early 1980s.

She was invited to appear on a local radio station to demonstrate her acquired mind skills, and the positive public reaction was so overwhelming that she became a local media personality. Record numbers of callers would consistently jam the telephone lines asking for her. Her low-key, non-sensational approach to people and subjects, surprises, fascinates, and delights her listening and viewing audiences. She is repeatedly asked to come back for additional appearances. On April 7, 2014, *The Donna Seebo Show* developed into Delphi Vision International Broadcasting, which now streams her programming to over 128 countries worldwide. In September of 2014, *Warriors for Peace* was introduced as a weekly show. Donna is considered one of the top broadcasters in the country by authors who have been interviewed by her. The primary theme of her eclectic program is Personal Empowerment. Guests are featured from all over the world, from all walks of life and various economic, professional, and social levels giving their knowledge and expertise to the listening audience. During the second half of the program, Donna shares her mental skills with those who call into the show. Informative and fun, Donna invites all of her listeners to join her weekdays where you and they can "Light Up Your Life with A Little Bit of Insight."

Another dimension to Donna's business and creative skills is writing. An accomplished author, she published an award-winning illustrated children's book, *God's Kiss*, along with a supporting and captivating audio book. Her second publication of her children's stories was *The Magic Hat*, followed by *Mind Magic, The Miracle of Eight Pennies*. She currently is working on a new children's publication, *The Woodcutter & The Tree*, and it will be released in the fall of this year.

Donna is also an exceptional public speaker. She is actively invited to make private and public appearances, speaking to large and small business groups and organizations. She is also exceptionally creative in developing programs that fit today's world of personal and professional development. Her specialty is developing programs that are interactive with those expected to be present in the audience. Personal and professional empowerment is a favorite among her themes. Donna Seebo has taken her own natural talents and developed them in multiple ways. Her life has been, and continues to be, a dynamic and successful journey with new directions being created every day. Writing, publishing, counseling, speaking, teaching, and hosting international talk shows, as well as guest appearances on national/international broadcasts displays her talents throughout the world. Likewise, her sparking personality, exceptional voice skills, and standard of excellence are an inspiration. Donna's accomplished, poised, warmth, sincerity, and sense of humor create a dynamic that makes it easy for everyone to feel and become at ease with her. I would be remiss after this introduction, to omit sharing the following overview of this incredible lady's corporate establishment which is available for public review and contact:

Donna Seebo

Delphi Vision International, Inc. International Mental Practitioner, Counselor, Speaker, Teacher, Award-Winning Author, Minister and Radio/TV Personality, Talk Show Host - *The Donna Seebo Show* and *Warriors for Peace*

Go to www.delphiinternational.com

The Donna Seebo Show page. Tap on player to listen live weekdays, 9:00–10:00 a.m., Pacific Time. *Warriors for Peace*, Wednesdays, 11:00 a.m.–noon, Pacific Time

On-demand programming available 24/7 - Tap on tower archive logo and you can choose the show you want to listen to. Callers welcome during second half of program.

Call-in 253.582.5597.

This international programming features authors, experts from around the world.

P.O. Box 97272, Lakewood, WA 98497-0272

www.delphiinternational.com or www.mrsseebosclassics.com

donna@delphiinternational.com

Our lives are filled with unforeseen opportunities to meet and to get to know people. Donna Seebo became one of those déjà vu notable encounter experiences for me and perhaps it may be for you.

B.G. "Jug" Burkett, Combat Veteran and Author

The son of an Air Force colonel, Jug Burkett said that growing up, his heroes "were not sports figures like Mickey Mantle and Willie Mays, but the fighter pilots who had blasted the German Luftwaffe out of the sky!" Life, observing and honoring my father and as a "military brat," he said, imbued in him an understanding that the United States Military was the guardian of the freedoms enjoyed by all of us within our country. He later joined the Army himself and served as did his father before him.

I first met Jug in Dallas at a book review given by him on his documented researched history of Vietnam War personalities entitled, *Stolen Valor*. His revelations in this now famous publication were an eye-opening shock to me and I am sure to the many others who have read his work, such as me, who also served two tours of duty in Vietnam. I introduced myself to Jug following his presentation and book signing, where I purchased a copy. I waited until he completed the book signing and responding to the many questions by those in attendance; then I introduced myself. I immediately found a gentle, soft-spoken, and humble man. He was far from what I expected after listening to him describe the research and arduous task of writing such a revealing story.

I will briefly summarize his *Stolen Valor* and then more on this exceptional newfound friend. Jug tells the story of visiting the U.S. Naval Academy Museum once and spotted a Navy chief petty officer in uniform with several rows of ribbons. He said that he immediately noted among the ribbons, at the very top, was the Navy Cross. Recognizing that the Navy Cross is the United States Navy's second-highest decoration awarded for valor in combat to a member of the Navy, Marine Corps, or the Coast Guard, having served in Vietnam himself, Jug said that he was curious as to where and when this Navy chief earned the distinction of such a medal of valor. He said that he approached the chief, introduced himself, and asked about the Navy Cross ribbon on his uniform. The chief flushed, he said, immediately turned away and walked out of the building as fast as he could. Jug was astute enough to note the chief's name tag. Later, he contacted the Navy, identified himself and shortly discovered that this particular Navy non-commissioned officer had not been awarded the Navy Cross. He did his duty, he said, by advising the Navy that he met this man and that he was wearing the highly distinctive and meritorious Navy Cross ribbon on his uniform.

Having served in the Army and in Vietnam combat himself, this was *not* the first incident of this kind. He told me, and I acknowledged the same, that he had frequently observed men wearing Vietnam Veteran caps, T-shirts, jackets, etc., and, out of curiosity when he approached them asked, "When, or where, were you in 'Nam'?"

He said, surprisingly, many turned and walked quickly away. I shared with him my same experiences. I told him that just recently, I had spotted a young fellow in Wal-Mart wearing a Vietnam Veteran's cap and whom I believed to be far too young to have served in Vietnam that many years ago. When I asked him the traditional question, he blurted, "None of your damned business," and moved away as quickly as he could into the store crowd.

I shared another similar experience about when I saw a young man wearing such a cap, and I couldn't resist asking him when he was there. He similarly spouted, "What's it to you?" and quickly took off. Jug and I chatted and lamented for quite a while, which indicated that he wanted to talk and share his feelings and to seek mine, about such instances and flagrant misrepresentations and violations.

Jug said that he began to ponder the argument that the image of the Vietnam Veteran was tarnished by a combination of media coverage, veteran imposter, US citizen's anger against the draft, and even the perception of the veteran as a victim. The lingering thoughts prompted him to move forward toward more research, to seek out examples of his thoughts and perceptions. After a period of discovery and finding more than he had even suspected, he launched into an ever more concentrated pursuit of "seek and find" abuses. After months of documentation, Jug began to draft his findings and conclusions. His book, *Stolen Valor*, looks deeply into the diagnoses of post-traumatic stress disorder (PTSD) in Vietnam Veterans and how it is treated by the Veteran's Administration. He also discusses the abuses and the faking by many, who claim to have PTSD, as well as the converse rise of war atrocity accusations against Vietnam Veterans. Jug also concludes a further analysis of the effects of many whom he suspects to be Vietnam War Veteran imposters. His book reveals several movie "stars" who claimed to have served in Vietnam. His discoveries also delve into the mislabeling of the Vietnam War, particularly by the news media, as one of the causes of homelessness veterans.

An equally disturbing part of Jug's research findings revealed the widespread wearing of Vietnam War medals, ribbons, and badges by servicemen and even civilians who did not serve, much less even earn them. Using the Freedom of Information Act (FOIA), he was successful in retrieving records of individuals who claimed they served in Vietnam during the War but did not. He also used the FOAI process to disclose and denounce those who did not have records to support their military service, badges, ribbons, and medals. The findings and analysis Jug found also revealed that minorities participated in rates similar or slightly lower than their percentage of the populations of the background of possible veteran imposter. His research also discovered and confirmed what he previously believed to be a myth about the effects of Agent Orange, the herbicide and defoliant chemical used by the U.S. military to defoliate the dense Vietnam jungles to make warfighting on the ground easier for our troops. He largely proved that the profiling of pilots who flew the Agent Orange delivery missions in Vietnam and who had claimed numerous illnesses had not had a particular increase in health effects as a result.

After our meeting, I invited Jug to participate in several book signing presentations which were enjoyed by all in attendance. One of the highlights of those presentations was to take him to my alma mater, Texas A&M University-Commerce for an Air Force reunion where he spoke and opened the eyes of both students and faculty about the realities of war and those who served.

While on this subject of personal interest many in our country, I wish to share a few undisputed facts, cited by President Richard Nixon: "No event in American history is more misunderstood than the Vietnam War. It was misreported then, and it is misremembered now. Rarely have so many people been so wrong about so much. Never have the consequences of their misunderstanding been so tragic."

One of the important major results of B.G. Burkett's *Stolen Valor* is the following act of Congress: The Stolen Valor Act of 2013 (Pub.L. 113–12; H.R. 258) is a United States federal law that was passed by the 113th United States Congress. The law amends the federal criminal code to make it a crime for a person to fraudulently claim having received a valor award specified in the Act, with the intention of obtaining money, property, or other tangible benefit by convincing another that he or she received the award.

B.G. "Jug" Burkett, one of my exceptional encounters in life, resides in Dallas, Texas, and continues to serve our nation by researching and extracting the fiction from the facts that affect our brave Military Service men and women.

Manuel L. English, PhD

I received a phone call one day in the spring of 2010 from a secretary at the Brazos River Authority where I serve on the Board of Directors. She told me that a "Dr. English, from the Seattle, Washington, area," was trying to get in touch with me and wished to have my telephone number. I didn't recognize his name but told her that it was okay to provide him my number. A day or so later, I received a call from "Manny" English, who said that he had conducted considerable research, looking for published authors from Texas and had come across some of my works. He said that he had wished to contact me regarding discussing the possibility of working together on a manuscript notion of his about Texas. Manny shared with me that he was a native Texan and had many concerns about the ongoing political situation within the United States and he thought that, if I shared his feelings, I might wish to join him in creating a published work.

Manny's call surprised me, but after a lengthy telephone conversation and learning considerably about his background, I agreed that I would be pleased to discuss his initiative at his convenience. He moved fast and contacted me a few days later. He offered to meet me in Ft. Worth, if that was convenient, and we could discuss his writing notion. Meet, we did, a week later at the Naval Air Station, Ft. Worth, where Manny flew into, military space available, from Naval Air Station, Whidbey Island, near Seattle. During that first encounter, onward into an afternoon and evening discussion, I became fully informed, not only about his book-writing notion but also the incredible life story of a most unique man.

One of ten children, Manuel English left home at sixteen, lied about his age, and joined the Marine Corps. He served his four years tour of duty and chose to be honorably discharged in order to seek a job in civilian life. He said that he was unable to find anything to his satisfaction, so he decided to try military service again, and joined the Army. His Army enlistment came to an end, he reenlisted and was sent to Hawaii. It was there that he met the love of his life, a beautiful Canadian girl from Calgary. In a few short months, he and Jeanette were married and off on their life's journey. His discharge from the Army didn't result in his finding job satisfaction in the "outside world" until he discovered the "Military Service of choice, the U.S. Air Force!"

Life for Manny English took off, literally, in the Air Force. He was permitted to enroll in the Bootstrap Program, earned a bachelor's degree and a commission as an officer. He attended Medical Service Officer training and thereafter applied for a special master's degree program offered by the University of Oklahoma under the auspices of the Air Force. While his faithful Jeanette worked and raised two young girls that had come along the way, he completed his master's degree and promptly applied for an oversees tour. The Air Force sent Manny and his family to Mildenhall Air Force Base, England, where he was assigned duties as a hospital administrator. His quest to learn and to seek higher education led him to work further at Manchester University, where he successfully earned his doctoral degree in public institution management.

From England, Manny was assigned to Wilford Hall Air Force Medical Center in San Antonio as a hospital administrator. From there, he and his young family were sent to McChord Air Force Base, Washington, moving Jeanette closer to her native Canada. In the interim, another daughter and a son were born. After a period of time at McChord, he decided to retire from the Air Force and once again seek a life and career in the civilian world.

Retiring after twenty years active duty in three Military Services—the Marine Corps, Army, and the Air Force in 1964—likely set a record for service in uniform to our country. Teaching had always been Manny's first desire and he began his quest as an associate professor at the University of Puget Sound, Tacoma, Washington, teaching graduate and undergraduate courses in organizational theory/strategy and organizational behavior. From there, he became an adjunct professor at California State University, teaching management. Moving on, he became a professor of management at Eastern Washington University, and coordinator of the university's International Business Programs. He also taught organizational theory and organizational behavior to graduate and undergraduate students. Back to the University of Washington, he served as a professor of management in the School of Business.

Not one to sit still, Manny leaped off to Europe with the family, to accept a position as professor of management with the Executive MBA Program at the American University of Bulgaria, in Sofia, teaching graduate school organizational theory. In 1995, he moved on to Riyadh, Saudi Arabia, to become the administrator and chief executive officer of the Security Forces Hospital, a 476-bed teaching hospital with multiple specialty services and a staff of 2,500. There, Manny was charged with the responsibility of developing and implementing a strategic plan for moving the hospital to the next operational level. The process called for opening a new wing, recruiting an internationally competitive group of physicians and other hospital personnel, and instituting various quality processes and procedures from the senior level administration of the hospital down to operational levels.

Lured back to Seattle, Manny became president and chief executive officer, Northwest Lions Foundation for Sight & Hearing. Founded in 1969, the Northwest Lions Foundation supported forty thousand children and adults within its sight and hearing programs. A complex medical facility, it included an internationally renowned eye bank, a mobile health screening unit, various research grants, and charitable giving programs, as well as a newborn hearing screening partnership with Northwest hospitals. As the CEO, Manny English led the quadrupling of program services, including mobile health screening and a Hearing Aid Bank.

Always looking ahead to the next opportunity and challenge, Manny found time to put his thoughts on paper. He has since written dozens of articles on hospital and business management, published in professional journals in the United States and Europe. A published author and poet, he authored "An Imaginative Existence," in 2010, a provocative essay on "causation, manifestation, and finality of being," Amazon Publications. An award-winning poet, he is a member of the Poetry Society of Texas 2014.

Manny approached me with a notion to develop a novel reflecting the history of Texas, applying our great state's philosophy of "freedom for our people first" to the ongoing drift toward socialism under the present administration in Washington. His idea was interesting, and the more we discussed the present politics and growing unrest in the country, the more his story idea appealed to me. We spent two days developing an outline for a story plot. Manny would research and document Texas history from its beginnings, statehood, and unrelenting quest for independence. I agreed to create and develop a fictional story arising out of actual Texas history, statehood to pseudo-characters serving in state offices today. We agreed to exchange ideas back and forth via e-mail and phone conversations and meet again in a month. I enjoyed developing the scenario of Texas threatening to exercise its "right" to secede and to become the Republic of Texas once again. Manny did an excellent job of documenting the state's history, which made for a factual appendix to the story.

We concluded our project during a third meeting and Manny proceeded to attract a publisher and *Texas: A Free Nation Under God* was published in 2011. We became close friends during and more so following our book-writing exercise; our wives and families visited one another in their home state of Washington and they visited Texas.

As we are frequently reminded, behind every successful man, there is a dedicated, strong, and committed wife. Jeanette English, I was to learn and also witness, fulfilled all of those character traits as much or more so, than any wife could. I have summarized Manny English's incredible rise out of the depths of a meager existence, lack of early education opportunities or direction to become a scholar, education professor, and successful business executive. Standing steady as a rock, unwavering and working hard to support Manny's pursuits, while raising four children rising to their own personal successes, was ever-faithful Jeanette.

To this special lady and also a special notable encounter's additional credit, I want to acknowledge that, among those accomplishments mentioned, she is also a published author. *Infidel Behind the Paradoxical Veil* describes a Western woman's experience and observations while living in Saudi Arabia. Along with her children and accompanying Manny during his year as administrator of the Special Forces Hospital in Riyadh, Jeanette English witnessed firsthand Saudi women, who by Shariah law and culture, are considered to be the far weaker sex. Jeanette candidly unmasks a unique experience exposing the enigmatic rules imposed on Saudi women. She describes their never-ending struggle for equality and freedom of choice in their restrictive lives. Jeanette was forced to wear the hijab, study the Koran, and spoke with Saudi women, which allowed her inquisitive nature to look behind the veil that most Westerners only read about. An excellent book and candid portrayal by one who lived and witnessed the story.

Manny and Jeanette English, exceptional encounters who have become enduring friends!

7

Notable Entertainer
Encounters

As previously highlighted, serving in the United States Air Force had many redeeming benefits beyond the pleasure of serving my country. I wish also at the outset of this segment to note and emphasize, that while the following encounter adventures were enjoyable, we were also at war at the time. My flight guys, aircraft support troops, and I were engaged in many more harried activities than those that are shared herein. I have previously described many of those adventures in other writings. The brief encounter interludes described herein were a break from the surrounding realities of war and combat. I was afforded the opportunities, many, if not most, by coincidence or accident, to meet many incredible well-known personalities and entertainers from one genre to another. The first notable of these encounters began while I was stationed at Korat Air Base, Thailand, during Vietnam. Other encounters continued to occur as the Air Force guided me along my career path and onward into a more sedate life following military service. Neither will I delve too deeply into the personal lives or backgrounds of these encounters since most do not need an introduction. Most of these encounters were also very brief due to the impromptu situations. I will begin with three recognized personalities, at least of the time and to many of you, old enough to remember, and who went out of their way to entertain our troops during Vietnam.

Bob Hope, Korat Air Base, Thailand

During Christmastime in 1966, Hollywood entertainers were traveling all around Southeast Asia: Vietnam, Thailand, etc. Among those were Bob Hope and his incredible Christmas for the Troops shows. He came to Korat and presented us with a typical wonderful Bob Hope Special. Unfortunately, that opportunity did not afford the opportunity for an up close and personal "notable encounter." But, Bob Hope's show and troupe were the best ever: my second opportunity and special blessing to see this true patriot perform! This was the second opportunity to enjoy Bob Hope and his incredible show and tribute to the military men and women serving overseas. The first time was immediately after the Cuban Crisis, and he came to Ramey Air Force Base, Puerto Rico, bringing his entire entourage to honor us. We had just completed four days of flying twenty-four-hour B-52 bomber alert missions in response to Russia's military intrusion into Cuba. Once Mr. Khrushchev capitulated and agreed to withdraw from Cuba, we all relaxed and in came Bob Hope to help us celebrate.

As mentioned, many encounters with people occur "out of the blue" as we frequently termed such surprises in the Air Force. I was serving as director of operations, 388th Combat Support Group, based at Korat Air Base, in central Thailand. In addition to overseeing Base Operations and a multitude of other related activities, I was in charge of a flight of four ancient World War II vintage C-47 Gooney Bird transport aircraft. The term "transport" is highly overstated; the interior of the old birds was essentially bare. There were no passenger seats, only drop-down web bench seats on either side of the hollow cabin, with seat belts attached to the iron bench frames. We were on call 24/7 to fly to most anywhere in Southeast Asia to deliver or pick up people, parts, and, worst of all, casualties. The unexpected was ever-present. I frequently flew the missions myself along with one of the other pilots who was on standby.

Lionel Hampton, Korat Air Base, Thailand

Shortly after that Christmas season, the USO brought Lionel Hampton to Korat Air Base to entertain the young enlisted troops at their various club house gathering places. I received a call late one evening during his show to ask if I could provide an aircraft to transport him and his band ensemble to Bangkok after their performance. I agreed, and the hour being late, I called one of the standby pilots to accompany me. We met Lionel and his band members at the aircraft, and my most pleasant recall of that event was how gracious he was. I introduced myself, and he gave me a warm handshake, apologizing for "interrupting" our evening to fly them to Bangkok. The crew chief got the small band party and their instruments loaded up, and we taxied out and took off for Bangkok International Airport.

I was vaguely aware of Lionel Hampton and his musical talents and successes but never that close to his music. Neither is it unusual to scramble about and do research on someone after you meet them. Lionel Hampton was an American jazz icon: vibraphonist, pianist, percussionist, bandleader, and actor. Along the way, he worked with musicians from Teddy Wilson, Benny Goodman, and Buddy Rich to Charlie Parker, Charles Mingus, and Quincy Jones. Long after I was privileged to meet him, he was inducted into the Alabama Jazz Hall of Fame in 1992 and awarded the National Medal of Arts in 1996.

During our brief flight, Hampton came up to the cockpit, patted me on the shoulder, and thanked us graciously for flying them to Bangkok. We chatted about the area and the tragedy of the ongoing Vietnam War; he asked numerous questions about Thailand, the people and their culture. He said that he was scheduled to visit each of the other four U.S. Air Force bases in Thailand during their tour. I thanked him for his and his band's service in entertaining our young troops. Once on the ground at Bangkok, Lionel thanked us again for transporting him; he gave me, the other pilot, and the crew chief big bear hugs and goodbye handshakes. He was a pleasurable encounter.

Jayne Mansfield, Korat, Thailand

Another such impromptu call occurred late one evening in early June 1967. I was aware that Jayne Mansfield and her entertainment entourage were on the base entertaining at the non-commissioned officers' and the airmen's clubs. That was the USO's usual event scheduling. They concentrated on entertaining the young enlisted men and women. Neither was it unusual to have USO shows on the base at most anytime, day or night, whatever their schedule and transportation dictated. They usually flew in on their own contract aircraft, and we were seldom called upon to provide support. On that particular night, however, I was called by the Command Post duty officer as I had during Lionel Hampton's visit, and asked if I could provide airlift support to Bangkok for the Jayne Mansfield show group. Their scheduled aircraft had been canceled. There was a war going on and chaos was, more often than not, routine. I told the duty officer that I could take care of it; we would see the group to Bangkok. I called Dick Osborne, my operations officer, and asked him to go with me. I then called Maintenance Control and asked them to get an aircraft ready. My roommate, John Dillon, who was the Wing Executive Officer, was in the room when I received the call. I asked if he would like to "go along on a journey with Jayne Mansfield?"

He jumped at the offer! "Go along on a flight with Jayne Mansfield? Yahoo!"

John and I got into my jeep and drove to the flight line. Dick Osborne met us there along with the crew chief and ground crew. Dick and I got aboard and into our cockpit seats. I asked John and the crew chief to escort the group aboard the aircraft when they arrived. Once all were on board and strapped into their seats, the crew chief gave me the okay. I started engines and taxied out for take-off. Once we were safely airborne, the crew chief told the passengers that they could move around the cabin, but that it would be a brief forty-five-minute flight.

Suddenly, this incredible heavy perfumed aroma penetrated the cockpit; I looked over my right shoulder, and there she was, a large bundle of long blond hair hanging down off her shoulders. The cockpit was dark except for the dim instrument lights, but I could imagine Dick Osborne's eyes bulged wide open

"Hello, boys," our VIP passenger said in a soft Southern drawl.

I replied, "Hello, welcome aboard, Ms. Mansfield; we're delighted to have the opportunity to deliver you to Bangkok."

She replied back in her soft drawl, something like, "How do you like flying airplanes?" Or, something as such.

I had a sudden impulse, not that I haven't such before when a notion hit me. I said, "Dick, jump out of your seat and let Ms. Mansfield come in."

Dick unbuckled his seat belt and climbed out of the compact cockpit and helped Jayne Mansfield into the copilot's seat. I told him to put his headset on her, which he did, and then I spoke to her over the intercom. We chatted for a brief moment about how the plane operated, etc. Then, I had another impulse. We were required to report periodically to Ground Control Intercept (GCI) sites for safety and security along our routes of flight.

I called the GCI site (Call sign "Dressy Lady," by sheer coincidence!). "Dressy Lady, this is Air Force 1234 (I don't recall our actual call sign), checking in."

I received an immediate response, "Roger, Air Force 1234, I understand you have some hot cargo on board."

I replied, "Roger that. Would you like to speak with our VIP passenger?"

In response came a loud rowdy gaggle of background yelling and a shout, "Yes, sir!"

My "new copilot" heard the loud response and smiled. I reached over, showed her the radio mike button and told her to speak to the troops.

And, she said, "Hello, boys, how are you doing down there, and are you working very hard?"

The same response came back, laughing and yelling, "Yes, ma'am, we are!"

She spoke on, snickering and having fun with the guys on the ground for a few minutes. Then I had to sign them off and ask her to go back to the cabin and get ready to land.

We landed at Bangkok International Airport, and I taxied up to where there was a bus and cars waiting. We saw them off the plane, and her manager invited us to come to their hotel for a presentation that Jayne was going to perform that evening. I thanked him, but declined in the interest of "better judgment," to get the aircraft back home. This was at the dismay of my crew guys, and especially John! He had enjoyed an adventure of a lifetime, riding in the cabin and chatting with Jayne Mansfield and her group. We headed back to Korat with another "war story" to post in our log books.

That became an event and fun adventure to remember. But then, one morning, a week or ten days later, I had lost count, as I was getting dressed for the day, a bulletin came in on the Armed Forces Radio station that I had tuned in, listening to "yesterday's news" back home. The announcer said that there was breaking news: "Actress Jayne Mansfield and several others had been killed in an automobile accident near New Orleans, Louisiana, the evening before on June 29, 1967."

I all but froze as the words sunk in. I sat on the side of my bed for a minute, recalling our recent transporting event with her, and then I went next door to our hootch shower/restroom where my roommate, John, had just showered and was shaving. When I told him about the news I had just heard, he stopped shaving and stared at the mirror in shock. We finally chatted about the news for a few minutes and reflected on it all for days thereafter.

The details of the tragic accident finally drifted over to us in Thailand. It seemed that Jayne Mansfield, along with several others, had been on their way to New Orleans from Biloxi, Mississippi, where she had been performing at a local nightclub. Ronald B. Harrison, a nightclub employee, was driving Jayne Mansfield, her lawyer, Samuel S. Brody, along with three of her children, and her ex-husband Mickey Hargitay, in a 1966 Buick Electra. They were apparently directly behind a flatbed trailer-truck on a dark stretch of road. As the truck ahead approached a machine off the highway, emitting a thick white fog used to spray mosquitoes, the truck apparently slowed down suddenly due to his loss of visibility. The Buick Electra slammed into the rear of the trailer-truck. Jayne Mansfield,

Harrison, and Brody were all killed. Her children, eight-year-old Mickey, six-year-old Zoltan, and three-year-old Marie survived, along with Mickey Hargitay. The children had apparently been sleeping on the rear seat; they were injured but survived. Truly sad ending to this encounter.

Brenda Lee, Korat, Thailand

The final entertainer encounter in Southeast Asia was not as pleasant as the previous two. Earlier in the day in late August 1967, I had been requested to set up a flight to transport entertainer Brenda Lee, her manager and small band combo to Bangkok. The request had come to me via the USO office in Bangkok and was due their transportation shortage. We were asked to fly the group from Korat to Bangkok immediately following her early shows at the enlisted clubs, and that she needed to be in Bangkok by 8:00 p.m. for a night-club engagement there. I arranged for the flight with two pilots and a crew chief, and all were prepared to go.

I received a call from my commander around six thirty that evening, and he asked if I had arranged for such a flight. I told him that I had. He then said, "You can't make that trip, Chris; your aircraft is out of commission."

I was only slightly surprised. "Sir?" I asked. "Colonel, we're good to go, to take the group to Bangkok. Is something going on?"

"I don't want them flown to Bangkok on our aircraft," he replied sharply. "Chris, I asked that gal's manager if they would come by the officer's club after her last performance at the NCO club and put on a short presentation during happy hour for the fighter pilots, and he declined, telling me that they have a commitment at a club in Bangkok. So, let them find their own transportation."

"Yes, sir," I replied. That was that.

I cogitated as to how to deal with this one. I drove to base operations a little before 7:00 p.m. and "they" were already there, milling around the foyer. I recognized the young lady that had to be Brenda Lee and the fellow I presumed to be her manager. I approached them

and introduced myself, shook hands with both Brenda Lee and her manager.

I told him that we were not going to be able to provide airlift for them to Bangkok due to a "higher priority."

Her manager froze and looked at me with, "What are you telling us?"

I said, "Sir, the aircraft scheduled to take you to Bangkok cannot go."

He screamed back at me, "How in the hell do you think we are going to get there? We have a performance scheduled in two hours!"

I shrugged my shoulders and told him that I was sorry. I looked at Brenda Lee, and she had a blank, tired expression on her face as if she cared less. I doubt if she did care very much. At that time, she was all of twenty-two years old and in a crazy place and world.

I told him that he could make use of any of our communications systems there in base operations to make arrangements. He shrugged, turned, and walked away.

I departed and left a very uncomfortable situation, certainly not one that I wanted to be involved in. I learned the next day that the manager was able to muster a bus locally and I suppose made their way to Bangkok—very late, of course.

Not a pleasant encounter.

Roy Rogers and Dale Evans, Cheyenne, Wyoming

When I received orders to go to F.E. Warren Air Force Base near Cheyenne, Wyoming, in 1973, I had no idea what lay ahead in that great western state and community. I was far too absorbed in moving into a new position to even consider the surroundings. It wasn't long after though that we were adopted by one of the most military-friendly and welcoming cities in my career. Western hospitality and social activities were at the top of the local native's priorities.

We arrived in the dead of a frigid cold December of that year, and I don't think that it began to thaw until late spring. Suddenly, the beautiful western plains began to reveal themselves, and Cheyenne came bustling alive with activity. Cheyenne Frontier Days was the talk of the town. And, that year's super star performers were to be Roy Rogers and Dale Evans! I gave it little thought: a rodeo, a lot of celebrating and stage show. The city fathers were most cordial and, early on, I received an invitation and complimentary VIP tickets to any and everything we wished to attend. So attend we did. On the special entertainment night with Roy and Dale, the front row seats were great, and their show was excellent.

Let me retreat for a few paragraphs and provide proper recognition of Cheyenne Frontier Days, known around the United States, if not the world, as one of the greatest western cowboy reunions, rodeos, and entertainment events of all time. The outdoor rodeo and western celebration has been held annually since 1897. It bills itself as the "World's Largest Outdoor Rodeo and Western Celebration," and draws upwards to two hundred thousand attendees each year. The city goes out in every way to welcome its guests. Prior to the annual kickoff on the first Friday in July, the annual walking of the steers down main street is the first event inspired by the cattle drives of the Old West. Thereafter, the rodeo begins and lasts for ten rowdy days

A special annual event within the program is an air show featuring the United States Air Force Thunderbirds Air Demonstration Team, which takes place on the first Wednesday. The Air Force and the Thunderbirds share a long history with Cheyenne Frontier Days as they made their public debut there in 1953 and have continued to perform regularly since. The ground portion of the show, along with static displays and flying of other aircraft, also makes for a special event. F.E. Warren Air Force Base and Cheyenne have enjoyed a long history of working together. The U.S. Cavalry developed Fort D.A. Russell in 1867, the same year Cheyenne was founded. The Fort transitioned to the Air Force in 1947. The base conducts an open house and tours during Frontier Days.

The historic home tours are a special highlight along with military reenactments and orientations on the missile system operations headquartered there. Living in one of the historic homes was a special venture treat at F.E. Warren. Quarters 8, built in 1895, was provided to me upon arrival. The three-story brick home, some 5000 square feet in size, had been kept completely modernized over the years with every modern convenience, including a mega-sized furnace in the basement that provided ample heating during the frequent minus twenty-degree winter days.

Following the evening's rodeo and show by Roy Rogers and Dale Evans, we were invited to what I found to be a traditional after rodeo social hosted by rancher Ed Murray, whom I also got to know well and appreciate during my F.E. Warren assignment days. Approximately a hundred friends of Ed's gathered at his ranch a few miles from Cheyenne. Ed's ranch was not only a large cattle spread but a beautiful home and a unique Hollywood set type store front block long village. The village street was lined on both sides with store fronts reflecting shops, hotel, saloons, etc. It was something to behold.

As the guests mingled about, drinking sodas and beer, Ed Murray called me aside and asked me to watch for the arrival of a limousine, and asked if I would go out and greet his guests. When the black limo pulled up, I walked out, opened the right rear door, and out stepped Dale Evans dressed in her bright-colored western togs and boots. I introduced myself and shook her hand. As the ladies gathered around Dale, I walked around and greeted Roy Rogers, who responded with a strong cowboy handshake grip. The ladies escorted Dale over to a gathering area while I walked along with Roy. Ed Murray met us and introduced my Air Force position and rank to Roy Rogers. That introduction initiated a lengthy conversation reflecting Roy Rogers's interest in the military and his quizzing me about our mission and work at F.E. Warren.

We were all impressed with how literally down to earth the two carried themselves, casually milling around, shaking hands and chatting with all the guests.

That event became a most pleasant memorable evening and a notable encounter with two delightful American entertainers.

Barbara Mandrell, Cheyenne, Wyoming

A very busy and rapid year ensued after the first Cheyenne Frontier Days event, and suddenly it was that time again. I was in command of the 90th Strategic Missile Wing with its 1000 Minuteman intercontinental missiles deployed over 10,000 square miles of Wyoming, Colorado, and South Dakota. The job made for what seemed to be, and frequently was, a 24/7 operation, but it was challenging "fun."

Frontier Days rolled around again with the same Cheyenne area hoopla of getting ready. Actually, they worked at it year-round! We attended the entertainment night rodeo with Barbara Mandrell as the featured star. Afterward, we were again invited to Ed Murray's ranch for the after-show gathering. Barbara Mandrell was very gracious, being a Texas girl originally from Houston, this was no surprise.

Briefly, Barbara was several years older than her two sisters and took to music and the steel guitar early in her life under her father's talented tutelage. She became recognized early in her life. At age thirteen, she played the steel guitar for Patsy Cline. She also went on tour with Patsy Cline, Johnny Cash, and George Jones. She married her husband, Ken Dudney, after graduating from high school, and the rest became a successful musical and show business career. Her husband, Ken, became the drummer for her band, and her two younger sisters joined in to form the Mandrell Family Band.

Ken Dudney later received a commission in the Navy and became a fighter pilot while Barbara moved onward with her talented family's band and music. Ken was with her for that Cheyenne show and there that evening at Ed's ranch reception. I enjoyed a pleasant chat with him, talking about flying and telling aviator "war stories."

I also learned that the entertainment personalities that were invited each year to participate in Frontier Days had to meet certain characteristics, and this proved to be the case during the two events that occurred while stationed in Cheyenne. This was another pleasant encounter experience with "Hollywood people" who turned out to be little different than the folks in Cheyenne who invited them.

Tennessee Ernie Ford, Offutt Air Force Base, Nebraska

As highlighted previously in my profile of leaders was General Russell E. Dougherty. General Dougherty was most proud of his World War II B-29 Bombadier, Lieutenant Ernest J. Ford. Always full of surprises, General Dougherty invited his former bombardier, "Tennessee Ernie Ford," to attend his last commander's conference at SAC Headquarters, Offutt Air Force Base, Nebraska, in the spring of 1977. All of us in attendance had an opportunity to meet this notable entertainer. He was gracious, friendly, and humorous to each who met him, shook his hand, and enjoyed a friendly chat.

A radio announcer with WOPI-AM in Bristol, Tennessee, and a classical singer with the Cincinnati Conservatory of Music, Ernie Ford joined the Army Air Corps at the outbreak of World War II. He was commissioned and became a B-29 bombadier. He was assigned to the flight crew commanded by Major Russell E. Dougherty. They flew bombing missions over Japan during the war with Ford later becoming a bombadier instructor at George Air Force Base, California. After the war, Tennessee Ernie Ford became and remains to this day a legendary baritone singer and entertainer, whom I proudly add to my notable encounters.

Charlton Heston, Los Alamos, New Mexico

Among the various responsibilities I assumed as an associate director, Los Alamos National Laboratory, was coordinating the support for documenting experimental testing of classified nuclear weapons systems. Harry, a most creative producer/director who planned and coordinated all necessary documentation requirements with laboratory directorates, was assigned to me. Perhaps the most creative of his initiatives was to solicit one of the most well-known and articulate voices in Hollywood to do voice-over descriptions of film productions. He shocked me one day when he confidently strode into my office and told me that he had arranged for a reception to welcome his latest technical film production "voice." He went on to tell me that he wanted to invite the laboratory director and other senior laboratory officers to the reception that would be held at the University House, our central reception center. I said, "Fine; by the way, who is this new documentary 'voice' that you are so excited about?"

"Oh, yes, sir," he smirked with a smile, "'Chuck' Heston is our new consultant. He and his wife, Lydia, will be visiting the lab for a couple days to orient him on our work and I wanted to make them feel welcome."

"Where is he from?" I asked.

"Oh, sir," he grinned. "You must be familiar with Charlton Heston, the Hollywood actor."

I could have smacked him. "Okay, smarty," I said. "How about a security clearance and all the attendant paperwork necessary to bring someone into the lab?"

"All taken care of, sir," he said, again smirking confidently.

The reception for Charlton Heston and his wife, Lydia, was a delightful event. He was able to slip the Hestons on site to the reception and Heston, himself, to the next day's orientation.

They were a delightful couple, down to earth, cordial, friendly, and personable. Heston had also done his homework as commented early about President George H.W. Bush. He walked around the room on arrival, shaking hands, acknowledging and repeating each name. He came up to me, I introduced myself, and he responded, "I know you, General." I was only "slightly" surprised and taken aback! I thought later that he was not only a very bright and talented actor, and perhaps used the name recognition gimmick to disarm people. Whatever, it took me by surprise!

The encounter was the beginning of a most successful operation that continued on for several years. I was privileged to interact with Charlton Heston each time he visited the laboratory, and the scientists and technical development people were delighted with his support to them.

I'll not delve into the background of this super patriot, actor, and special notable encounter whom it was my privilege to meet and work with, known so well to all.

I must add a footnote to the Charlton Heston encounter, however. Harry, my technical film coordinator, came in one day several months later and said that they had an urgent requirement to wrap up a technical experiment documentary. He would love to have Charlton Heston do the voice-over, but that he was involved in his own work in Hollywood and couldn't come to the lab. He could, however, meet our team somewhere in the Los Angeles area, if they could rendezvous with him there for a day. They also needed a classified facility within which to conduct the work.

I promptly called a former colleague of mine who happened to be the commander of an Air Force facility near Los Angeles. I asked if we could possibly use his classified facilities conference room for our project. I explained that our voice-over consultant would meet us there. Being just a bit more than arrogant, he told me that he was reluctant to permit anyone to use his facilities due to the sensitivity of his activities. I went on to explain that all of our laboratory people and the consultant had the proper security clearances and that this was an urgent Department of Energy priority. He remained reluctant as I continued to pressure him for the *favor* to support the requirement.

Finally, before I could drop the key word on him, he asked, "Who is this consultant, anyway, Chris? And, why is he so important that he can't come to your place?"

That was it. I said, "Oh, I should have told you his name—Charlton Heston."

Dead silence for a millisecond, "Chris, I'm sorry! By all means, I will do anything we need to do here to support you. Can I arrange for a helicopter and go pick him up?"

I thanked him for his cooperation and gracious support and all went well from there on . . .

Barbara Walters, Saudi Arabia

Operation Desert Shield gave way to Desert Storm in January 1991, and the Gulf War to drive Iraqi forces out of Kuwait was underway. The operation lasted for a bloody forty-two days before

President George H.W. Bush declared a cease-fire. By that time most all of the Iraqi forces had either been killed, surrendered, or fled back inside their own border.

Andrew Corporation had provided on loan to the U.S. Army four prototype high frequency (HF) direction finding (DF) systems, nicknamed "Dakota." As the war came to a close, I was asked to go to Riyadh, Saudi Arabia, and to determine the disposition of the four Dakota HF/DF systems. They were valued at approximately one million dollars each. The quandary within the company was to either donate the equipment to the U.S. Army or transport the systems back to Dallas, with the overriding expense of the latter as an issue. Charlie Clarke, a good friend and company colleague/engineer, accompanied me on the journey.

Charlie and I flew to London and connected with a Saudi Airline flight to Riyadh via Jeddah. The Saudi Airliner was an encounter within itself. The Boeing 767 was palatially decorated within the interior much like a mid-eastern palace might be. The cabin was adorned with heavy colorful drapes and the carpet in the aisles were like walking on soft cotton. A heavily decorated prayer table was centered in the aisle of the first class compartment. Charlie and I were unable to secure seats beside one another, which I thought might be by design since we were both Americans. I was seated next to a Saudi gentleman, attired in full native dress: a thawb, ankle length robe, the ghutrah headdress, and an agal. I attempted to speak to him when I took my seat on the aisle, but he did not look up nor respond.

An hour or so into the six-hour flight, I overheard a female voice that I thought I recognized. She appeared to be two rows forward and across the aisle from my seat. I listened as I continued to hear her muffled voice. After a while, I got up from my seat, strolled up the aisle, and glanced over at the lady sitting on the inside seat next to a gentleman on the aisle. She had a heavy scarf over her head, but I caught a glimpse of her face.

I knew that I had recognized her voice: Barbara Walters of TV commentator fame. I walked back to where Charlie was seated and told him about my discovery. We had a VIP on board!

When we landed at Jeddah for the purpose of going through customs and immigration, I got up, collected my roller bag, and moved toward the exit and ended up just behind Ms. Walters and her escort. She had her face covered with a light scarf in addition to the heavy one over her head. We disembarked into a trolley bus to deliver us to the terminal. She walked in cautiously and sat down by herself on a center seat in the trolley. So, bold me, I walked over and sat down facing her on an opposite row of seats. I said to her, "Your disguise is great, but otherwise, you are a dead giveaway."

She was slightly startled and replied through her facial scarf, "Did you recognize me?"

I said, "Yes, your beautiful voice gave you away."

She pulled back her scarf and smiled. "Thank you." She then commented on the warnings she had been given when traveling in Saudi Arabia and how critical they are about dress, particularly for women.

I asked her why she was traveling there in the first place, and she said that she had a television interview scheduled with General Schwarzkopf. The interview was to be several segments in length.

I identified myself as being retired Air Force and she warmed up to the conversation, being very pleasant and responsive.

Her manager joined us and told her that there would be about an hour stop in Jeddah to go through a customs shakedown, check passports, etc., and then onward to Riyadh.

We arrived at the terminal and disembarked into a chaos of people and noise. Charlie and I visited with her and her manager for some length of time until our checked baggage arrived and we separated to track our pieces through customs. And customs inspection it was! The inspectors opened each bag and ran their gloved hands through every article of clothing and otherwise therein. I wondered at the time how Ms. Walters felt about having all of her carefully packed "delicate" clothing handled, piece by piece?

That visit concluded an impromptu pleasant encounter along another journey.

Anita Bryant, Branson, Missouri

We were in Branson, Missouri, in September 1997, and saw an advertisement showcasing *The Anita Bryant Show*. Having read stories about her over the years, we decided to attend her presentation. The music and her performance was upbeat and excellent. At the end of the show, they announced that she would be conducting a book review of her then recent publication, *A New Day*. I always enjoy attending book reviews to observe and learn! The review and book signing was held in a small comfortable room with her sitting behind a table lined with her book. Her book review was the *most* personal and revealing description of one's past life we had ever heard. She discussed what many of us feel, in one way or the other, or perhaps at some time in our own lives, which included depression, fear, anxiety, and grief.

I was so impressed by her personal and apparent sincere in-depth reflections that I purchased her book. She sat behind the table as people lined up to purchase her book. We were at the end of the line and when we arrived, she said, "Sit down, you've been waiting too long."

We sat down next to the table and she held out her hand to greet us. "Thank you for coming," she said. "I hope you enjoyed our show."

"We did," I replied, "and especially the in-depth review of your book, which I would like to purchase."

"Thank you," she smiled. "Did you serve in the military?"

"Yes, I did," I replied. "Thirty-one years in the Air Force."

"Wonderful!" she said. "Thank you for your service. I am a military brat and I always want to know about anyone who served our country."

She continued talking as she scribed a note in her book and handed it to me. I handed her attendant the money for the book and Anita said, "No, thank you. This is my gift to you for your service to our country. Bless you."

I thanked her and we departed, considerably impressed by this lady who displayed more genuine depth and sincerity than I had ever witnessed in a celebrity.

Her autographed comments on the fly page of the book: "9-2-97 . . . To Chris Adams, Thank you with love for your service. Anita Bryant, Phil (Philippians) 4–13."

I commend her book to you, even after these years, and conclude that was an evening and an event that became yet another unexpected encounter, and one with a remarkably notable lady.

Johnny Mann and Burton Gilliam, Dallas, Texas

Good friends, Terry and Alyce Price, invited us to a special musical event at the Preston Hollow Presbyterian Church in Dallas, in the Spring of 2013. Terry had been the minister of music at Preston Hollow for years, as well as associated with the Dallas Philharmonic and other music affiliations around the world. I didn't know what we were in store for on that particular evening until the program began, and the Master of Ceremonies, Burton Gilliam, stepped to the lectern. You may or may not recognize his name, but if you saw the movies *Paper Moon, Blazing Saddles, Honeymoon in Vegas*, or a dozen others to his credit, you will remember this incredible comedian. His most noted was the cowboy cut-up character in *Blazing Saddles*.

I began to become slightly uncomfortable when I recognized my biography being described in elaborate terms by Gilliam and then his calling my name to stand and be recognized. From there he moved on to others in the massive congregation and finally, the true guest of honor, Johnny Mann, of the John Mann Singers fame. I had already noticed the fellow in a bright red sport coat sitting directly in front of us who turned out to be Johnny Mann and his wife.

My friend, Terry, had already extended an invitation to attend what he described a small reception, after the musical presentation. When the program ended, Terry and Alyce guided us to his car and drove us to the mega-beautiful home of their friends in Preston Hollow. Once inside, we were surprised to be greeted not only by the home's host and hostess, but Johnny Mann, his wife, Betty, along with Burton Gilliam, his wife, Susan, and a few others. It turned out to be quite an evening. Johnny Mann and Betty were the most gracious, humble, and down home people you would ever wish to meet and visit with. Gilliam, former Coast Guardsman, Dallas firefighter, movie star, was the same comic cut-up you would expect. He kept the gathering alive throughout!

I'll not belabor the wonderful conversations and chatting that lasted for over two hours or longer, except to encourage you to Google up both of these notable personalities to refresh your memories or to discover much more about them. Burton Gilliam and his wife, Susan, reside comfortably in Allen, Texas, where he continues his acting career along with participating in numerous television commercials.

I received a surprise package in the mail a few weeks after that evening that contained a book, *The Music Mann, My Life in Song*, by Johnny Mann. His special autograph note read, "I and our country thank you! Blessings, Johnny Mann."

This encounter with special people concludes with the sad note that Johnny Mann passed away just one year after that evening on June 28, 2014.

8

Notable Enduring
Encounters

When I began to think about developing this work, I also had some concern that I might have difficulty in remembering details and the various circumstances surrounding some encounters. However, just the opposite occurred. I found recalling and refreshing my memory of these notable encounters with incredible people of my past brought about surreal feelings in many instances, placing me virtually back to the exact time, the situation, and the place where it occurred.

In closing, I especially wish to recall and honor the memories of several special patriots whom I enjoyed the pleasure of knowing and serving alongside, particularly during the Cold War era, which we sometimes forget absorbed forty-five years of our lives; it persists today, for that matter.

These true patriots were the combat crew members, with whom I enjoyed the pleasure of sharing the good times and frequent challenging times, for thirteen continuous years. When I reported to the Strategic Air Command 95th Bombardment Wing(H) at Biggs Air Force Base, El Paso, Texas, in December 1953, I didn't have a clue where I was headed or what lie ahead in the years to come. I was a young lieutenant, fresh out of basic pilot training and assigned to SAC B-36 Combat Crew S-05.

Aircraft Commander, Captain John D. "Jake" Kaplan, welcomed this "shave tail" aboard and promptly put me to work, "studying and learning." The mighty B-36 was the largest strategic nuclear bomber ever built, perhaps even one of the most complex. I will leave it to the reader to Google up the history and lore of this mighty air machine.

It is my personal pleasure to recognize my fellow combat crew members on the B-36 crew on which I served for six years, as well as those on two additional weapons system combat crews for seven

The names of these unsung heroes will likely not be recognized except by their families. They were faceless men of service and honor with whom I was privileged to serve alongside during frequent complex and difficult times. Their names, positions, and service rise to equal any and all notable encounters:

SAC B-36 Combat Crew S-05, 1953–1959

Captain John D. "Jake" Kaplan, Aircraft Commander; First Lieutenant Chris Adams, First Pilot; Second Lieutenant Bill Vlach, copilot; Radar Navigator, Captain John Eder; Navigator, Captain Paul Kilmain; Co-observor, Lieutenant Alonzo Haines; Flight Engineer, Captain Earl Land; Second Engineer, T/Sgt. Frank Rodriquez; Radio Operator, M/Sgt. Al Driesdale; Second Radio Operator/Forward Turret Gunner; Senior Tail Gunner: Jim Lashley.

I would be remiss if I did not inject a brief story about Jake Kaplan and his incredible leadership and confidence-building skills. We were returning to our home base, Biggs AFB, one late night from a fourteen-hour training mission: practice bomb runs over Salt Lake City, Denver, and Dallas. A couple hours before arriving back at Biggs, Jake had me take his left, aircraft commander's seat, in the cockpit, so that he could get up and stretch after the long flight day, and Bill Vlach took my seat. This was a usual training routine for both myself and Bill, "taking charge of the aircraft," on the tail end of a flight. As we approached Biggs, I looked back to see where Jake was, and he was nowhere in sight. I finally called the radio operator, Al Driesbach, and asked him to tell the AC that we were approaching the field for approach and landing. In a few minutes, Jake came up the flight deck and sat down behind me on the jump seat. I looked over my shoulder, saw him, and I began to unbuckle my seat belt and harness. He tapped me on the shoulder and shook his, pointing straight ahead, as if to say, *stay in the seat and keep on flying*. I was puzzled. I had only made approaches and landings in the big ten-engine B-36 monster from the right pilot's seat under his supervision. We had already received clearance to land and I looked back at him again. He had his traditional stern look on his face, as best I could see in the dark cockpit. He pointed again, straight ahead, and nodded for me to stay seated. This was to be a true test. I knew that he meant for me to make the landing. I glanced over at Bill and he had the same shock on his face as I felt! I proceeded to reduce power on the engines, gave Bill and the flight engineers instructions for landing as well as the rest of the crew.

I made my first "solo" B-36 landing, perhaps the most memorable aircraft landing before or after, in my lifetime. Memories . . .

SAC B-52 Combat Crew S-02, 1960–1963

Major Arthur Chadborne, Aircraft Commander; Captain Chris Adams, Pilot; Captain Hal Meyers, Radar Navigator; Captain John Kresl, Navigator; Tail Gunner, Lief Johnson.

SAC Minuteman ICBM Combat Crew L-14, 1963–1966

Major Chris Adams, Combat Crew Commander.

Lieutenant Allen Tiedman, Deputy Crew Commander.

Combat crew duty in Strategic Air Command was by far the most disciplined training regime that anyone serving in the United States military could have ever experienced. I know, as many of you from other military services and duties will argue with me, and SAC guys took a lot of "ribbing" about being in SAC, but most will also admit that the stories they had heard from SAC "crew dogs" would agree that the "General Curtis LeMay" standard of discipline and training program during the Cold War days was not only the most demanding and requiring, but the most exacting and precise one might ever experience. Enough on that, and not to create an argument with my fighter pilot or other Service friends, except to close in sharing that for those who missed the opportunity of servitude under General Curtis LeMay, missed a great deal in their military lives.

Notable Tribute

I wish to conclude with a serious measure of thought and reflection about the notable wives and families of those valiant heroes in uniform who served our nation over the years, the forty-five-year Cold War, before and after. Of each, it can truly be said, they also served! It was common knowledge especially throughout the Military Services, that the greatest burdens of the Cold War frequently fell upon the families of those in uniform. Combat crew members and the support personnel were frequently away when they were needed most.

Having been personally acquainted with literally thousands of the Cold Warriors, their wives and families, over the years, while being there myself; with the challenges of keeping homes and families intact while their husbands were either far away on a deployment, ground alert, in a missile launch control center, or in an SLBM submarine at sea, I marveled at their resilience and the steadfast loyalty to their husband's jobs and responsibilities. Most took the long days, alert duty, and prolonged separations in stride, seldom complaining. They became mother and father to the kids, took care of the upkeep of house and home, paid the bills, and nurtured the family automobile when it needed repair. In spite of all the pressures and anxiety, the stability among military families was exceptionally high.

Looking back at the stressful and challenging times, many Strategic Air Command wives pointed to the Cuban Crisis as the most frightening period of their military service lives of the time. Of course, later on, Vietnam surged into an even more life-threatening situation, lasting for more than ten years. Military combat crew members, ground forces and support personnel alike, took each of these challenges as they were called to duty with their respective bomber, fighter, tanker, reconnaissance, submarine, and missile weapons systems. Combat units were moved out to forward bases and overseas locations. The men were frequently forbidden to tell their families where they were going or when they would return. All the other deployed airmen and sailors, likewise, disappeared to forward operating bases around the world and the Navy SLBM subs disappeared beneath the seas. The only related source of information for families, came from the radio, TV and newspapers, and none of the various media outlets had an inkling of what was really happening with the military forces. The "war of nerves" that frequently pervades the country through the media during crisis situations only add to family fears and concern.

As a B-52 pilot and Wing Command Post Controller at Ramey AFB, Puerto Rico, when the Cuban Crisis began to unravel, President Kennedy directed B-52 airborne alert missions to commence immediately. Bomber combat crews were either in the air or on ground-alert with aircraft fully generated, nuclear weapons loaded, and ready to take whatever actions so directed. The consequences of the situation, unquestioned among the combat crew force, did not fully impact overseas families until the casualty assistance people began collecting personal affairs information and requesting each family to pack for potential immediate evacuation if necessary. At that point, the true specter and fear of war became a reality.

I was continuously amazed, as were others, that there was virtually no panic among the wives and children—they simply went about their necessary preparations, "just in case." Rumors were always a part of military life and the lives of the families, especially during such tense periods when their husbands were deployed across the world for several months at a time or potential crises such as that with Cuba and even more so during Vietnam. Wives frequently responded to stressful situations by participating in support groups, led by other wives, many with special education and training to deal with unpredictable circumstances. Those who stepped forward were exceptionally beneficial in providing counsel a comfort to the younger wives when husbands were away, rumors flying about, or when a tragic accident happened. They all bonded as a family of one—relying upon and supporting one another.

Someone once said to me early in my career, "The Air Force always gets two for the price of one." And, the same held true for all the other Military Services. Only "one," the military spouse, gets paid for serving, but both, along with the children, also clearly serve. I would have been remiss if I did not acknowledge the true bravery and spirit of the wives and families of the Cold War warriors. And while this has been but a brief acknowledgment of that special group of silent and unsung heroes—the wives and families—who carried out perhaps the most difficult duties of all, it is a heartfelt tribute to each. They also served!

> *The bravest are the tenderest; the loving are the daring.*
> *—Henry Wadsworth Longfellow*

Books by Chris Adams

Inside the Cold War: A Cold Warrior's Reflections (1999)
Red Eagle: A Cold War Espionage Story (2000)
Ideologies in Conflict: A Cold War Docu-Story (2001)
Profiles in Betrayal: The Enemy Within (2002)
The Betrayal Mosaic: A Cold War Spy Story (2004)
Out of Darkness: The Last Russian Revolution (2006)
Deterrence: An Enduring Strategy (2009)
Requiem of a Spy (2018)
Texas: A Free Nation Under God with Manuel English (2011)
Dallas: Lone Assassin or Pawn with Mary Ward (2013)
Final Approach: A Flight Through Life (2015)

About
the Authors

Author: *Notable Encounters*, Chris Adams

C hris Adams is a retired Air Force major general and former Chief of Staff, Strategic Air Command. He is also a former Associate Director, Los Alamos National Laboratory, and Vice President, Government Systems, Andrew Corporation. He has worked around the world, including the United Kingdom, China, South Korea, Australia, Saudi Arabia, and five years in Russia and the Post-Cold War Soviet Union. He is the author of eleven books; documentaries and spy novels, all of which drawn from his vast experiences. Among his recognitions and awards are Distinguished Alumnus, Tarleton State University and Texas A&M University-Commerce, the United States Distinguished Service Medal, two Legions of Merit, Vietnam Service Medal with four Battle Stars, the

Daughters of the American Revolution Medal of Honor, and is listed in Who's Who in America.

Co-author: *Notable Encounters*, Paulette Bridges

Paulette Bridges is a former adjunct professor, Texas Wesleyan University; supervisor of student teachers; sales consultant, Houghton Mifflin and Harcourt Publishers and ESL; school principal; publications editor; extraordinary and skilled manuscript editor. BS, University of Houston; Masters Degree in Education, Stephen F. Austin State University. Married, four children and eight grandchildren.

CPSIA information can be obtained
at www.ICGtesting.com
Printed in the USA
FSHW020028190219
55769FS

9 781644 160701